W9-BPK-297

Modern Critical Views

Modern Critical Views

ANTON CHEKHOV

Edited and with an introduction by
Harold Bloom
Sterling Professor of the Humanities
Yale University

CHELSEA HOUSE PUBLISHERS
Philadelphia

Public Library, New Brunswick, N. J. 08901

© 1999 by Chelsea House Publishers, a division of
Main Line Book Co.

Introduction © 1999 by Harold Bloom

All rights reserved. No part of this publication may be
reproduced or transmitted in any form or by any means
without the written permission of the publisher.

Printed and bound in the United States of America

10   9   8   7   6   5   4   3   2   1

∞ The paper used in this publication meets the minimum
requirements of the American National Standard for
Permanence of Paper for Printed Library Materials,
Z39.48-1984

Library of Congress Cataloging-in-Publication Data

Anton Chekhov / edited and with an introduction by
Harold Bloom.
        p. 262   cm.—(Modern critical views)
     Includes bibliographical references and index.
     ISBN 0-7910-4783-0
     1. Chekhov, Anton Pavlovich, 1860-1904—Criticism
and interpretation.   I. Bloom, Harold.   II. Series.
PG3458.Z8A523   1998
891.72'3—dc21   98-6614
                                                   CIP

Contents

Editor's Note

This volume brings together a representative selection of the best critical essays available in English on the plays and short stories of Anton Chekhov.

My Introduction is an overview of Chekhov's four major plays, taking note of their relationship to *Hamlet*. Novelist Virginia Woolf commences the sequence of commentary with a sensitive review of a 1920 London performance of *The Cherry Orchard*.

The wonderful reminiscences of Chekhov by Maxim Gorky follow, giving us the best sense of Chekhov as a person ever made available.

Eric Bentley provides his fine observations on *Uncle Vanya*, showing that all plot devices function superbly both as form and content, after which Raymond Williams emphasizes Chekhov's innovations in dramatic form.

The mystical Lev Shestov illuminates Chekhov's inwardness, his secular spirituality, while Francis Fergusson, considering *The Cherry Orchard*, shows that Chekhov reduces "the dramatic art to its ancient root."

Rufus W. Mathewson Jr. considers Chekhov's influence upon modern short fiction, while the poet Howard Moss gives us the gift of the subtlest and most Chekhovian reading that *Three Sisters* ever has received.

Martin Esslin concentrates upon Chekhov's place within modern drama, after which Charles May gives a general overview of Chekhov's relation to the modern short story.

Peter Szondi briefly meditates upon renunciation in Chekhov's dramas, and in David Cole's examination of *The Sea Gull*, the acts of reading within the play are seen as central to characterization.

Michael C. Finke studies "At Sea," Chekhov's first published story, finding in it the writer's lifelong obsession with *Hamlet*.

Robert Louis Jackson's analysis of Chekhov's story "The Enemies" finds in it the ancient Greek understanding that character is fate, while Liza Knapp's account of the famous story "Ward Six" emphasizes how directly Chekhov works upon his readers' sensibilities.

This volume closes with Gary Saul Morson's exegesis of *Uncle Vanya*, where the high theatricality of the play is stressed.

Introduction

Chekhov's best critics tend to agree that he is essentially a dramatist, even as a writer of short stories. Since the action of his plays is both immensely subtle and absolutely ineluctable, the stories also are dramatic in Chekhov's utterly original way. D.S. Mirsky, in his helpful *History of Russian Literature*, rather severely remarks upon "the complete lack of individuality in his characters and in their way of speaking." That seems unjust, but a critic, like myself, who reads no Russian perhaps cannot dispute Mirsky, who also indicts Chekhov's Russian:

> It is colorless and lacks individuality. He had no feeling for words. No Russian writer of anything like his significance used a language so devoid of all raciness and verve. This makes Chekhov (except for topical allusions, technical terms and occasional catch-words) so easy to translate; of all Russian writers, he has the least to fear from the treachery of translators.

It is difficult to believe that this helps account for the permanent popularity of Chekhov's plays in the English-speaking theater, or of his stories with readers of English. Chekhov, as Mirsky also says, is uniquely original and powerful at one mode of representation in particular: "No writer excels him in conveying the mutual unsurpassable isolation of human beings and the impossibility of understanding each other." Mirsky wrote this in 1926, and presumably in ignorance of Kafka, before the advent of Beckett, but they verge upon vision or phantasmagoria; Chekhov seems to represent a simpler and more available reality, but by no means a cruder one.

The best critical observation on Chekhov that I have encountered is a remark that Gorky made about the man rather than the stories and plays: "It seems to me that in the presence of Anton Pavlovich, everyone felt an unconscious desire to be simpler, more truthful, more himself." That is the effect upon me of rereading "The Student" or "The Lady with Dog," or of attending a performance of *Three Sisters* or *The Cherry Orchard*. That hardly means we will be made any better by Chekhov, but on some level we will wish we could be better. That desire, however repressed, seems to me an aesthetic rather than a moral phenomenon. Chekhov, with his artist's wisdom, teaches us implicitly that literature is a form of desire and wonder and not a form of the good.

II

As a modern version of *Hamlet*, *The Seagull* surpasses Pirandello's *Henry IV* and even Beckett's *Endgame*, precisely because its *Hamlet* is so hopelessly weak. I do not mean by this that *The Seagull* is of the dramatic eminence of *Endgame*, or even of *Henry IV*; it is not, and seems to me the weakest and most contrived of Chekhov's four major plays. Its use of *Hamlet*, however, is shrewd and effective, and despite *The Seagull's* limitations, few comedies stage better or remain as authentically funny.

Trigorin, in one of Chekhov's frightening ironies, appears to be a self-parody on Chekhov's own part. One hardly knows who is funnier, more outrageously deceptive, and ultimately self-deceived, the novelist or the actress. Trigorin begins by savoring Nina's naive but sincere offer to be ruined by him, which he, Arkadina, and we know he is going to take up anyway. That makes wholly and deliciously rancid Trigorin's deliberations: "Why do I hear so much sorrow in this cry sent by someone so pure in soul? Why does it wring so much pain in my own heart?" But even better is his address to Arkadina, beginning: "If you wanted to, you could be extraordinary." And yet better is the ferocious hilarity of the exchange after the actress has fallen upon her knees, with Arkadina assuring Trigorin that he is "Russia's one and only hope," and the submissive writer collapsing into: "Take me, carry me off, but just don't let me go one single step away from you." These beauties deserve, and will go on deserving, one another, and Chekhov has achieved the highest comedy with them, rather clearly modeling these extravagant charmers upon his own relation to various actresses.

Wherever it is pure comedy, *The Seagull* seems to me magnificent. Unfortunately, it has two aesthetic disasters, the unfortunate Konstantin, bad writer and mama's boy, who inconsiderately delays shooting himself until the very end of the play, and the aspiring actress Nina, Trigorin's eager victim, whose endless vows of high-mindedness always make me wish a director would interject a rousing chorus or two of Noel Coward's "Don't put your daughter on the stage, Mrs. Worthington—don't put your daughter on the stage!" One sees what Chekhov meant to do with Nina, and Ibsen might have gotten away with it, but Chekhov was too good a comedian not to subvert his own presentation of Nina's idealism. That does not quite save Chekhov, and us, from having to hear Nina proclaim, "Know how to bear your cross and have faith." Subtlest of writers, Chekhov did not make that mistake again in a drama.

III

Eric Bentley, in his superb essay on *Uncle Vanya*, observes that "what makes Chekhov seem most formless is precisely the means by which he achieves strict form—namely, the series of tea-drinkings, arrivals, departures, meals, dances, family gatherings, casual conversations of which his plays are made." This only apparent formlessness, as Bentley goes on to show, allows Chekhov to naturalize such unrealistic conventions as the tirade and "self explaining soliloquies" spoken with others present but with no reference to others. "Naturalizing the unrealistic" is indeed a summary of Chekhov's dramatic art except that Chekhov's deep wisdom is always to remind us how strange "the realistic" actually is. One might venture, quite naively, that Chekhov's most indisputable power is the impression we almost invariably receive, reading his stories or attending his plays, that here at last is the truth of our existence. It is as though Chekhov's quest had been to refute Nietzsche's declaration that we possess art lest we perish from the truth.

Uncle Vanya, as it happens, is my earliest theatrical memory except for the Yiddish theater, since I saw the Old Vic production when I was a teenager. Alas, I have forgotten Laurence Olivier as Astrov, and even those three extraordinary actresses—Joyce Redman, Sybil Thorndike, Margaret Leighton—but that is because I was so permanently mesmerized by Ralph Richardson as Vanya, a performance eclipsed in my memory only by seeing Richardson, years later, as Falstaff. I have seen *Uncle Vanya* several times since, but in less splendid productions, and like *The Seagull*, it seems to survive any director. The audience discovers what Vanya and Sonya and even Astrov discover: our ordinary existence has a genuine horror in it, however we mask the recognition lest we become mad or violent. Sonya's dark, closing tirade can neither be forgotten nor accepted, and makes us reflect that *The Seagull* and *The Cherry Orchard* are subtitled as comedies in four acts, and *Three Sisters* as a drama in four acts, but *Uncle Vanya*, a play where all life must be lived vicariously, has the ironic subtitle "Scenes from Country Life in Four Acts."

Serebryakov is an effective if simplistic representation of all those qualities of obtuseness, vainglory, and ignorance that are the curse of the academic profession at all times and in all places. We are confronted again by the singular power of Chekhov's armory of ironies; it is the low intellectual and spiritual quality of Professor Serebryakov that helps reveal to Vanya and Sonya, Astrov and Yelena, their own lucid consciousnesses and ranges of significant emotion, a revelation that only serves to make a bad enough life still worse for all of them. You shall know the truth and the truth shall make you despair would be the gospel of Anton Chekhov, except that this gloomy genius insists upon being cheerful. As Bentley says, your fate is unsettled because that is how Chekhov sees the truth.

The highest tribute that can be made to *Uncle Vanya* is that the play partakes of the madness of great art; to describe it is to believe that attending it or reading it would be depressing, but the aesthetic dignity of this drama produces a very different effect, somber but strong, a dirge for the unlived life. If *Uncle Vanya* is not quite of the order of *Three Sisters* and *The Cherry Orchard*, still it surpasses *The Seagull* and is imperishable.

IV

Three Sisters seems to me, as to many other readers, Chekhov's masterpiece, outdoing even the grand epilogue to his work in *The Cherry Orchard* and such magnificent stories as "The Darling," "The Lady with Dog," and "The Bishop." But *Three Sisters* is darker even than *Uncle Vanya*, though more vitalistic in that darkness. Howard Moss, in a preternaturally Chekhovian essay on the play, began by noting that "the inability to act becomes the action of the play." That suggests to me a particular tradition in tragedy, one that includes the *Prometheus Bound* of Aeschylus and the Book of Job, and Job's inheritors in Milton's *Samson Agonistes* and Shelley's *The Cenci*. Since *Three Sisters* is not a tragedy, but deliberately only "a drama," of no genre, we are left perplexed by the play's final effect upon us, which does appear to be a Chekhovian ambiguity.

Moss's comparison to *Hamlet* applies throughout *Three Sisters* far more adequately than in *The Seagull*, though there the use of *Hamlet* is overt. Chekhov's three sisters—Olga, Masha, and Irina—together with their brother Andrey, make up a kind of fourfold parody of the prince of Denmark, rather in the way that the Karamazov brothers Ivan, Mitya, Alyosha, and the bastard Smerdyakov—make up a sort of necessarily indeliberate parody of Blake's primordial man, Albion, by way of the Four Zoas who constitute him.

Moss justly remarks that Olga is the least interesting of the three sisters, but that is only because Masha and Irina are so profoundly fascinating, and are more at home in the erotic realm than she is. Yet Olga has her own enchantments for the playgoer or reader, being both motherly and exceedingly fragile, incarnating the good, but unable to defend it, whether in herself or others.

An Ibsenite terror, much as we adore her, Masha gives everyone, on stage and in the audience, more truth than anyone can hope to bear, and she certainly is almost too much for her lover, the weak but imaginative Vershinin, who seems to be another of Chekhov's remarkably unflattering self-portraits. We do not know very much about some of the greatest writers of the past, but what we do know about some of the titans, such as Milton and Wordsworth, does not make us love them. Chekhov, of all the major writers, would appear to have been the best human being, something we could hardly know from his various self-presentations.

Masha is more intricate than Irina, but matched by her in vitality. What we remember best about Irina though is her grim metaphor in which she calls herself a locked piano to which she herself has lost the key. She is very young, but maturation will not make her able to return the passions that she so frequently provokes, and even if she reached the Moscow of her visions, her heart would not spring open there. Greatly deluded, Irina takes the erotic place of her dead mother, being her visual representative in the play, yet otherwise strangely unconnected to her. As for Andrey, he is less than his sisters, being little more than an amiable aesthete and his fierce wife's willing victim. Yet he is the artist among the four, even as Masha is the intellectual, Irina the dreamer, and Olga the benign embodiment of maternal care. All of them self-defeating, all worthy of love, all yearners for culture, kindness, and the spirit, the four Prozorovs are quite enough to break the heart of any playgoer.

Hamlet, particularly in Act 5, is beyond our love, and very nearly beyond even the most transcendental of our apprehensions. The sisters' suffering affects us so greatly because, unlike Hamlet, they are within the limits of the possible for us. Alas, they are incapable of learning to live to the full within the limits of the possible for themselves. The sisters' self-frustration remains as much a mystery as their failure to resist their rapacious sister-in-law, Natasha. Moss, again almost more Chekhovian than Chekhov was, insists that they are survivors and not losers, too alive to be quite mortal: "They may languish in life but they refuse to die in art, and with a peculiar insistence—an irony only good plays manage to achieve because it is only on the stage that the human figure is always wholly represented and representative." Chekhov would have agreed, but Tolstoy, as Moss well knows, would not. The sisters lament that they do not know enough, which Moss translates as their stasis, their inability to be elsewhere, to be different, to be in Moscow or in the world of open vision. So profound is Chekhov's play that I suspect the sisters must be right. They embody the truth but cannot know it, yet surely that is just as well. Unlike Vanya, they go on living not wholly without hope.

The Cherry Orchard is far less intricate in texture than *Three Sisters*, but like that greater play it is of no genre, though Chekhov insisted upon his subtitle: "A Comedy in Four Acts." Whatever Chekhov's intentions, we attend or read the drama now and are compelled to find in it the author's pastoral elegy both for himself and his world. There are strong elements of farce in *The Cherry Orchard*, and the merchant Lopakhin, though he has some complex elements, could be at home in a relatively pure farce. But the distinguished and doom-eager protagonist, Lyubov Andreevna Ranevsskaya, who is fated to lose the cherry orchard, is a figure of immense pathos, stylized yet intensely moving, and she prevents the play from being farce or pure comedy. *The Cherry Orchard* is a lyric meditation—theatrical through and through but a theater-poem, as Francis Fergusson usefully called it.

Genre hardly matters in Chekhov anyway, since like Shakespeare he excelled in the representation of change, or even impending change, and the dramatic image of a crossing or transition necessarily participates in the nature of what Emerson splendidly termed "shooting the gulf" or "darting to an aim." Chekhov is not much interested in the aim or in change as such, so I am impressed by Fergusson's complete phrase for *The Cherry Orchard*: "A Theater-Poem of the suffering of change." The pathos of change in this play is strangely similar to the pathos of stasis in *Three Sisters*, so it seems clear that Chekhov by "change" does not mean anything so vulgar or reductive as social and economic, let alone political metamorphoses. Lopakhin, before the play ends, is almost as much a figure of pathos as Lyubov. It is true that her life has been one long disaster: an alcoholic husband, dead of drink; an endless love affair with a scoundrel, who stole from her and abandoned her; the death by drowning of her little boy; the coming sale of her ancestral property. In contrast to this self-destructive and charming gentlewoman, Lopakhin is a very tough soul archetype of the self-made man. Son of a muzhik, Lopakhin has considerable cruelty in him, but his deep feeling is for Lyubov, with whom we can surmise he always will be, quite hopelessly, in love. But then, so are we, with its endlessly mobile and magnificent woman, this large-souled vision of passion on the old, grand, high scale. In his elegy for himself, the lover of women Anton Chekhov has given us his most vivid representation of an embodied Sublime in Lyubov.

Yet Lopakhin is even more interesting, and perhaps enables us to encounter a more profound pathos. The one respect in which *The Cherry*

Orchard could be termed an advance over the astonishing *Three Sisters* is that in his masterpiece Chekhov had to give us Natasha as a very negative figure. I do not agree with Robert Brustein when he sees Natasha's victory as "the triumph of pure evil" and says she is "without a single redeeming trait." Unlike the sisters, whose vitality is thwarted, the uncultured Natasha is extending the life of the Prozorov family; she is peopling the house with babies, though it is unclear whether they are Prozorovs or the children of her offstage lover, one Protopopov, whose splendid name is that of a contemporary literary critic whom Chekhov despised. In any case, Lopakhin is no Natasha; he is not a villain, but a good man, though clownish and hard, and there is something curiously Shakespearean in his complex mixture of force and nostalgia, his pragmatic workmanship and his reverence for, almost awe of, the glorious Lyubov.

It is almost as frustrating to attempt a description of the aesthetic effects of *The Cherry Orchard* as it is to venture an analysis of the almost absurdly rich *Three Sisters*. Chekhov, in his two finest plays, writes a theatrical poetry that relies upon perspectives unlike any achieved before him. Consider only the famous and weirdly poignant end of Act 3, Lopakhin's great moment, which calls for an extraordinary actor. Chekhov wrote it for Stanislavsky himself, who declined the part. Charles Laughton played it in London in 1933, and I always envision him as Lopakhin when I reread the play. One sees him handling that persuasive antithetical movement from Lopakhin proclaiming, "Music, start playing!" to his tenderly rough reproach to the bitterly weeping Lyubov, until he himself passes to tears, with the immense, "Oh, if only this would pass by as quickly as possible, if only we could hurry and change our life somehow, this unhappy, helter-skelter way we live." The change he wants he cannot have—to be married to Lyubov, eternally too high above him—and his clownish exit ("I can pay for everything!") reverberates darkly as we listen to Anya's ineffectual and self-deceiving but sincere and loving consolation of her mother. We see why Chekhov, in his letters, described Lopakhin as a gentle and honest person, and as a man who did not shout. Chekhov, confronting change, humanized it, and goes on humanizing us.

VIRGINIA WOOLF

The Cherry Orchard

Although every member of the audience at the Art Theatre last week had probably read Chekhov's *The Cherry Orchard* several times, a large number of them had, perhaps, never seen it acted before. It was no doubt on this account that as the first act proceeded the readers, now transformed into seers, felt themselves shocked and outraged. The beautiful, mad drama which I had staged often enough in the dim recesses of my mind was now hung within a few feet of me, hard, crude, and over-emphatic, like a cheap coloured print of the real thing. But what right had I to call it the real thing? What did I mean by that? Perhaps something like this.

There is nothing in English literature in the least like *The Cherry Orchard*. It may be that we are more advanced, less advanced, or have advanced in an entirely different direction. At any rate, the English person who finds himself at dawn in the nursery of Madame Ranevskaia feels out of place, like a foreigner brought up with entirely different traditions, But the traditions are not (this, of course, is a transcript of individual experience) so ingrained in one as to prevent one from shedding them not only without pain but with actual relief and abandonment. True, at the end of a long railway journey one is accustomed to say goodnight and go to bed. Yet on this occasion, since everything is so strange, the dawn rising and the birds beginning to sing in the cherry-trees, let us gather round the coffee-cups; let us talk

From *The New Statesman*, July 24, 1920.

about everything in the whole world. We are all in that queer emotional state
when thought seems to bubble into words without being spoken. The
journey is over and we have reached the end of everything where space seems
illimitable and time everlasting. Quite wrongly (since in the production
approved by Chekhov the birds actually sing and the cherries are visible on
the trees) I had, on my imaginary stage, tried to give effect to my sense that
the human soul is free from all trappings and crossed incessantly by thoughts
and emotions which wing their way from here, from there, from the furthest
horizons—I had tried to express this by imagining an airy view from the
window with ethereal pink cherries and perhaps snow mountains and blue
mist behind them. In the room the characters spoke suddenly whatever
came into their heads, and yet always vaguely, as if thinking aloud. There
was no "comedy of manners"; one thought scarcely grazed, let alone struck
sparks from, another; there was no conflict of individual wills. At the same
time the characters were entirely concrete and without sentimentality. Not
for an instant did one suppose that Madame Ranevskaia was wrapping up a
mystic allusion to something else when she spoke. Her own emotions were
quite enough for her. If what was said seemed symbolical, that was because
it was profound enough to illumine much more than an incident in the life
of one individual. And, finally, though the leap from one thought to another
was so wide as to produce a sense of dangerous dislocation, all the separate
speeches and characters combined to create a single impression of an overwhelming kind.

The actors at the Art Theatre destroyed this conception, first, by the
unnatural emphasis with which they spoke; next by their determination to
make points which brought them into touch with the audience but destroyed
their harmony with each other; and, finally, by the consciousness which hung
about them of being well-trained English men and women ill at ease in an
absurd situation, but determined to make the best of a bad business. One
instance of irrepressible British humour struck me with considerable force.
It occurred in the middle of Charlotte's strange speech in the beginning of
the second act. "I have no proper passport. I don't know how old I am; I
always feel I am still young," she begins. She goes on, "When I grew up I
became a governess. But where I come from and who I am, I haven't a
notion. Who my parents were—*very likely they weren't married*—I don't
know." At the words I have italicised, Dunyasha bounced away from her to
the other end of the bench, with an arch humour which drew the laugh it
deserved. Miss Helena Millais seemed to be delighted to have this chance of
assuring us that she did not believe a word of this morbid nonsense, and that
the old jokes still held good in the world of sanity round the corner. But it
was Miss Ethel Irving who showed the steadiest sense of what decency

requires of a British matron in extremity. How she did it, since she spoke her part accurately, it is difficult to say, but her mere presence upon the stage was enough to suggest that all the comforts and all the decencies of English upper-class life were at hand, so that at any moment her vigil upon the bench might have been appropriately interrupted by a manservant bearing a silver tray. "The Bishop is in the drawing-room, m'lady." "Thank you, Parker. Tell his Lordship I will come at once." In that sort of play, by which I mean a play by Sheridan or Oscar Wilde, both Miss Irving and Miss Millais would charm by their wit, spirit and competent intellectual outfit. Nor, though the quotation I have made scarcely proves it, have we any cause to sneer at English comedy or at the tradition of acting which prevails upon our stage. The only question is whether the same methods are as applicable to *The Cherry Orchard* as they are to *The School for Scandal*.

But there are four acts in *The Cherry Orchard*. How it may have been with the other readers I do not know, but before the second act was over some sort of compromise had been reached between my reader's version and the actor's one. Perhaps in reading one had got the whole too vague, too mad, too mystical. Perhaps as they went on the actors forgot how absurd such behaviour would be thought in England. Or perhaps the play itself triumphed over the deficiencies of both parties. At any rate, I felt less and less desire to cavil at the acting in general and more and more appreciation of the acting of Mr. Cancellor, Mr. Dodd, Mr. Pearson and Miss Edith Evans in particular. With every word that Mr. Felix Aylmer spoke as Pishchick one's own conception of that part plumped itself out like a shrivelled skin miraculously revived. But the play itself—that was what overwhelmed all obstacles, so that though the walls rocked from floor to ceiling when the door was shut, though the sun sank and rose with the energetic decision of the stage carpenter's fist, though the scenery suggested an advertisement of the Surrey Hills rather than Russia in her wildness, the atmosphere of the play wrapped us round and shut out everything alien to itself. It is, as a rule, when a critic does not wish to commit himself or to trouble himself that he refers to atmosphere. And, given time, something might be said in greater detail of the causes which produced this atmosphere—the strange dislocated sentences, each so erratic and yet cutting out the shape so firmly, of the realism, of the humour, of the artistic unity. But let the word atmosphere be taken literally to mean that Chekhov has contrived to shed over us a luminous vapour in which life appears as it is, without veils, transparent and visible to the depths. Long before the play was over we seemed to have sunk below the surface of things and to be feeling our way among submerged but recognisable emotions. "I have no proper passport. I don't know how old I am; I always feel I am still young"—how the words go sounding on in one's mind—how the whole play resounds with such sentences, which reverberate, melt into each other, and pass far away out beyond everything! In short, if it is permissible to use such vague language, I do not know how better to describe the sensation at the end of *The Cherry Orchard*, than by saying that it sends one into the street feeling like a piano played upon at last, not in the middle only but all over the keyboard and with the lid left open so that the sound goes on.

This being so, and having felt nothing comparable to it from reading the play, one feels inclined to strike out every word of criticism and to implore Madame Donnet to give us the chance of seeing play after play, until to sit at home and read plays is an occupation for the afflicted only, and one to be viewed with pity, as we pity blind men spelling out their Shakespeare with their fingers upon sheets of cardboard.

Virginia Woolf

MAXIM GORKY

Fragments of Recollections

Once he invited me to the village Koutchouk-Koy where he had a tiny strip of land and a white, two-storied house. There, while showing me his "estate," he began to speak with animation: "If I had plenty of money, I should build a sanatorium here for invalid village teachers. You know, I would put up a large, bright building—very bright, with large windows and lofty rooms. I would have a fine library, different musical instruments, bees, a vegetable garden, an orchard. . . . There would be lectures on agriculture, mythology. . . . Teachers ought to know everything, everything, my dear fellow."

He was suddenly silent, coughed, looked at me out of the corners of his eyes, and smiled that tender, charming smile of his which attracted one so irresistibly to him and made one listen so attentively to his words.

"Does it bore you to listen to my fantasies? I do love to talk of it. . . . If you knew how badly the Russian village needs a nice, sensible, educated teacher! We ought in Russia to give the teacher particularly good conditions, and it ought to be done as quickly as possible. We ought to realize that without a wide education of the people, Russia will collapse, like a house built of badly baked bricks. A teacher must be an artist, in love with his calling; but with us he is a journeyman, ill educated, who goes to the village to teach children as though he were going into exile. He is starved, crushed, terrorized by the fear of losing his daily bread. But he ought to be the first

From *Reminiscences of Anton Chekhov*. © 1921 by B.W. Huebsch, Inc.

man in the village; the peasants ought to recognize him as a power, worthy of attention and respect; no one should dare to shout at him or humiliate him personally, as with us every one does—the village constable, the rich shop-keeper, the priest, the rural police commissioner, the school guardian, the councilor, and that official who has the title of school-inspector, but who cares nothing for the improvement of education and only sees that the circulars of his chiefs are carried out. . . . It is ridiculous to pay in farthings the man who has to educate the people. It is intolerable that he should walk in rags, shiver with cold in damp and draughty schools, catch cold, and about the age of thirty get laryngitis, rheumatism, or tuberculosis. We ought to be ashamed of it. Our teacher, for eight or nine months in the year, lives like a hermit: he has no one to speak a word to; without company, books, or amusements, he is growing stupid, and, if he invites his colleagues to visit him, then he becomes politically suspect—a stupid word with which crafty men frighten fools. All this is disgusting; it is the mockery of a man who is doing a great and tremendously important work. . . . Do you know, whenever I see a teacher, I feel ashamed for him, for his timidity, and because he is badly dressed . . . it seems to me that for the teacher's wretchedness I am myself to blame—I mean it."

He was silent, thinking; and then, waving his hand, he said gently: "This Russia of ours is such an absurd, clumsy country."

A shadow of sadness crossed his beautiful eyes; little rays of wrinkles surrounded them and made them look still more meditative. Then, looking round, he said jestingly: "You see, I have fired off at you a complete leading article from a radical paper. Come, I'll give you tea to reward your patience."

That was characteristic of him, to speak so earnestly, with such warmth and sincerity, and then suddenly to laugh at himself and his speech. In that sad and gentle smile one felt the subtle skepticism of the man who knows the value of words and dreams; and there also flashed in the smile a lovable modesty and delicate sensitiveness. . . .

We walked back slowly in silence to the house. It was a clear, hot day; the waves sparkled under the bright rays of the sun; down below one heard a dog barking joyfully. Chekhov took my arm, coughed, and said slowly: "It is shameful and sad, but true: there are many men who envy the dogs."

And he added immediately with a laugh: "To-day I can only make feeble speeches . . . It means that I'm getting old."

I often heard him say: "You know, a teacher has just come here—he's ill, married . . . couldn't you do something for him? I have made arrange-ments for him for the time being." Or again: "Listen, Gorky, there is a teacher here who would like to meet you. He can't go out, he's ill. Won't you come and see him? Do." Or: "Look here, the women teachers want books to be sent to them."

Sometimes I would find that "teacher" at his house; usually he would be sitting on the edge of his chair, blushing at the consciousness of his own awkwardness, in the sweat of his brow picking and choosing his words, trying to speak smoothly and "educatedly"; or, with the ease of manner of a person who is morbidly shy, he would concentrate himself upon the effort not to appear stupid in the eyes of an author, and he would simply belabor Anton Chekhov with a hail of questions which had never entered his head until that moment.

Anton Chekhov would listen attentively to the dreary, incoherent speech; now and again a smile came into his sad eyes, a little wrinkle appeared on his forehead, and then, in his soft, lusterless voice, he began to speak simple, clear, homely words, words which somehow or other immediately made his questioner simple: the teacher stopped trying to be clever, and therefore immediately became more clever and interesting. . . .

I remember one teacher, a tall, thin man with a yellow, hungry face and a long, hooked nose which drooped gloomily towards his chin. He sat opposite Anton Chekhov and, looking fixedly into Chekhov's face with his black eyes, said in a melancholy bass voice:

"From such impressions of existence within the space of the tutorial session there comes a psychical conglomeration which crushes every possibility of an objective attitude towards the surrounding universe. Of course, the universe is nothing but our presentation of it. . . ."

And he rushed headlong into philosophy, and he moved over its surface like a drunkard skating on ice.

"Tell me," Chekhov put in quietly and kindly, "who is that teacher in your district who beats the children?"

The teacher sprang from his chair and waved his arms indignantly: "Whom do you mean? Me? Never! Beating?"

He snorted with indignation.

"Don't get excited," Anton Chekhov went on, smiling reassuringly; "I'm not speaking of you. But I remember—I read it in the newspapers— there is some one in your district who beats the children."

The teacher sat down, wiped his perspiring face, and, with a sigh of relief, said in his deep bass:—

"It's true . . . there was such a case . . . it was Makarov. You know, it's not surprising. It's cruel, but explicable. He's married . . . has four children . . . his wife is ill . . . himself consumptive . . . his salary is 20 roubles, the school like a cellar, and the teacher has but a single room—under such circumstances you will give a thrashing to an angel of God for no fault . . . and the children—they're far from angels, believe me."

And the man, who had just been mercilessly belaboring Chekhov with his store of clever words, suddenly, ominously wagging his hooked nose, began to speak simple, weighty, clear-cut words, which illuminated, like a fire, the terrible, accursed truth about the life of the Russian village.

When he said good-bye to his host, the teacher took Chekhov's small, dry hand with its thin fingers in both his own, and, shaking it, said:—

"I came to you as though I were going to the authorities, in fear and trembling . . . I puffed myself out like a turkey-cock . . . I wanted to show you that I was no ordinary mortal. . . . And now I'm leaving you as a nice, close friend who understands everything. . . . It's a great thing—to understand everything! Thank you! I'm taking away with me a pleasant thought: big men are simpler and more understandable . . . and nearer in soul to us fellow men than all those wretches among whom we live. . . . Good-bye; I will never forget you."

His nose quivered, his lips twisted into a good-natured smile, and he added suddenly:

"To tell the truth, scoundrels too are unhappy—the devil take them."

When he went out, Chekhov followed him with a glance, smiled, and said:

"He's a nice fellow. . . . He won't be a teacher long."

"Why?"

"They will run him down—whip him off."

He thought for a bit, and added quietly:

"In Russia an honest man is rather like the chimney-sweep with whom nurses frighten children."

I think that in Anton Chekhov's presence every one involuntarily felt in himself a desire to be simpler, more truthful, more one's self; I often saw how people cast off the motley finery of bookish phrases, smart words, and all the other cheap tricks with which a Russian, wishing to figure as a European, adorns himself, like a savage with shells and fish's teeth. Anton Chekhov disliked fish's teeth and cock's feathers; anything "brilliant" or foreign, assumed by a man to make himself look bigger, disturbed him; I noticed that, whenever he saw any one dressed up in this way, he had a desire to free him from all that oppressive, useless tinsel and to find underneath the genuine face and living soul of the person. All his life Chekhov lived on his own soul; he was always himself, inwardly free, and he never troubled about what some people expected and others—coarser people—demanded of Anton Chekhov. He did not like conversations about deep questions, conversations with which our dear Russians so assiduously comfort themselves, forgetting that it is ridiculous, and not at all amusing, to argue about velvet costumes in the future when in the present one has not even a decent pair of trousers.

Beautifully simple himself, he loved everything simple, genuine, sincere, and he had a peculiar way of making other people simple.

Once, I remember, three luxuriously dressed ladies came to see him; they filled his room with the rustle of silk skirts and the smell of strong scent; they sat down politely opposite their host, pretended that they were interested in politics, and began "putting questions":—

Anton Pavlovitch, what do you think? How will the war end?"

Anton Pavlovitch coughed, thought for a while, and then gently, in a serious and kindly voice, replied:

"Probably in peace."

"Well, yes . . . certainly. But who will win? The Greeks or the Turks?"

"It seems to me that those will win who are the stronger."

"And who, do you think, are the stronger?" all the ladies asked together.

"Those who are the better fed and the better educated."

"Ah, how clever," one of them exclaimed.

"And whom do you like best?" another asked.

Anton Pavlovitch looked at her kindly, and answered with a meek smile:

"I love candied fruits . . . don't you?"

"Very much," the lady exclaimed gayly.

"Especially Abrikossov's," the second agreed solidly. And the third, half closing her eyes, added with relish:

"It smells so good."

And all three began to talk with vivacity, revealing, on the subject of candied fruit, great erudition and subtle knowledge. It was obvious that they were happy at not having to strain their minds and pretend to be seriously interested in Turks and Greeks, to whom up to that moment they had not given a thought.

When they left, they merrily promised Anton Pavlovitch:

"We will send you some candied fruit."

"You managed that nicely," I observed when they had gone.

Anton Pavlovitch laughed quietly and said:

"Every one should speak his own language."

On another occasion I found at his house a young and prettyish crown prosecutor. He was standing in front of Chekhov, shaking his curly head, and speaking briskly:

"In your story, 'The Conspirator,' you, Anton Pavlovitch, put before me a very complex case. If I admit in Denis Grigoriev a criminal and conscious intention, then I must, without any reservation, bundle him into prison, in the interests of the community. But he is a savage; he did not realize the criminality of his act. . . . I feel pity for him. But suppose I regard him as a man who acted without understanding, and suppose I yield to my feeling of pity, how can I guarantee the community that Denis will not again unscrew the nut in the sleepers and wreck a train? That's the question. What's to be done?"

He stopped, threw himself back, and fixed an inquiring look on Anton Pavlovitch's face. His uniform was quite new, and the buttons shone as self-confidently and dully on his chest as did the little eyes in the pretty, clean, little face of the youthful enthusiast for justice.

"If I were judge," said Anton Pavlovitch gravely, "I would acquit Denis."

"On what grounds?"

"I would say to him: you, Denis, have not yet ripened into the type of the deliberate criminal; go—and ripen."

The lawyer began to laugh, but instantly again became pompously serious and said:

"No, sir, the question put by you must be answered only in the interests of the community whose life and property I am called upon to protect. Denis is a savage, but he is also a criminal—that is the truth."

"Do you like gramophones?" suddenly asked Anton Pavlovitch in his soft voice.

"O yes, very much. An amazing invention!" the youth answered gayly.

"And I can't stand gramophones," Anton Pavlovitch confessed sadly.

"Why?"

"They speak and sing without feeling. Everything seems like a caricature . . . dead. Do you like photography?"

It appeared that the lawyer was a passionate lover of photography; he began at once to speak of it with enthusiasm, completely uninterested, as Chekhov had subtly and truly noticed, in the gramophone, despite his admiration for that "amazing invention." And again I observed how there looked out of that uniform a living and rather amusing little man, whose feelings towards life were still those of a puppy hunting.

When Anton Pavlovitch had seen him out, he said sternly:

"They are like pimples on the seat of justice—disposing of the fate of people."

And after a short silence:

"Crown prosecutors must be very fond of fishing . . . especially for little fish."

He had the art of revealing everywhere and driving away banality, an art which is only possible to a man who demands much from life and which comes from a keen desire to see men simple, beautiful, harmonious. Banality always found in him a discerning and merciless judge.

Some one told in his presence how the editor of a popular magazine, who was always talking of the necessity of love and pity, had, for no reason at all, insulted a railway guard, and how he usually acted with extreme rudeness towards his inferiors.

"Well," said Anton Pavlovitch with a gloomy smile, "but isn't he an aristocrat, an educated gentleman? He studied at the seminary. His father wore bast shoes, and he wears patent-leather boots."

And in his tone there was something which at once made the "aristocrat" trivial and ridiculous.

"He's a very gifted man," he said of a certain journalist. "He always writes so nobly, humanely, ... lemonadely. Calls his wife a fool in public . . . the servants' rooms are damp and the maids constantly get rheumatics."

"Don't you like N. N., Anton Pavlovitch?"

"Yes, I do—very much. He's a pleasant fellow," Anton Pavlovitch agrees, coughing. "He knows everything. . . reads a lot . . . he hasn't returned three of my books . . . he's absent-minded. To-day he will tell you that you're a wonderful fellow, and to-morrow he will tell somebody else that you cheat your servants, and that you have stolen from your mistress's husband his silk socks . . . the black ones with the blue stripes."

Some one in his presence complained of the heaviness and tediousness of the "serious" sections in thick monthly magazines.

"But you mustn't read those articles," said Anton Pavlovitch. "They are friends' literature—written for friends. They are written by Messrs. Red, Black, and White. One writes an article; the other replies to it; and the third reconciles the contradictions of the other two. It is like playing whist with a dummy. Yet none of them asks himself what good it is to the reader."

Once a plump, healthy, handsome, well-dressed lady came to him and began to speak *à la Chekhov*:—

"Life is so boring, Anton Pavlovitch. Everything is so gray: people, the sea, even the flowers seem to me gray. . . . And I have no desires . . . my soul is in pain . . . it is like a disease."

"It is a disease," said Anton Pavlovitch with conviction, "it is a disease; in Latin it is called *morbus imitatis*."

Fortunately the lady did not seem to know Latin, or, perhaps, she pretended not to know it.

"Critics are like horse-flies which prevent the horse from plowing," he said, smiling his wise smile. "The horse works, all its muscles drawn tight like the strings on a doublebass, and a fly settles on his flanks and tickles and buzzes . . . he has to twitch his skin and swish his tail. And what does the fly buzz about? It scarcely knows itself; simply because it is restless and wants to proclaim: 'Look, I too am living on the earth. See, I can buzz, too, buzz about anything.' For twenty-five years I have read criticisms of my stories, and I don't remember a single remark of any value or one word of valuable advice. Only once Skabitchevsky wrote something which made an impression on me . . . he said I would die in a ditch, drunk."

Nearly always there was an ironical smile in his gray eyes, but at times they became cold, sharp, hard; at such times a harder tone sounded in his soft, sincere voice, and then it appeared that this modest, gentle man, when he found it necessary, could rouse himself vigorously against a hostile force and would not yield.

But sometimes, I thought, there was in his attitude towards people a feeling of hopelessness, almost of cold, resigned despair.

"A Russian is a strange creature," he said once. "He is like a sieve; nothing remains in him. In his youth he fills himself greedily with anything which he comes across, and after thirty years nothing remains but a kind of gray rubbish. . . . In order to live well and humanly one must work—work with love and with faith. But we, we can't do it. An architect, having built a couple of decent buildings, sits down to play cards, plays all his life, or else is to be found somewhere behind the scenes of some theatre. A doctor, if he has a practice, ceases to be interested in science, and reads nothing but *The Medical Journal*, and at forty seriously believes that all diseases have their origin in catarrh. I have never met a single civil servant who had any idea of the meaning of his work: usually he sits in the metropolis or the chief town of the province, and writes papers and sends them off to Zmiev or Smorgon for attention. But that those papers will deprive some one in Zmiev or Smorgon of freedom of movement—of that the civil servant thinks as little as an atheist of the tortures of hell. A lawyer who has made a name by a successful defense ceases to care about justice, and defends only the rights of property, gambles on the Turf, eats oysters, figures as a connoisseur of all the arts. An actor, having taken two or three parts tolerably, no longer troubles to learn his parts, puts on a silk hat, and thinks himself a genius. Russia is a land of insatiable and lazy people: they eat enormously of nice things, drink, like to sleep in the day-time, and snore in their sleep. They marry in order to get their house looked after and keep mistresses in order to be thought well of in society. Their psychology is that of a dog: when they are beaten, they whine shrilly and run into their kennels; when petted, they lie on their backs with their paws in the air and wag their tails."

Pain and cold contempt sounded in these words. But, though contemptuous, he felt pity, and, if in his presence you abused any one, Anton Pavlovitch would immediately defend him.

"Why do you say that? He is an old man . . . he's seventy." Or: "But he's still so young . . . it's only stupidity."

And, when he spoke like that, I never saw a sign of aversion in his face.

When a man is young, banality seems only amusing and unimportant, but little by little it possesses a man; it permeates his brain and blood like poison or asphyxiating fumes; he becomes like an old, rusty signboard: something is painted on it, but what?—You can't make out.

Anton Pavlovitch in his early stories was already able to reveal in the dim sea of banality its tragic humor; one has only to read his "humorous" stories with attention to see what a lot of cruel and disgusting things, behind the humorous words and situations, had been observed by the author with sorrow and were concealed by him.

He was ingenuously shy; he would not say aloud and openly to people: "Now do be more decent"; he hoped in vain that they would themselves see how necessary it was that they should be more decent. He hated everything banal and foul, and he described the abominations of life in the noble language of a poet, with the humorist's gentle smile, and behind the beautiful form of his stories people scarcely noticed the inner meaning, full of bitter reproach.

The dear public, when it reads his "Daughter of Albion," laughs and hardly realizes how abominable is the well-fed squire's mockery of a person who is lonely and strange to every one and everything. In each of his humorous stories I hear the quiet, deep sigh of a pure and human heart, the hopeless sigh of sympathy for men who do not know how to respect human dignity, who submit without any resistance to mere force, live like fish, believe in nothing but the necessity of swallowing every day as much thick soup as possible, and feel nothing but fear that some one, strong and insolent, will give them a hiding.

No one understood as clearly and finely as Anton Chekhov, the tragedy of life's trivialities, no one before him showed men with such merciless truth the terrible and shameful picture of their life in the dim chaos of bourgeois every-day existence.

His enemy was banality; he fought it all his life long; he ridiculed it, drawing it with a pointed and unimpassioned pen, finding the mustiness of banality even where at the first glance everything seemed to be arranged very nicely, comfortably, and even brilliantly—and banality revenged itself upon him by a nasty prank, for it saw that his corpse, the corpse of a poet, was put into a railway truck "For the Conveyance of Oysters."

That dirty green railway truck seems to me precisely the great, triumphant laugh of banality over its tired enemy; and all the "Recollections" in the gutter press are hypocritical sorrow, behind which I feel the cold and smelly breath of banality, secretly rejoicing over the death of its enemy.

Reading Anton Chekhov's stories, one feels oneself in a melancholy day of late autumn, when the air is transparent and the outline of naked trees, narrow houses, grayish people, is sharp. Everything is strange, lonely, motionless, helpless. The horizon, blue and empty, melts into the pale sky and its breath is terribly cold upon the earth which is covered with frozen mud. The author's mind, like the autumn sun, shows up in hard outline the monotonous roads, the crooked streets, the little squalid houses in which tiny, miserable people are stifled by boredom and laziness and fill the houses with an unintelligible, drowsy bustle. Here anxiously, like a gray mouse, scurries "The Darling," the dear, meek woman who loves so slavishly and who can love so much. You can slap her cheek and she won't even dare to utter a sigh aloud, the meek slave. . . . And by her side is Olga of "The Three Sisters": she too loves much, and submits with resignation to the caprices of the dissolute, banal wife of her good-for-nothing brother; the life of her sisters crumbles before her eyes, she weeps and cannot help any one in anything, and she has not within her a single live, strong word of protest against banality.

And here is the lachrymose Ranevskaya and the other owners of "The Cherry Orchard," egotistical like children, with the flabbiness of senility. They missed the right moment for dying; they whine, seeing nothing of what is going on around them, understanding nothing, parasites without the power of again taking root in life. The wretched little student, Trofimov, speaks eloquently of the necessity of working—and does nothing but amuse himself, out of sheer boredom, with stupid mockery of Varya who works ceaselessly for the good of the idlers.

Vershinin dreams of how pleasant life will be in three hundred years, and lives without perceiving that everything around him is falling into ruin before his eyes; Solyony, from boredom and stupidity, is ready to kill the pitiable Baron Tousenbach.

There passes before one a long file of men and women, slaves of their love, of their stupidity and idleness, of their greed for the good things of life; there walk the slaves of the dark fear of life; they straggle anxiously along, filling life with incoherent words about the future, feeling that in the present there is no place for them.

At moments out of the gray mass of them one hears the sound of a shot:

Ivanov or Triepliev has guessed what he ought to do, and has died.

Many of them have nice dreams of how pleasant life will be in two hundred years, but it occurs to none of them to ask themselves who will make life pleasant if we only dream.

In front of that dreary, gray crowd of helpless people there passed a great, wise, and observant man; he looked at all these dreary inhabitants of his country, and, with a sad smile, with a tone of gentle but deep reproach, with anguish in his face and in his heart, in a beautiful and sincere voice, he said to them:

"You live badly, my friends. It is shameful to live like that."

ERIC BENTLEY

Craftsmanship in Uncle Vanya

The Anglo-American theater finds it possible to get along without the services of most of the best playwrights. Æschylus, Lope de Vega, Racine, Molière, Schiller, Strindberg—one could prolong indefinitely the list of great dramatists who are practically unknown in England and America except to scholars. Two cases of popularity in spite of greatness are, of course, Shakespeare and Shaw, who have this in common: that they can be enjoyed without being taken seriously. And then there is Chekhov.

It is easy to make over a play by Shaw or by Shakespeare into a Broadway show. But why is Chekhov preserved from the general oblivion? Why is it that scarcely a year passes without a major Broadway or West End production of a Chekhov play? Chekhov's plays—at least by reputation, which in commercial theater is the important thing—are plotless, monotonous, drab, and intellectual: find the opposites of these four adjectives and you have a recipe for a smash hit.

Those who are responsible for productions of Chekhov in London and New York know the commodity theater. Some of them are conscious rebels against the whole system. Others are simply genuine artists who, if not altogether consciously, are afflicted with guilt; to do Chekhov is for them a gesture of rebellion or atonement, as to do Shakespeare or Shaw is not. It is as if the theater remembers Chekhov when it remembers its conscience.

From *In Search of Theater*. © 1953 by Eric Bentley.

The rebels of the theater know their Chekhov and love him; it is another question whether they understand him. Very few people seem to have given his work the careful examination it requires. Handsome tributes have been paid Chekhov by Stanislavsky, Nemirovich-Danchenko, and Gorky, among his countrymen; and since being taken up by Middleton Murry's circle thirty years ago, he has enjoyed a high literary reputation in England and America. The little book by William Gerhardi and the notes and *obiter dicta* of such critics as Stark Young and Francis Fergusson are, however, too fragmentary and impressionistic to constitute a critical appraisal. They have helped to establish more accurate general ideas about Chekhov's art. They have not inquired too rigorously in what that art consists.

I am prompted to start such an enquiry by the Old Vic's engrossing presentation of *Uncle Vanya* in New York. Although *Vanya* is the least well known of Chekhov's four dramatic masterpieces, it is—I find—a good play to start a critical exploration with because it exists in two versions—one mature Chekhov, the other an immature draft. To read both is to discover the direction and intention of Chekhov's development. It is also to learn something about the art of rewriting when not practiced by mere play-doctors. There is a lesson here for playwrights. For we are losing the conception of the writer as an artist who by quiet discipline steadily develops. In the twentieth century a writer becomes an event with his first best-seller, or smash hit, and then spends the rest of his life repeating the performance—or vainly trying to.

Chekhov's earlier version—*The Wood Demon*—is what Hollywood would call a comedy drama: that is, a farce spiced with melodrama. It tells the story of three couples: a vain Professor and his young second wife, Yelena; Astrov, the local doctor, who is nicknamed the Wood Demon because of his passion for forestry, and Sonya, the Professor's daughter by his first marriage; finally, a young man and woman named Fyodor and Julia. The action consists to a great extent in banal comedic crisscrossing of erotic interests. Julia's brother seems for a time to be after Sonya. Yelena is coveted rather casually by Fyodor and more persistently by Uncle Vanya, the brother of the Professor's first wife. Rival suitors, eternal triangles, theatric adultery! It is not a play to take too seriously. Although in the third act there is a climax when Uncle Vanya shoots himself, Chekhov tries in the last and fourth act to re-establish the mode of light comedy by pairing off all three couples before bringing down the curtain on his happy ending.

Yet even in *The Wood Demon* there is much that is "pure Chekhov." The happy ending does not convince, because Chekhov has created a situation that cannot find so easy an outcome. He has created people who cannot possibly be happy ever after. He has struck so deep a note that the play cannot quite, in its last act, become funny again.

The death of Vanya is melodrama, yet it has poignancy too, and one might feel that, if it should be altered, the changes should be in the direction of realism. The plot centers on property. The estate was the dowry off Vanya's sister, the Professor's first wife. Vanya put ten years' work into paying off the mortgage. The present owner is the daughter of the first marriage, Sonya. The Professor, however, thinks he can safely speak of "our estate" and propose to sell it, so he can live in a Finnish villa on the proceeds. It is the shock of this proposal, coming on top of his discovery that the Professor, in whom he has so long believed is an intellectual fraud—coming on top of his infatuation with Yelena—that drives Vanya to suicide. And if this situation seems already to be asking for realistic treatment, what are we to say to the aftermath? Yelena leaves her husband, but is unable to sustain this "melodramatic" effort. She comes back to him, defeated yet not contrite: "Well, take me, statue of the commander, and go to hell with me in your twenty-six dismal rooms!"

The Wood Demon is a conventional play trying, so to speak, to be something else. In *Uncle Vanya*, rewritten, it succeeds. Perhaps Chekhov began by retouching his ending and was led back and back into his play until he had revised everything but the initial situation. He keeps the starting-point of his fable, but alters the whole outcome. Vanya does not shoot himself; he fires his pistol at the Professor, and misses. Consequently the last act has quite a different point of departure. Yelena does not run away from her husband. He decides to leave, and she goes with him. Astrov, in the later version, does not love Sonya; he and she end in isolation. Vanya is not dead or in the condemned cell; but he is not happy.

To the Broadway script-writer, also concerned with the rewriting of plays (especially if in an early version a likable character shoots himself), these alterations of Chekhov's would presumably seem unaccountable. They would look like a deliberate elimination of the dramatic element. Has not Prince Mirsky told us that Chekhov is an undramatic dramatist? The odd thing is only that he could be so dramatic *before* he rewrote. The matter is worth looking into.

Chekhov's theater, like Ibsen's, is psychological. If Chekhov changed his story, it must be either because he later felt that his old characters would act differently or because he wanted to create more interesting characters. The four people who emerge in the later version as the protagonists are different from their prototypes in *The Wood Demon*, and are differently situated. Although Sonya still loves Astrov, her love is not returned. This fact is one among many that make the later ending Chekhovian: Sonya and Astrov resign themselves to lives of labor without romance. Vanya is not resolute enough for suicide. His discontent takes form as resentment against the author of his misery. And yet, if missing his aim at such close quarters be an accident, it is surely one of those unconsciously willed accidents that Freud wrote of. Vanya is no murderer. His outburst is rightly dismissed as a tantrum by his fellows, none of whom dreams of calling the police. Just as Vanya is the kind of man who does not kill, Yelena is the kind of woman who does not run away from her husband, even temporarily.

In the earlier version the fates of the characters are settled; in the later they are unsettled. In the earlier version they are settled, moreover, not by their own nature or by force of circumstance, but by theatrical convention. In the later, their fate is unsettled because that is Chekhov's view of the truth. Nobody dies. Nobody is paired off. And the general point is clear: life knows no endings, happy or tragic. (Shaw once congratulated Chekhov on the discovery that the tragedy of the Hedda Gablers is, in real life, precisely that they do *not* shoot themselves.) The special satiric point is also familiar: Chekhov's Russians are chronically indecisive people. What is perhaps not so easy to grasp is the effect of a more mature psychology upon dramaturgy. Chekhov has destroyed the climax in his third act and the happy consummation in his fourth. These two alterations alone presuppose a radically different dramatic form.

II

The framework of the new play is the attractive pattern of arrival and departure: the action is what happens in the short space of time between the arrival of the Professor and his wife on their country estate and their departure from it. The unity of the play is discovered by asking the question: what effect has the visit upon the visited—that is, upon Vanya, Sonya, and Astrov? This question as it stands could not be asked of *The Wood Demon*, for in that play the Professor and Yelena do not depart, and Vanya is dead before the end. As to the effect of the Professor's arrival, it is to change and spoil everything. His big moment—the moment when he announces his intention to sell the estate—leads to reversal in Aristotle's sense, the decisive point at which the whole direction of the narrative turns about. This is Uncle Vanya's suicide. Vanya's futile shots, in the later version, are a kind of mock reversal. It cannot even be said that they make the Professor change his mind, for he had begun to change it already—as soon as Vanya protested. Mechanical, classroom analysis would no doubt locate the climax of the play in the shooting. But the climax is an anticlimax. If one of our script-writers went to work on it, his "rewrite" would be *The Wood Demon* all over again, his principle of revision being exactly the opposite of Chekhov's. What Chekhov is after, I think, is

not reversal but recognition—also in Aristotle's sense, "the change from ignorance to knowledge." In Aristotle's sense, but with a Chekhovian application.

In the Greeks, in much French drama, and in Ibsen, recognition means
the discovery of a secret which reveals that things are not what all these years
they have seemed to be. In *Uncle Vanya*, recognition means that what all these
years seemed to be so, though one hesitated to believe it, really is so and will
remain so. This is Vanya's discovery and gradually (in the course of the
ensuing last act) that of the others. Thus Chekhov has created a kind of
recognition which is all his own. In Ibsen the terrible thing is that the surface
of everyday life is a smooth deception. In Chekhov the terrible thing is that
the surface of everyday life is itself a kind of tragedy. In Ibsen the whole
surface of life is suddenly burst by volcanic eruption. In Chekhov the crust is
all too firm; the volcanic energies of men have no chance of emerging. *Uncle
Vanya* opens with a rather rhetorical suggestion that this *might* be so. It ends
with the knowledge that it certainly *is* so, a knowledge shared by all the characters who are capable of knowledge—Astrov, Vanya, Sonya, and Yelena.
This growth from ignorance to knowledge is, perhaps, our cardinal experience of the play (the moment of recognition, or experimental proof, being
Vanya's outburst *before* the shooting).

Aristotle says that the change from ignorance to knowledge produces
"love or hate between the persons destined by the poet for good or bad
fortune." But only in *The Wood Demon*, where there is no real change from
ignorance to knowledge, could the outcome be stated in such round terms.
Nobody's fortune at the end of *Uncle Vanya* is as good or bad as it might be;
nobody is very conclusively loving or hating. Here again Chekhov is avoiding
the black and the white, the tragic and the comic, and is attempting the
halftone, the tragicomic.

If, as has been suggested, the action consists in the effect of the presence
of the Professor and Yelena upon Sonya, Vanya, and Astrov, we naturally ask:
what *was* that effect? To answer this question for the subtlest of the characters—Astrov—is to see far into Chekhov's art. In *The Wood Demon* the effect is
nil. The action has not yet been unified. It lies buried in the chaos of Chekhov's
materials. In *Uncle Vanya*, however, there is a thread of continuity. We are first
told that Astrov is a man with no time for women. We then learn (and there is
no trace of this in *The Wood Demon*) that he is infatuated with Yelena. In *The
Wood Demon*, Sonya gets Astrov in the end. In *Uncle Vanya*, when Astrov gives
up Yelena, he resigns himself to his old role of living without love. The old
routine—in this as in other respects—resumes its sway.

The later version of this part of the story includes two splendid scenes
that were not in *The Wood Demon*, even embryonically. One is the first of the
two climaxes in Act III—when Yelena sounds out Astrov on Sonya's behalf.

Astrov reveals that it is Yelena he loves, and he is kissing her when Vanya enters. The second is Astrov's parting from Yelena in the last act, a scene so subtle that Stanislavsky himself misinterpreted it: he held that Astrov was still madly in love with Yelena and was clutching at her as a dying man clutches at a straw. Chekhov had to point out in a letter that this is not so. What really happens is less histrionic and more Chekhovian. The parting kiss is passionless on Astrov's side. This time it is Yelena who feels a little passion. Not very much, though. For both, the kiss is a tribute to the Might-Have-Been.

Astrov's failure to return Sonya's love is not a result of the Professor's visit; he had failed to return it even before the Professor's arrival. The effect of the visit is to confirm (as part of the general Chekhovian pattern) the fact that what seems to be so *is* so; that what has been will be; that nothing has changed. How much difference has the visit made? It has made the case much sadder. Beforehand Astrov had maintained, and presumably believed, that he was indifferent to women. Afterward we know that it is Sonya in particular to whom he is indifferent. The "wood demon," devoted to the creative and the natural, can love only Yelena the artificial, the sterile, the useless. To Sonya, the good, the competent, the constructive, he is indifferent.

The Professor's visit clarifies Astrov's situation—indeed, his whole nature. True, he had already confessed himself a failure in some of the opening speeches of the play. The uninitiated must certainly find it strange (despite the august precedent of *Antony and Cleopatra*) that the play starts with a summary of the whole disaster. Yet the rest of the play, anything but a gratuitous appendix, is the proof that Astrov, who perhaps could not quite believe himself at the beginning, is right after all. The action of the play is his chance to disprove his own thesis—a chance that he misses, that he was bound to miss, being what he was. What was he, then? In the earlier version he had been known as the Wood Demon or Spirit of the Forest, and in *Uncle Vanya* the long speeches are retained in which he advances his ideal of the natural, the growing, the beautiful. Because he also speaks of great ennobling changes in the future of the race (not unlike those mentioned in the peroration of Trotsky's *Literature and Revolution*), he has been taken to be a prophet of a great political future for Russia in the twentieth century. But this would be wrenching his remarks from their context. Astrov is not to be congratulated on his beautiful dreams; he is to be pitied. His hope that mankind will some day do something good operates as an excuse for doing nothing now. It is an expression of his own futility, and Astrov knows it. Even in the early version he was not really a Wood Demon. That was only the ironical nickname of a crank. In the later version even the nickname has gone, and Astrov is even more of a crank. When Yelena arrives, he leaves his forest to rot.

Clearly they were no real fulfillment of his nature, but an old-maidish hobby, like Persian cats. They were *ersatz*, and as soon as something else seemed to offer itself, Astrov made his futile attempt at seduction. Freud would have enjoyed the revealing quality of his last pathetic proposal that Yelena should give herself to him in the depth of the forest.

The actor, of course, should not make Astrov *too* negative. If one school of opinion romanticizes all Chekhov characters who dream of the future, another, even more vulgar, sees them as weaklings and nothing else. Chekhov followed Ibsen in portraying the average mediocre man—*l'homme moyen sensuel*—without ever following the extreme naturalists in their concern with the utterly downtrodden, the inarticulate, the semihuman. His people are no weaker than ninety-nine out of every hundred members of his audience. That is to say, they are very weak, but there are also elements of protest and revolt in them, traces of will-power, some dim sense of responsibility. If his characters never reach fulfillment, it is not because they were always without potentialities. In fact, Chekhov's sustained point is precisely that these weeping, squirming, suffering creatures *might have been men*. And because Chekhov feels this, there is emotion, movement, tension, interplay, dialectic, in his plays. He never could have written a play like Galsworthy's *Justice*, in which the suffering creature is as much an insect as a man.

The Might-Have-Been is Chekhov's *idée fixe*. His people do not dream only of what could never be, or what could come only after thousands of years; they dream of what their lives actually could have been. They spring from a conviction of human potentiality—which is what separates Chekhov from the real misanthropes of modern literature. Astrov moves us because we can readily feel how fully human he might have been, how he has dwindled, under the influence of "country life," from a thinker to a crank, from a man of feeling to a philanderer. "It is strange somehow," he says to Yelena in the last scene, "we have got to know each other, and all at once for some reason—we shall never meet again. So it is with everything in this world." Such lines might be found in any piece of sentimental theater. But why is it that Chekhov's famous "elegiac note" is, in the full context, deeply moving? Is it not because the sense of death is accompanied with so rich a sense of life and the possible worth of living?

III

Chekhov had a feeling for the unity of the drama, yet his sense of the richness of life kept him clear of formalism. He enriched his dramas in ways that belong to no school and that, at least in their effect, are peculiar to himself.

While others tried to revive poetic drama by putting symbolist verse in the mouths of their characters, or simply by imitating the verse drama of the past, Chekhov found poetry within the world of realism. By this is meant not only that he used symbols. Symbolism of a stagy kind was familiar on the boulevards and still is. The Broadway title *Skylark* is symbolic in exactly the same way as *The Wild Duck* and *The Seagull*. It is rather the use to which Chekhov puts the symbol that is remarkable. We have seen, for instance, what he makes of his "wood demon." This is not merely a matter of Astrov's character. Chekhov's symbols spread themselves, like Ibsen's, over a large territory. They are a path to the imagination and to those deeper passions which in our latter-day drama are seldom worn on the sleeve. Thus if a symbol in Chekhov is explained—in the manner of the *raisonneur*—the explanation blazes like a denunciation. Yelena says:

> As Astrov was just saying, you are all recklessly destroying the forests and soon there will be nothing left on the earth. In the same way you recklessly destroy human beings, and soon, thanks to you, there will be no fidelity, no purity, no capacity for sacrifice left on the earth either! Why is it you can never look at a woman with indifference unless she is yours? That doctor is right: it's because there is a devil of destruction in all of you. You have no mercy on woods or birds or women or one another.

What a paradox: our playwrights who plump for the passions (like O'Neill) are superficial, and Chekhov, who pretends to show us only the surface (who, as I have said, writes the tragedy of the surface), is passionate and deep! No modern playwright has presented elemental passions more truly. Both versions of *Uncle Vanya* are the battleground of two conflicting impulses—the impulse to destroy and the impulse to create. In *The Wood Demon* the conflict is simple: Vanya's destructive passion reaches a logical end in suicide, Astrov's creative passion a logical end in happiness ever after. In *Uncle Vanya* the pattern is complex: Vanya's destructive passion reaches a pseudo-climax in his pistol-shots, and a pseudo-culmination in bitter resignation. Astrov's creative passion has found no outlet. Unsatisfied by his forests, he is fascinated by Yelena. His ending is the same as Vanya's—isolation. The destructive passions do not destroy; the creative passions do not create. Or, rather, both impulses are crushed in the daily routine, crushed by boredom and triviality. Both Vanya and Astrov have been suffering a gradual erosion and will continue to do so. They cry out. "I have not lived, not lived . . . I have ruined and wasted the best years of my life." "I have grown old, I have worked too hard, I have grown vulgar, all my feelings are blunted, and

I believe I am not capable of being fond of anyone." Chekhov's people never quite become wounded animals like the Greek tragic heroes. But through what modern playwright does suffering speak more poignantly?

At a time when Chekhov is valued for his finer shades, it is worth stressing his simplicity and strength, his depth and intensity—provided we remember that these qualities require just as prodigious a technique for their expression, that they depend just as much on details. Look at the first two acts of *Uncle Vanya*. While the later acts differ from *The Wood Demon* in their whole narrative, the first two differ chiefly in their disposition of the material. Act I of *The Wood Demon* is a rather conventional bit of exposition: we get to know the eleven principals and we learn that Vanya is in love with Yelena. In *Uncle Vanya* Chekhov gives himself more elbow-room by cutting down the number of characters: Julia and her brother, Fyodor and his father are eliminated. The act is no longer mere exposition in the naturalistic manner (people meeting and asking questions like "Whom did you write to?" so that the reply can be given: "I wrote to Sonya"). The principle of organization is what one often hears called "musical." (The word *poetic* is surely more accurate, but music is the accepted metaphor.) The evening opens, we might say, with a little overture in which themes from the body of the play are heard. "I may well look old!" It is Astrov speaking. "And life is tedious, stupid, dirty. Life just drags on." The theme of human deterioration is followed by the theme of aspiration: "Those who will live a hundred or two hundred years after us, for whom we are struggling now to beat out a road, will they remember and say a good word for us?" The overture ends; the play begins.

Analyses of the structure of plays seldom fail to tell us where the climax lies, where the exposition is completed, and how the play ends, but they often omit a more obtrusive factor—the *principle of motion*, the way in which a play copes with its medium, with time-sequence. In general, the nineteenth-century drama proceeded upon the principles of boulevard drama (as triumphantly practiced by Scribe). To deal with such a play, terms like *exposition*, *complication* and *denouement* are perfectly adequate because the play is, like most fiction, primarily a pattern of suspense. The "musical" principle of motion, however, does not reflect a preoccupation with suspense. That is why many devotees of popular drama are bored by Chekhov.

Consider even smaller things than the use of overture. Consider the dynamics of the first three lines in *Uncle Vanya*. The scene is one of Chekhov's gardens. Astrov is sitting with the Nurse. She offers him tea. She offers him vodka, but he is not a regular vodka-drinker. "Besides, it's stifling," he says; and there is a lull in the conversation. To the Broadway producer this is a good opening because it gives latecomers a chance to take their seats without missing anything. To Chekhov these little exchanges, these sultry pauses, are the bricks out of which a drama is built.

What makes Chekhov seem most formless is precisely the means by which he achieves strict form—namely, the series of tea-drinkings, arrivals, departures, meals, dances, family gatherings, casual conversations, of which his plays are made. As we have seen, Chekhov works with a highly unified action. He presents it, however, not in the centralized, simplified manner of Sophocles or Ibsen, but obliquely, indirectly, quasi-naturally. The rhythm of the play is leisurely yet broken and, to suspense-lovers, baffling. It would be an exaggeration to say that there is no story and that the succession of scenes marks simply an advance in our knowledge of a situation that does not change. Yet people who cannot interest themselves in this kind of development as well as in straightforward story-telling will not be interested in Chekhov's plays any more than they would be in Henry James's novels. Chekhov does tell a story—the gifts of one of the greatest raconteurs are not in abeyance in his plays—but his method is to let both his narrative and his situation leak out, so to speak, through domestic gatherings, formal and casual. This is his principle of motion.

The method requires two extraordinary gifts: the mastery of "petty" realistic material and the ability to go beyond sheer *Sachlichkeit*—materiality, factuality—to imagination and thought. (Galsworthy, for example, seems to have possessed neither of these gifts—certainly not the second.) Now, the whole Stanislavsky school of acting and directing is testimony that Chekhov was successfully *sachlich*—that is, not only accurate, but significantly precise, concrete, ironic (like Jane Austen). The art by which a special importance is imparted to everyday objects is familiar enough in fiction; on the stage, Chekhov is one of its few masters. On the stage, moreover, the *Sachlichkeit* may more often consist in a piece of business—I shall never forget Astrov, as played by Olivier, buttoning his coat—than in a piece of furniture. Chekhov was so far from being the average novelist-turned-dramatist that he used the peculiarly theatrical *Sachlichkeit* with the skill of a veteran of the footlights. The first entrance of Vanya, for instance, is achieved this way (compare it with the entrance of the matinee idol in a boulevard comedy):

> VANYA (comes out of the house; he has had a nap after lunch and looks rumpled; he sits down on the gardenseat and straightens his fashionable tie): *Yes.* . . . (Pause.) *Yes.* . . .

(Those who are used to the long novelistic stage-directions of Shaw and O'Neill should remember that Chekhov, like Ibsen, added stage-directions only here and there. But the few that do exist show an absolute mastery.)

How did Chekhov transcend mere *Sachlichkeit* and achieve a drama of imagination and thought? Chiefly, I think, by combining the most minute attention to realistic detail with a rigorous sense of form. He diverges widely from all the Western realists—though not so widely from his Russian predecessors such as Turgenev, whose *Month in the Country* could be palmed off as a Chekhov play on more discerning people than most drama critics—and his divergences are often in the preservation of elements of style and stylization, which naturalism prided itself it had discarded. Most obvious among these is the soliloquy. Chekhov does not let his people confide in the audience, but he does use the kind of soliloquy in which the character thinks out loud; and where there is no traditional device for achieving a certain kind of beginning or ending, he constructs for himself a set piece that will do his job. In *Uncle Vanya*, if there may be said to be an overture, played by Astrov, there may also be said to be a finale, played by Sonya. For evidence of Chekhov's theatrical talents one should notice the visual and auditory components of this final minute of the play. We have just heard the bells jingling as the Professor and his wife drive off, leaving the others to their desolation. "Waffles"—one of the neighbors—is softly tuning his guitar. Vanya's mother is reading. Vanya "passes his hand over" Sonya's hair:

> SONYA: *We must go on living!* (Pause.) *We shall go on living, Uncle Vanya! We shall live through a long, long chain of days and weary evenings; we shall patiently bear the trials that fate sends us; we shall work for others, both now and in our old age, and have no rest; and when our time comes we shall die without a murmur, and there beyond the grave we shall say that we have suffered, that we have wept, that our life has been bitter to us, and God will have pity on us, and you and I, uncle, dear uncle, shall see a life that is bright, lovely, beautiful. We shall rejoice and look back at these troubles of ours with tenderness, with a smile—and we shall have rest. I have faith, uncle, fervent, passionate faith.* (Slips on her knees before him and lays her head on his hands; in a weary voice) *We shall rest!* ("Waffles" softly plays on the guitar.) *We shall rest! We shall hear the angels; we shall see all heaven lit with radiance, we shall see all earthly evil, all our sufferings, drowned in mercy, which will fill the whole world, and our life will be peaceful, gentle, sweet like a caress. I have faith, I have faith.* (Wipes away his tears with her handkerchief.) *Poor, poor Uncle Vanya, you are crying.* (Through her tears) *You have had no joy in your life, but wait, Uncle Vanya, wait. We shall rest.* (Puts her arms around him.) *We shall rest!* (The watchman taps; Waffles plays softly; Vanya's mother

> makes notes on the margin of her pamphlet; the Nurse knits
> her stocking.) *We shall rest!* (Curtain drops slowly.)

The silence, the music, the watchman's tapping, the postures, the gestures, the prose with its rhythmic repetitions and melancholy import—these compose an image, if a stage picture with its words and music may be called an image, such as the drama has seldom known since Shakespeare. True, in our time the background music of movies and the noises-off in radio drama have made us see the dangers in this sort of theatricality. But Chekhov knew without these awful examples where to draw the line.

A weakness of much realistic literature is that it deals with inarticulate people. The novelist can of course supply in narrative and description what his milieu lacks in conversation, but the dramatist has no recourse—except to the extent that drama is expressed not in words but in action. Chekhov's realistic milieu, however, is, like Ibsen's, bourgeois and "intellectual"; a wide range of conversational styles and topics is therefore plausible enough. But Chekhov is not too pedantic about plausibility. He not only exploits the real explicitness and complication and abstractness of bourgeois talk; he introduces, or re-introduces, a couple of special conventions.

The first is the tirade or long, oratorically composed speech. Chekhov's realistic plays—unlike Ibsen's—have their purple patches. On the assumption that a stage character may be much more self-conscious and aware than his counterpart in real life, Chekhov lets his people talk much more freely than any other modern realist except Shaw. They talk on all subjects from book-keeping to metaphysics. Not always listening to what the other man is saying, they talk about themselves and address the whole world. They make what might be called self-explaining soliloquies in the manner of Richard III—except for the fact that other people are present and waiting, very likely, to make soliloquies of their own.

This is the origin of the second Chekhovian convention: each character speaks his mind without reference to the others. This device is perhaps Chekhov's most notorious idea. It has been used more crudely by Odets and Saroyan; and it has usually been interpreted in what is indeed its primary function: to express the isolation of people from one another. However, the dramaturgic utility of the idea is equally evident: it brings the fates of individuals before the audience with a minimum of fuss.

In Chekhov, as in every successful artist, each device functions both technically and humanly, serves a purpose both as form and as content. The form of the tirade, which Chekhov reintroduces, is one of the chief means to an extension of content; and the extension of content is one of the chief means by which Chekhov escapes from stolid naturalism into the broader realities that only imagination can uncover. Chekhov's people are immersed in facts, buried in circumstances, not to say in trivialities, yet—and this is what differentiates them from most dramatic characters—aware of the realm of ideas and imagination. His drama bred a school of acting which gives more attention to exact detail than any other school in history; it might also have bred a school of dramaturgy which could handle the largest and most general problems. Chekhov was a master of the particular and the general—which is another sign of the richness and balance of his mind.

IV

Obviously Chekhov is not a problem playwright in the vulgar sense. (Neither is Ibsen; neither is Shaw. Who is?) Nor is his drama *about* ideas. He would undoubtedly have agreed with Henry Becque: "The serious thing about drama is not the ideas. It is the absorption of the ideas by the characters, the dramatic or comic force that the characters give to the ideas." It is not so much the force Chekhov gives to any particular ideas as the picture he gives of the role of ideas in the lives of men of ideas—a point particularly relevant to *Uncle Vanya*. If Vanya might be called the active center of the play (in that he precipitates the crisis), there is also a passive center, a character whose mere existence gives direction to the action as a whole.

This is Professor Serebryakov. Although this character is not so satisfactory a creation as the professor in Chekhov's tale *A Tiresome Story*, and though Chekhov does too little to escape the cliché stage professor, the very crudeness of the characterization has dramatic point. Serebryakov is a simple case placed as such in contrast to Vanya and Astrov. His devotion to ideas is no more than a gesture of unearned superiority, and so he has become a valetudinarian whose wife truly says: "You talk of your age as though we were all responsible for it." Around this familiar and, after all, common phenomenon are grouped the others, each of whom has a different relation to the world of culture and learning. The Professor is the middle of the design; characters of developed awareness are, so to say, above him; those of undeveloped awareness below him. Above him are Vanya and Astrov, Yelena and Sonya—the men aware to a great extent through their superior intellect, the women through their finer feeling. Below him are three minor characters—Waffles, Vanya's mother, and the Nurse.

The Nurse, who is not to be found in *The Wood Demon*, stands for life without intellectuality or education. She sits knitting, and the fine talk passes her by. She stands for the monotony of country life, a monotony that she interprets as beneficent order. One of the many significant cross-references in the play is Vanya's remark at the beginning that the Professor's arrival has upset the household routine and the Nurse's remark at the end that now the meals will be on time again and all will be well.

Vanya's mother stands on the first rung of the intellectual ladder. She is an enthusiast for certain ideas, and especially for reading about them, but she understands very little. Less intelligent, less sensitive than Vanya, she has never seen through the Professor. Her whole character is in this exchange with her son:

> MOTHER: . . . *he has sent his new pamphlet.*
> VANYA: *Interesting?*
> MOTHER: *Interesting but rather queer. He is attacking what he himself maintained seven years ago. It's awful.*
> VANYA: *There's nothing awful in that. Drink your tea, maman.*
> MOTHER: *I want to talk.*
> VANYA: *We have been talking and talking for fifty years and reading pamphlets. It's about time to leave off.*
> MOTHER: *You don't like listening when I speak; I don't know why. Forgive my saying so, Jean, but you have so changed in the course of the last year that I hardly know you. You used to be a man of definite convictions, brilliant personality. . . .*

On a slightly higher plane than the tract-ridden Mother is the friend of the family, Waffles. If Vanya is the ruin of a man of principle, Waffles is the parody of one. Listen to his account of himself (it is one of Chekhov's characteristic thumbnail autobiographies):

> My wife ran away from me with the man she loved the day after our wedding on the ground of my unprepossessing appearance. But I have never been false to my vows. I love her to this day and am faithful to her. I help her as far as I can, and I gave her all I had for the education of her children by the man she loved. I have lost my happiness, but I still have my pride left. And she? Her youth is over, her beauty, in accordance with the laws of nature, has faded, the man she loved is dead. . . . What has she left?

Just how Waffles is able to keep his equilibrium and avoid the agony that the four principals endure is clear enough. His "pride" is a form of stupidity. For him, as for the Professor, books and ideas are not a window through which he sees the world so much as obstacles that prevent him seeing anything but themselves. The Professor's response to the crisis is a magnanimity that rings as false as Waffles's pride:

> Let bygones be bygones. After what has happened. I have gone through such a lot and thought over so many things in these few hours, I believe I could write a whole treatise on the art of living. . . .

Waffles also finds reflections of life more interesting than life itself. In *The Wood Demon* (where his character is more crudely drawn), having helped Yelena to run away, he shouts:

> If I lived in an intellectual center, they could draw a caricature of me for a magazine, with a very funny satirical inscription.

And a little later:

> Your Excellency, it is I who carried off your wife, as once upon a time a certain Paris carried off the fair Helen. I! Although there are no pockmarked Parises, yet there are more things in heaven and earth, Horatio, than are dreamt of in your philosophy!

In the more finely controlled *Uncle Vanya* this side of Waffles is slyly indicated in his attitude to the shooting:

> NURSE: *Look at the quarreling and shooting this morning—shameful!*
> WAFFLES: *Yes, a subject worthy of the brush of Aivazovsky.*

Aside from this special treatment of the modern intellectual and semi-intellectual, aside from explicit mention of various ideas and philosophies, Chekhov is writing "drama of ideas" only in the sense that Sophocles and Shakespeare and Ibsen were—that is to say, his plays are developed thematically. As one can analyze certain Shakespeare plays in terms of the chief concepts employed in them—such as Nature and Time—so one might analyze a Chekhov play in terms of certain large antitheses, such as (the list is compiled from *Uncle Vanya*) love and hate, feeling and apathy, heroism and lethargy, innocence and sophistication, reality and illusion, freedom and captivity, use and waste, culture and nature, youth and age, life and death. If one were to take up a couple of Chekhov's key concepts and trace his use of them through a whole play, one would find that he is a more substantial artist than even his admirers think.

Happiness and work, for instance. They are not exactly antitheses, but in *Uncle Vanya* they are found in by no means harmonious association. The outsider's view of Chekhov is of course that he is "negative" because he portrayed a life without happiness. The amateur's view is that he is "positive" because he preached work as a remedy for boredom. Both views need serious qualification. The word *work* shifts its tone and implication a good deal within the one play *Uncle Vanya*. True, it sometimes looks like the antidote to all the idleness and futility. On the other hand, the play opens with Astrov's just complaint that he is worked to death. Work has been an obsession, and is still one, for the Professor, whose parting word is: "Permit an old man to add one observation to his farewell message: you must work, my friends! you must work!" Vanya and Sonya obey him—but only to stave off desperation. "My heart is too heavy," says Vanya. "I must make haste and occupy myself with something. . . . Work! Work!" To Sonya, work is the noblest mode of self-destruction, a fact that was rather more than clear in *The Wood Demon*:

ASTROV: *Are you happy?*
SONYA: *This is not the time, Nikhail Lvovich, to think of happiness.*
ASTROV: *What else is there to think of?*
SONYA: *Our sorrow came only because we thought too much of happiness. . . .*
ASTROV : *So!* (Pause.)
SONYA: *There's no evil without some good in it. Sorrow has taught me this—that one must forget one's own happiness and think only of the happiness of others. One's whole life should consist of sacrifices. . . .*
ASTROV: *Yes . . .* (after a pause). *Uncle Vanya shot himself, and his mother goes on searching for contradictions in her pamphlets. A great misfortune befell you and you're pampering your self-love, you are trying to distort your life and you think this is a sacrifice. . . . No one has a heart. . . .*

In the less explicit *Uncle Vanya* this passage does not appear. What we do have is Sonya's beautiful lyric speech that ends the play. In the thrill of the words perhaps both reader and playgoer overlook just what she says—namely, that the afterlife will so fully make up for this one that we should learn not to take our earthly troubles too seriously. This is not Chekhov speaking. It is an overwrought girl comforting herself with an idea. In *The Wood Demon* Astrov was the author's mouthpiece when he replied to Sonya: "You are trying to distort your life and you think this is a sacrifice." The mature Chekhov has no direct mouthpieces. But the whole passage, the whole play, enforces the meaning: work for these people is not a means to happiness, but a drug that will help them to forget. Happiness they will never know. Astrov's yearnings are not a radical's vision of the future any more than the Professor's doctrine of work is a demand for a workers' state. They are both the daydreams of men who Might Have Been.

V

So much for *The Wood Demon* and *Uncle Vanya*. Chekhov wrote five other full-length plays. Three—*Ivanov, That Worthless Fellow Platonov*, and *The Wood Demon*—were written in his late twenties, and are experimental in the sense that he was still groping toward his own peculiar style. Two plays—*The Seagull* and *Uncle Vanya*—were written in his middle thirties; the last two plays—*The Three Sisters* and *The Cherry Orchard*—when he was about forty.

Chekhov's development as a playwright is quite different from that of Ibsen, Strindberg, or any of the other first-rate moderns. While they pushed tempestuously forward, transforming old modes and inventing new ones, perpetually changing their approach, endlessly inventing new forms, Chekhov moved quietly, slowly, and along one straight road. He used only one full-length structure: the four-act drama; and one set of materials: the rural middle class. For all that, the line that stretches from *Ivanov* (1887–9) to *The Cherry Orchard* (1903) is of great interest.

The development is from farce and melodrama to the mature Chekhovian *drame*. The three early plays are violent and a little pretentious. Each presents a protagonist (there is no protagonist in the four subsequent plays) who is a modern variant upon a great type or symbol. Ivanov is referred to as a Hamlet, Platonov as a Don Juan, Astrov as a Wood Demon. In each case it is a "Russian" variant that Chekhov shows—Chekhov's "Russians" like Ibsen's "Norwegian" Peer Gynt and Shaw's "Englishman" representing modern men in general. Those who find Chekhov's plays static should read the three early pieces: they are the proof that, if the later Chekhov eschewed certain kinds of action, it was not for lack of dramatic sense in the most popular meaning of the term. Chekhov was born a melo-dramatist and farceur; only by discipline and development did he become the kind of playwright the world thinks it knows him to be. Not that the later plays are without farcical and melodramatic elements; only a great mimic and caricaturist could have created Waffles and Gaev. As for melodrama, the pistol continues to go off (all but the last of the seven plays have a murder or suicide as climax or pseudo-climax), but the noise is taken further off-stage, literally and figuratively, until in *The Three Sisters* it is "the dim sound of a far-away shot." And *The Cherry Orchard*, the farthest refinement of

Chekhov's method, culminates not with the sharp report of a pistol, but with the dull, precise thud of an ax.

These are a few isolated facts, and one might find a hundred others to demonstrate that Chekhov's plays retain a relationship to the cruder forms. If, as Jacques Barzun has argued, there is a Balzac in Henry James, there is a Sardou in Chekhov. Farce and melodrama are not eliminated, but subordinated to a higher art, and have their part in the dialectic of the whole. As melodrama, *The Seagull*, with its tale of the ruined heroine, the glamorous popular novelist, the despairing artist hero, might have appealed to Verdi or Puccini. Even the story of *The Cherry Orchard* (the elegant lady running off to Paris and being abandoned by the object of her grand passion) hardly suggests singularity, highbrowism, or rarefaction.

In the later plays life is seen in softer colors; Chekhov is no longer eager to be the author of a Russian *Hamlet* or *Don Juan*. The homely Uncle Vanya succeeds on the title page the oversuggestive Wood Demon, and Chekhov forgoes the melodrama of a forest fire. Even more revealing; over-explicit themes are deleted. Only in *The Wood Demon* is the career of the Professor filled in with excessive detail (Heidelberg and all) or Astrov denounced as a socialist. Only in the early version does Vanya's mother add to her remark that a certain writer now makes his living by attacking his own former views: "It is very, very typical of our time. Never have people betrayed their convictions with such levity as they do now." Chekhov deletes Vanya's open allusion to the "cursed poisonous irony" of the sophisticated mind. He keeps the substance of Yelena's declaration that "the world perishes not because of murderers and thieves, but from hidden hatred, from hostility among good people, from all those petty squabbles," and deletes the end of the sentence: ". . . unseen by those who call our house a haven of intellectuals." He does not have Yelena explain herself with the remark: "I am an episodic character, mine is a canary's happiness, a woman's happiness." (In both versions Yelena has earlier described herself as an "episodic character." Only in *The Wood Demon* does she repeat the description. In *The Wood Demon* the canary image also receives histrionic reiteration. In *Uncle Vanya* it is not used at all.)

Chekhov does not tone things down because he is afraid of giving himself away. He is not prim or precious. Restraint is for him as positive an idea as temperance was for the Greeks. In Chekhov the toned-down picture—as I hope the example of *Uncle Vanya* indicates—surpasses the hectic, color scheme of melodrama, not only in documentary truth, but also in the deeper truth of poetic vision. And the truth of Chekhov's colors has much to do with the delicacy of his forms. Chekhov once wrote in a letter: "When a man spends the least possible number of movements over some definite action, that is grace"; and one of his critics speaks of a "'trigger' process, the release of enormous forces by some tiny movement." The Chekhovian form as we find it in the final version of *Uncle Vanya* grew from a profound sense of what might be called the *economy* of art.

We have seen how, while this form does not by any means eliminate narrative and suspense, it reintroduces another equally respectable principle of motion—the progress from ignorance to knowledge. Each scene is another stage in our discovery of Chekhov's people and Chekhov's situation; also in their discovering of themselves and their situation (in so far as they are capable of doing so). The apparent casualness of the encounters and discussions on the stage is Chekhov linking himself to "the least possible number of movements." But as there is a "definite action," as "large forces have been brought into play," we are not cheated of drama. The "trigger effect" is as dramatic in its way as the "buried secret" pattern of Sophocles and Ibsen. Of course, there will be people who see the tininess of the movements and do not notice the enormousness of the forces released—who see the trigger-finger move and do not hear the shot. To them, Chekhov remains a mere manufacturer of atmosphere, a mere contriver of nuance. To others he seems a master of dramatic form unsurpassed in modern times.

(1946)

RAYMOND WILLIAMS

Anton Chekhov

I regard the stage of today as mere routine and prejudice. When the curtain goes up and the gifted beings, the high priests of the sacred art, appear by electric light, in a room with three sides to it, representing how people eat, drink, love, walk, and wear their jackets; when they strive to squeeze out a moral from the flat vulgar pictures and the flat vulgar phrases, a little tiny moral, easy to comprehend and handy for home consumption; when in a thousand variations they offer me always the same thing over and over again—then I take to my heels and run, as Maupassant ran from the Eiffel Tower, which crushed his brain by its overwhelming vulgarity. . . . We must have new formulas. That's what we want. And if there are none, then it's better to have nothing at all.

This striking indictment of the naturalist theatre, an indictment which in seventy years has lost none of its force, is not, one had better begin by emphasizing, Chekhov's own. It is a speech which he gives to the young writer Constantine Treplef in *The Seagull*. Chekhov perhaps felt very much in this way (although from external evidence his literary position would seem to be more represented in *The Seagull* by Trigorin than by Treplef), but I do not wish to play the dangerous and tiresome game of identifications. The

From *Drama: From Ibsen to Brecht*. © 1968 by Raymond Williams.

outburst, which has a characteristic late nineteenth-century ring, is better worth quoting as a first step in the analysis of some of Chekhov's plays, and as a preface to some remarks on the relation of the naturalist drama to fiction, and on the "symbolism" which naturalist dramatists have developed.

"Ibsen, you know," Chekhov wrote to A. S. Vishnevsky, "is my favourite author". And this affiliation is a point which the critic can no longer doubt. It is true that in England the public projections of Ibsen and Chekhov are very dissimilar. So acute an Ibsenite as William Archer could see nothing in *The Cherry Orchard* but empty and formless time-wasting. The devotees of Chekhov in the theatres of England, on the other hand, acclaim his work as "really lifelike and free from any tiresome moralizing". Taken over, as he has been, by a sentimental sect, he has even been welcomed, astonishingly, as "naturalism without politics". In this connection, one might hazard a supplementary remark to the sentence quoted from Chekhov's letter: "*The Wild Duck*, you know, is my favourite play"; and imagine Chekhov saying, as Ibsen said of *The Wild Duck*:

> The characters, I hope, will find good and kind friends . . .
> not least among the player-folk, to whom they all, without excep-
> tion, offer problems worth the solving.

For the buttress of Chekhov's popularity in England has been his popularity with that kind of actor and atmosphere, with "the high priests of the sacred art".

In Ibsen's *The Wild Duck* the crucial point for an evaluation of the play is a study of the function of the title-symbol. The same is true of *The Seagull*, where the "symbol", indeed, has passed even beyond the confines of the work to become the emblem of a new movement in the theatre. Chekhov introduces the seagull in the second act, at a point where Treplef's play has failed, and where his beloved Nina is about to pass from his influence to that of the more famous Trigorin:

> [*Enter* TREPLEF *hatless, with a gun and a dead seagull.*]
> TREPLEF: Are you alone?
> NINA: Yes.
> [TREPLEF *lays the bird at her feet.*]
> NINA: What does that mean?
> TREPLEF: I have been brute enough to shoot this seagull. I lay
>   it at your feet.
> [*She takes up the seagull and looks at it.*]
> TREPLEF: I shall soon kill myself in the same way. . . .

NINA: You have grown nervous and irritable lately. You express yourself incomprehensibly in what seem to be symbols. This seagull seems to be another symbol, but I'm afraid I don't understand. I am too simple to understand you.

It is an incapacity—this failure to understand the symbol—which, it becomes clear, the author does not intend the audience to share. Trigorin makes the next point:

A subject for a short story. A girl—like yourself, say—lives from her childhood on the shores of a lake. She loves the lake like a seagull, and is happy and free like a seagull. But a man comes along by chance and sees her and ruins her, like this seagull, just to amuse himself.

Since this is exactly what Trigorin is going to do to Nina—we are often reminded of this prophecy—the point will doubtless be regarded as subtle. It is a subtlety which stops perhaps a little short of the diabolic—at the deadly.

When Nina has been seduced and abandoned by Trigorin she writes regularly to Treplef:

TREPLEF: Her imagination was a little disordered. She signed herself "Seagull". In Pushkin's "Rusalka" the miller says he is a raven, so she said in her letters that she was a seagull.

And when Trigorin comes on a visit:

SHAMRAYEF: We've still got that thing of yours, Boris.
TRIGORIN: What thing?
SHAMRAYEF: Constantine shot a seagull one day, and you asked me to have it stuffed for you.
TRIGORIN: Did I? I don't remember.

Immediately afterwards Nina returns to see Treplef:

NINA: . . . I am a seagull . . . no, that's wrong. I am an actress. Yes, yes . . . I am a seagull. No, that's wrong. . . . Do you remember you shot a seagull? "A man comes along by chance and sees her, and, just to amuse himself, ruins her. . . . A subject for a short story." . . .

As she leaves, the stuffed seagull is brought in and placed on the table, with Trigorin still murmuring:

I don't remember. No. I don't remember.

At this moment Treplef shoots himself. ("I am still adrift in a welter of images and dreams. . . . I have been brute enough to shoot this seagull")

Now in Ibsen's *The Wild Duck* Hedvig, when told to shoot the wild duck, shoots herself. She identifies herself with the bird. In *The Seagull* the story of Nina's seduction and ruin is similarly identified with the bird. In *The Wild Duck* the bird is also used to define other characters and the whole atmosphere of the play. Similarly, in *The Seagull*, the bird and its death, and its stuffed resurrection, are used to indicate something about Treplef, and the general death of freedom which pervades the play. In this comparison, I am not attempting to prove plagiarism. All authors steal (it is only, it seems, in an industrial society, that this has been reckoned as wrong), and a good trick is always worth playing twice. I am trying, rather, to assess the function and validity of the device. The function is surely clear. The seagull emphasizes, as a visual symbol—a piece of stage property—the action and the atmosphere. It is a device for emotional pressure, for inflating the significance of the related representational incidents. After *Ivanov* (1887) and *The Wood Spirit* (1888), which had both failed, Chekhov, we are told by Princess Nina Andronikova Toumanova,

> for seven long years gave up the stage, although the search for a new dramatic form unceasingly occupied his mind. He meditated upon a realistic play in which he could introduce a symbol as a means of communicating to the audience his deeper and inner thoughts.

This is the frank orthodox description of the form. The symbol, as we now know, came to hand biographically, and Chekhov commented on the seagull which his friend Levitan had shot:

> Another beautiful living creature is gone, but two dumb-bells returned home and had supper.

In the play the symbol is illustrative, and the centre of emotional pressure. I have described it as "inflating the significance of the incidents", which may seem to beg the question. But this very characteristic naturalist device is clearly a substitute for adequate expression of the central experience of the play in language. It is a *hint* at profundity. At a simple illustrative level it is precise. The correspondences, as we have seen, are established explicitly and with great care. At any other level, and at the symbolic level at which it is commonly assumed to operate, it is essentially imprecise; any serious analysis must put it down as mainly a lyrical gesture.

The Seagull is a very good example of the problem with which the talented dramatist, in a predominantly naturalist period, is faced. The substance of his play is settled as a representation of everyday life; and the qualities which Chekhov saw in everyday life were frustration, futility, delusion, apathy. This weary atmosphere, moreover, was characterized by an inability to speak out—an inability of which almost every notable writer in the last seventy years has complained. Major human crises are resolved in silence, or are indicated by the slightest of commonplace gestures.

> Let us [Chekhov wrote to Suvorin] just be as complex and as simple as life is. People dine and at the same time their happiness is made or their lives are broken.

Fidelity to the representational method, therefore, compels the author to show people dining, to depict their conversation in minor commonplaces. But if he is seriously concerned with experience, he cannot leave it at this. Either one or more of his characters may—for some reason—have an ability to speak out, to indicate the underlying pattern. In *The Seagull*, Trigorin, particularly, and Treplef, who are both writers, possess this faculty. Even then the author may not be satisfied; a total pattern has to be indicated, for since the characters are conceived as absolute, as "real persons", their statements may be merely personal and idiosyncratic. Here, in the final attempt to resolve the difficulty, is introduced such a device as that of the seagull.

That is an early play, and Chekhov was to go beyond it. But in one respect, this relation between what is felt and what can be said is decisive in all his work. There is no modern dramatist whose characters are more persistently concerned with explicit self-revelation: the desire and the need to tell the truth about oneself are overpowering. Yet this self-revelation can be very different in purpose and effect, as the following examples show:

> TREPLEF: Who am I? What am I? Sent down from the University without a degree through circumstances for which the editor cannot hold himself responsible, as they say; with no talents, without a farthing, and according to my passport a Kiev artisan; for my father was officially reckoned a Kiev artisan although he was a famous actor. So that when these actors and writers in my mother's drawing-room graciously bestowed their attention on me, it seemed to me that they

were merely taking the measure of my insignificance; I guessed their thoughts and felt the humiliation.

(*The Seagull*)

UNCLE VANYA: I am intelligent, brave, and strong. If I had lived normally I might have become another Schopenhauer, or Dostoyevsky.   (*Uncle Vanya*)

OLGA: I'm always having headaches from having to go to the High School every day and then teach till evening. Strange thoughts come to me, as if I were already an old woman. And really, during these four years that I have been working here, I have been feeling as if every day my strength and youth have been squeezed out of me, drop by drop. And only one desire grows and grows in strength. . . . To Moscow, as soon as possible.   (*The Three Sisters*)

SHIPUCHIN: As I was saying, at home I can live like a tradesman, a *parvenu*, and be up to any games I like, but here everything must be *en grand*. This is a Bank. Here every detail must *imponiren*, so to speak, and have a majestic appearance.   (*The Anniversary*)

GAYEF: I'm a good Liberal, a man of the eighties. People abuse the eighties, but I think I may say that I've suffered for my convictions in my time. It's not for nothing that the peasants love me. We ought to know the peasants, we ought to know with what . . .

ANYA: You're at it again, Uncle.   (*The Cherry Orchard*)

Treplef and Olga are outlining their explicit situation; their speeches are devices of the author's exposition, which, because of the large number of characters he handles, is frequently awkward, as in *The Three Sisters*. There is also, with Olga and Treplef, a sentimental vein (with real persons it would be called self-pity) which depends on their explicitness. While retaining the manner of conversation, they are doing more, or attempting more, than conversation can ever do. In Uncle Vanya, this has become the full sentimentality, as it is also in Gayef. But in Gayef, the device is satiric. We are evidently *not* "intended to accept the character's sentimental interpretation of himself". Shipuchin is a more unequivocal comic figure, but then *The Anniversary*—a short piece—is a less equivocal play: it is farce without strings. One's doubts about even the best of Chekhov's plays are doubts about the strings.

But then, as this response becomes clear, we have to put the critical question in a different way. We have to discover the relation between this particular convention—of an explicit self-revelation, at times awkward and sentimental, at other times negotiated as satire or farce—and Chekhov's actual structure of feeling. And what we then see is an important change, from both Ibsen and Strindberg. It is not the passionate overt conflict of early Strindberg, nor the savage internal inquiry, the fixed distortions of an alienated group, of Strindberg's later world. Again, in the comparison with Ibsen, there is a crucial difference, beyond the surface similarities. Chekhov saw, as clearly as Ibsen, the frustration and stagnation of the available forms of social life; his difference, in his mature work, is that he does not set against these, even in defeat and failure, an actively liberating individual. In *Ivanov* this liberal structure is still present: an isolated, struggling man, against the habits of his group; breaking, and breaking others in his fall. For that structure, the dramatic methods of Ibsen were still relevant, and in *The Seagull*, where again a break is being attempted, by Treplev, they are still partly relevant. But in *The Three Sisters* and *The Cherry Orchard* something new has happened: it is not the liberating individual against the complacent group; it is that the desire for liberation has passed into the group as a whole, but at the same time has become hopeless, inward-looking—in effect a defeat before the struggle has even begun. Chekhov, that is to say, is not writing about a generation of liberal struggle against false social forms, but about a generation whose whole energy is consumed in the very process of becoming conscious of their own inadequacy and impotence. The dramatic conventions of liberal struggle had been clear: the isolation of the individual; his contrast with his group; and then an action which took this forward—not to the point of change, which Ibsen could not see happening, but to the point where the effort and the resistance, the vocation and the debt, reached deadlock: the hero died still climbing and struggling, but with the odds against him. As we have seen, this deadlock was never merely external: the limiting consciousness of the false society—"we are all ghosts . . . all of us so wretchedly afraid of the light"—was seen, by Ibsen, as inevitably entering the consciousness of the man who was struggling: the deadlock with a false society was re-enacted as a deadlock within the self. The methods of Ibsen's last plays, particularly, are related to this internal deadlock.

It was from this point that Chekhov began. He attempted the same action, and made it end in suicide. But he came to see this as "theatrical": a significant description of one of those crucial moments when a structure of feeling is changing, and when the conventions appropriate to it come suddenly to seem empty. As Chekhov explores his world, he finds not deadlock—the active struggle in which no outcome is possible—but stalemate—the collective recognition, as it were before the struggle, that this is so. Virtually everyone wants change; virtually no-one believes it is possible. It is the sensibility of a generation which sits up all night talking about the need for revolution, and is then too tired next morning to do anything at all, even about its own immediate problems.

This world, this new structure of feeling, is very powerfully created in *The Three Sisters* and in *The Cherry Orchard*. In *The Three Sisters* it is the longing to make sense of life, to have a sense of a future, in a stagnant and boring military-provincial society. In *The Cherry Orchard* it is an attempt to come to terms with the past: to live without owning the orchard and its servants. In neither situation is any real success possible: what happens is not to change the situation, but to reveal it. The counter-movement, against what would be simple fantasy (the desire to be in Moscow, although they would be the same people there) or simple nostalgia (the desire to have the orchard and yet to be free to go away), is an emphasis on redemption, effort, work. Characteristically, these cannot materialize as events; they can only be spoken about:

> They will forget our faces, voices, and even how many there were of us, but our sufferings will turn into joy for those who will live after us. . . . Your orchard frightens me. When I walk through it in the evening or at night, the rugged bark on the trees glows with a dim light, and the cherry-trees seem to see all that happened a hundred and two hundred years ago in painful and oppressive dreams. Well, we have fallen at least two hundred years behind the times. We have achieved nothing at all as yet; we have not made up our minds how we stand with the past; we only philosophise, complain of boredom, or drink vodka. It is so plain that before we can live in the present, we must first redeem the past, and have done with it; and it is only by suffering that we can redeem it, only by strenuous unremitting toil.

Characteristically, this last speech is by Trophimov, who does practically no work. This does not mean that he is wrong, or that what he says can be disregarded: it is the dominant emotion of the play. But there is this precise paradox, in Trophimov and in the others, between what can be said and what can be done; what is believed and what is lived.

Inevitably, such a man, such a situation, such a generation can seem comic; it is easy to laugh at them and at what Chekhov calls their "neurotic whining". At the same time, to get even the strength to see what is wrong, to sit up talking to try to get it clear, can be, in such a time, a major effort. In its inadequacy and yet its persistence it is heroism of a kind, an ambivalent kind. It is then this feeling—this structure of feeling—that Chekhov sets himself to dramatize.

The consequences in method are important. First, there will be no isolated, contrasting characters; the crucial emotion is that of a group. Second, there will, so far as possible, be no action: things will happen, but as it were from outside: what happens within the group is mainly gesture and muddle. Third, the contradictory character, of the group and its feelings, has to be conveyed in the tone: a kind of nobility, and a kind of farce, have to co-exist. (This is not, by the way, a cue for the usual question: are we supposed to laugh or cry at such people and such situations? That is a servile question: we have to decide our response for ourselves. The point is, always, that the characters and situations can be seen, are written to be seen, in both ways; to decide on one part of the response or the other is to miss what is being said).

As we come to see that this is what Chekhov is doing, we are faced with very difficult critical problems. He is attempting to dramatize a stagnant group, in which consciousness has turned inward and become, if not wholly inarticulate, at least unconnecting. He is attempting to dramatize a social consequence—a common loss—in private and self-regarding feeling. It is, inevitably, a very difficult balance, a very difficult method, to achieve.

Now certainly, Chekhov's representation of living action is impressive. The structure is more finely and more delicately constructed than that of any of his contemporaries. The same method achieves, in his fiction, very valuable results. But the method, I would say, is ultimately fictional. In the bare, economical, and inescapably explicit framework of drama the finest structure of incident and phrase, left to itself, appears crude. The convention of general description, which in the novel is essentially a whole structure of feeling, is very difficult to achieve, in this kind of play. And then the miniatures are left suspended; there is a sense, as in Ibsen's *The Wild Duck*, of disintegration, which springs directly from this absence. A gap must be filled, and to the rescue, as before, comes the unifying pressure of a device of atmosphere. It is a poor compromise. The characters, which in fiction are more than their separated selves, now dissociate, outline themselves, by the conditions of dramatic presentation. Delineation degenerates to slogan and catchphrase, to the mumbled "and all the rest of it" with which old Sorin ends his every speech in *The Seagull*. For of such is a "character" built. The just comment is Strindberg's, in the Preface to *Lady Julie*:

> A character on the stage came to signify a gentleman who was fixed and finished; nothing was required, but some bodily defect—a club-foot, a wooden leg, a red nose; or the character in question was made to repeat some such phrase as "That's capital", "Barkis is willin'", or the like.

Nothing is more surprising, in the genuine detail of experience which

Chekhov so finely achieves, than the appearance—the repeated appearance—of that kind of fixed, external device of personality. Moreover, that separable "personality" is the more contradictory in that what Chekhov is essentially expressing is a *common* condition. It is this that is missed or weakened when personality declines to an idosyncrasy or a "human vignette".

On the other hand, Chekhov attempted to develop a new kind of dialogue which, paradoxically, would express disintegration without weakening the sense of a common condition. Such dialogue is very hard to read and to play, and it is, I think, only intermittently successful. But where it does succeed, something very original and in its own way powerful has come into modern drama. An unfamiliar rhythm is developed, in which what is being said, essentially, is not said by any one of the characters, but, as it were inadvertently, by the group. This is not easy to illustrate, since the printed convention, separating and assigning the speeches, usually breaks it up. The major example, I think, is the second act of *The Cherry Orchard*, which as a theme for voices, a condition and an atmosphere created by hesitation, implication, unconnected confession, is more complete and powerful than anything else Chekhov wrote. A briefer example, from *The Three Sisters*, may allow the method to be seen more clearly (I omit the names of the speakers so that the form of a connected dialogue—connected, paradoxically, to show disconnection—can be followed):

> We do not seem to understand each other. How can I convince you? Yes, laugh. Not only after two or three centuries, but in a million years, life will still be as it was; life does not change, it remains for ever, following its own laws which do not concern us, or which, at any rate, you will never find out. Migrant birds, cranes for example, fly and fly, and whatever thoughts, high or low, enter their heads, they will still fly and not know why or where. They fly and will continue to fly, whatever philosophers come to life among them; they may philsophise as much as they like, only they will fly . . .
>> Still, is there a meaning?
>> A meaning? Now the snow is falling. What meaning?
>> It seems to me that a man must have faith, or must search for a faith, or his life will be empty, empty. To live and not to know why the cranes fly, why babies are born, why there are stars in the sky. Either you must know why you live, or everything is trivial, not worth a straw.
>> Still, I am sorry that my youth has gone.
>> Gogol says: life in this world is a dull matter, my masters.

And I say it's difficult to argue with you, my masters. Hang it all.

Balzac was married at Berdichev. That's worth making a note of. Balzac was married at Berdichev.

Balzac was married at Berdichev.

The die is cast. I've handed in my resignation.

As we listen to this, it is obvious that what is being expressed is not a dealing between persons, or a series of self-definitions; it is a common, inadvertent mood—questioning, desiring, defeated. To the degree that we separate the speeches out, and see them as revealing this or that particular character, the continuing rhythm, at once tentative and self-conscious, superficially miscellaneous and yet deeply preoccupied, is quickly lost. And of course, in performance, such continuity, such timing, is very difficult to sustain, if each actor sees himself as acting a separate part. It is the final paradox, in Chekhov's work, that the local identifying features, of the members of his dramatic group, are truly superficial, yet are the constant cues. What comes through or can come through is a very different voice—the human voice within and beyond the immediate negotiation and self-presentation. But within his conventions, and this is usually accentuated in performance, this human voice is intermittent and inadvertent; an unusual silence has to be imposed, if it is ever to be properly heard.

What Chekhov does then, in effect, is to invent a dramatic form which contradicts most of the available conventions of dramatic production. To perform him with any success at all, as we know from the record, Stanislavsky and Nemirovich-Danchenko had to find new methods of acting and design: to substitute an altered internal, suggestive method for what had been explicit, presented, articulate. It was a major development in the theatre, and is still, after seventy years, influential. But it is no surprise to find Chekhov dissatisfied, when he saw what was being done. In his persistent honesty, his scrupulous fineness of detail, he was presenting problems which could only ever be partially solved. The inherited conventions were either crude and loud, or, where they were refined to express individuality, were only partly relevant to his purposes. What happened in the theatre was that another kind of talent—a producer's talent—took over his work and found a way of presenting it, but, as can be seen from Stanislavsky's notes on his production of *The Seagull*, by adding and altering, to achieve a stageable effect. It is a significant moment, in the history of modern drama, for it shows a writer of genius beginning to create a new dramatic form, but in ways so original and so tentative that it is in constant danger of breaking down, and another kind of art has to be invented to sustain it. It is now seen as the triumph, but must also be seen as the crisis, of the naturalist drama and theatre.

Anton Chekhov: (*Creation from the Void*)

Résigne-toi, mon coeur, dors ton sommeil de brute.
—Charles Baudelaire

Chekhov is dead; therefore we may now speak freely of him. For to speak of an artist means to disentangle and reveal the 'tendency' hidden in his works, an operation not always permissible when the subject is still living. Certainly he had a reason for hiding himself, and of course the reason was serious and important. I believe many felt it, and that it was partly on this account that we have as yet had no proper appreciation of Chekhov. Hitherto in analysing his works the critics have confined themselves to commonplace and *cliché*. Of course they knew they were wrong: but anything is better than to extort the truth from a living person. Mihailovsky alone attempted to approach closer to the source of Chekhov's creation, and as everybody knows, turned away from it with aversion and even with disgust. Here, by the way, the deceased critic might have convinced himself once again of the extravagance of the so-called theory of 'art for art's sake.' Every artist has his definite task, his life's work, to which he devotes all his forces. A tendency is absurd when it endeavours to take the place of talent, and to cover impotence and lack of content, or when it is borrowed from the stock of ideas which

From *All Things Are Possible and Penultimate Words and Other Essays.* © 1977 by Ohio University Press.

happen to be in demand at the moment. 'I defend ideals, therefore every one must give me his sympathies.' Such presences we often see made in literature, and the notorious controversy concerning 'art for art's sake' was evidently maintained upon the double meaning given to the word 'tendency' by its opponents. Some wished to believe that a writer can be saved by the nobility of his tendency; others feared that a tendency would bind them to the performance of alien tasks. Much ado about nothing: ready-made ideas will never endow mediocrity with talent; on the contrary, an original writer will at all costs set himself his own task. And Chekhov had his *own* business, though there were critics who said that he was the servant of art for its own sake, and even compared him to a bird, carelessly flying. To define his tendency in a word, I would say that Chekhov was the poet of hopelessness. Stubbornly, sadly, monotonously, during all the years of his literary activity, nearly a quarter of a century long, Chekhov was doing one alone: by one means or another he was killing human hopes. Herein, I hold, lies the essence of his creation. Hitherto it has been little spoken of. The reasons are quite intelligible. In ordinary language what Chekhov was doing is called crime, and is visited by condign punishment. But how can a man of talent be punished? Even Mihailovsky, who more than once in his lifetime gave an example of merciless severity, did not raise his hand against Chekhov. He warned his readers and pointed out the 'evil fire' which he had noticed in Chekhov's eyes. But he went no further. Chekhov's immense talent overcame the strict and rigorous critic. It may be, however, that Mihailovsky's own position in literature had more than a little to do with the comparative mildness of his sentence. The younger generation had listened to him uninterruptedly for thirty years, and his word had been law. But afterwards every one was bored with eternally repeating: "Aristides is just, Aristides is right.' The younger generation began to desire to live and to speak in its own way, and finally the old master was ostracised. There is the same custom in literature as in Tierra del Fuego. The young, growing men kill and eat the old. Mihailovsky struggled with all his might, but he no longer felt the strength of conviction that comes from the sense of right. Inwardly, he felt that the young were right, not because they knew the truth—what truth did the economic materialists know?—but because they were young and had their lives before them. The rising star shines always brighter than the setting, and the old must of their own will yield themselves up to be devoured by the young. Mihailovsky felt this, and perhaps it was this which undermined his former assurance and the firmness of his opinion of old. True, he was still like Gretchen's mother in Goethe: he did not take rich gifts from chance without having previously consulted his confessor. Chekhov's talent too was taken to the priest, by whom it was evidently rejected as suspect; but Mihailovsky no longer had the courage to set himself against public opinion. The younger generation prized Chekhov for his talent, his immense talent, and it was plain they would not disown him. What remained for Mihailovsky? He attempted, as I say, to warn them. But no one listened to him, and Chekhov became one of the most beloved of Russian writers.

Yet the just Aristides was right this time too, as he was right when he gave his warning against Dostoevsky. Now that Chekhov is no more, we may speak openly. Take Chekhov's stories, each one separately, or better still, all together: look at him at work. He is constantly, as it were, in ambush, to watch and waylay human hopes. He will not miss a single one of them, not one of them will escape its fate. Art, science, love, inspiration, ideals—choose out all the words with which humanity is wont, or has been in the past, to be consoled or to be amused—Chekhov has only to touch them and they instantly wither and die. And Chekhov himself faded, withered and died before our eyes. Only his wonderful art did not die—his art to kill by a mere touch, a breath, a glance, everything whereby men live and wherein they take their pride. And in this art he was constantly perfecting himself, and he attained to a virtuosity beyond the reach of any of his rivals in European literature. Maupassant often had to strain every effort to overcome his victim. The victim often escaped from Maupassant, though crushed and broken, yet with his life. In Chekhov's hands, nothing escaped death.

II

I must remind my reader, though it is a matter of general knowledge, that in his earlier work Chekhov is most unlike the Chekhov to whom we became accustomed in late years. The young Chekhov is gay and careless, perhaps even like a flying bird. He published his work in the comic papers. But in 1888 and 1889, when he was only twenty-seven and twenty-eight years old, there appeared *The Tedious Story* and the drama *Ivanov*, two pieces of work which laid the foundations of a new creation. Obviously a sharp and sudden change had taken place in him, which was completely reflected in his works. There is no detailed biography of Chekhov, and probably will never be, because there is no such thing as a full biography—I, at all events, cannot name one. Generally biographies tell us everything except what it is important to know. Perhaps in the future it will be revealed to us with the fullest details who was Chekhov's tailor; but we shall never know what happened to Chekhov in the time which elapsed between the completion of his story *The Steppe* and the appearance of his first drama. If we would know, we must rely upon his works and our own insight.

Ivanov and *The Tedious Story* seem to me the most autobiographical of all his works. In them almost every line is a sob; and it is hard to suppose that a man could sob so, looking only at another's grief. And it is plain that his grief is a new one, unexpected as though it had fallen from the sky. Here it is, it will endure for ever, and he does not know how to fight against it.

In *Ivanov* the hero compares himself to an overstrained labourer. I do not believe we shall be mistaken if we apply this comparison to the author of the drama as well. There can be practically no doubt that Chekhov had overstrained himself. And the overstrain came not from hard and heavy labour; no mighty overpowering exploit broke him: he stumbled and fell, he slipped. There comes this nonsensical, stupid, all but invisible accident, and the old Chekhov of gaiety and mirth is no more. No more stories for *The Alarm Clock*. Instead a morose and overshadowed man, a 'criminal' whose words frighten even the experienced and the omniscient.

If you desire it, you can easily be rid of Chekhov and his work as well. Our language contains two magic words: 'pathological,' and its brother 'abnormal.' Once Chekhov had overstrained himself, you have a perfectly legal right, sanctified by science and every tradition, to leave him out of all account, particularly seeing that he is already dead, and therefore cannot be hurt by your neglect. That is if you desire to be rid of Chekhov. But if the desire is for some reason absent, the words 'pathological' and 'abnormal' will have no effect upon you. Perhaps you will go further and attempt to find in Chekhov's experiences a criterion of the most irrefragable truths and axioms of this consciousness of ours. There is no third way: you must either renounce Chekhov, or become his accomplice.

The hero of *The Tedious Story* is an old professor; the hero of *Ivanov* a young landlord. But the theme of both works is the same. The professor had overstrained himself, and thereby cut himself off from his past life and from the possibility of taking an active part in human affairs. Ivanov also had overstrained himself and become a superfluous, useless person. Had life been so arranged that death should supervene simultaneously with the loss of health, strength and capacity, then the old professor and young Ivanov could not have lived for one single hour. Even a blind man could see that they are both broken and are unfit for life. But for reasons unknown to us, wise nature has rejected coincidence of this kind. A man very often goes on living after he has completely lost the capacity of taking from life that wherein we are wont to see its essence and meaning. More striking still, a broken man is generally deprived of everything except the ability to acknowledge and feel his position. Nay, for the most part in such cases the intellectual abilities are refined and sharpened and increased to colossal proportions. It frequently happens that an average man, banal and mediocre, is changed beyond all recognition when he falls into the exceptional situation of Ivanov or the old professor. In him appear signs of a gift, a talent, even of genius. Nietzsche once asked: 'Can an ass be tragical?' He left his question unanswered, but Tolstoy answered for him in *The Death of Ivan Ilych*. Ivan Ilych, it is evident from Tolstoy's description of his life, is a mediocre, average character, one of those men who pass through life avoiding anything that is difficult or problematical, caring exclusively for the calm and pleasantness of earthly existence. Hardly had the cold wind of tragedy blown upon him, than he was utterly transformed. The story of Ivan llych in his last days is as deeply interesting as the life-story of Socrates or Pascal.

In passing I would point out a fact which I consider of great importance. In his work Chekhov was influenced by Tolstoy, and particularly by Tolstoy's later writings. It is important, because thus a part of Chekhov's 'guilt' falls upon the great writer of the Russian land. I think that had there been no *Death of Ivan Ilych*, there would have been no *Ivanov*, and no *Tedious Story*, nor many others of Chekhov's most remarkable works. But this by no means implies that Chekhov borrowed a single word from his great predecessor. Chekhov had enough material of his own: in that respect he needed no help. But a young writer would hardly dare to come forward at his own risk with the thoughts that make the content of *The Tedious Story*. When Tolstoy wrote *The Death of Ivan Ilych*, he had behind him *War and Peace*, *Anna Karenina*, and the firmly established reputation of an artist of the highest rank. All things were permitted to him. But Chekhov was a young man, whose literary baggage amounted in all to a few dozen tiny stories, hidden in the pages of little known and uninfluential papers. Had Tolstoy not paved the way, had Tolstoy not shown by his example, that in literature it was permitted to tell the truth, to tell everything, then perhaps Chekhov would have had to struggle long with himself before finding the courage of a public confession, even though it took the form of stories. And even with Tolstoy before him, how terribly did Chekhov have to struggle with public opinion. 'Why does he write his horrible stories and plays?' everyone asked himself. 'Why does the writer systematically choose for his heroes situations from which there is not, and cannot possibly be, any escape?' What can be said in answer to the endless complaints of the old professor and Katy, his pupil? This means that there is, essentially, something to be said. From times immemorial, literature has accumulated a large and varied store of all kinds of general ideas and conceptions, material and metaphysical to which the masters have recourse the moment the over-exacting and over-restless human voice begins to be heard. This is exactly the point. Chekhov himself, a writer and an educated man, refused in advance every possible consolation, material or metaphysical. Not even in Tolstoy, who set no great store by philosophical systems, will you find such keenly expressed disgust for every kind of conceptions and ideas as in Chekhov. He is well aware that conceptions ought to be esteemed and respected, and he reckons his inability to bend the knee before that which educated people consider holy as a defect against which he must struggle with all his strength. And he does struggle with all his strength against this defect. But not only is the struggle unavailing; the longer Chekhov lives, the weaker grows the power of lofty words over him, in spite of his own reason and his conscious will. Finally, he frees himself entirely from ideas of every kind, and loses even the notion of connection between the happenings of life. Herein lies the most important and original characteristic of his creation. Anticipating a little, I would here point to his comedy, *The Sea-Gull*, where, in defiance of all literary principles, the basis of action appears to be not the logical development of passions, nor the inevitable connection between cause and effect, but naked accident, ostentatiously nude. As one reads the play, it seems at times that one has before one a copy of a newspaper with an endless series of news paragraphs, heaped upon one another, without order and without previous plan. Sovereign accident reigns everywhere and in everything, this time boldly throwing the gauntlet to all conceptions. In this, I repeat, is Chekhov's greatest originality, and this, strangely enough, is the source of his most bitter experiences. He did not want to be original: he made superhuman efforts to be like everybody else: but there is no escaping one's destiny. How many men, above all among writers, wear their fingers to the bone in the effort to be unlike others, and yet they cannot shake themselves free of *cliché*—yet Chekhov was original against his will! Evidently originality does not depend upon the readiness to proclaim revolutionary opinions at all costs. The newest and boldest idea may and often does appear tedious and vulgar. In order to become original, instead of inventing an idea, one must achieve a difficult and painful labour; and, since men avoid labour and suffering, the really new is for the most part born in man against his will.

III

'A man cannot reconcile himself to the accomplished fact: neither can he refuse so to reconcile himself: and there is no third course. Under such conditions "action" is impossible. He can only fall down and weep and beat his head against the floor.' So Chekhov speaks of one of his heroes; but he might say the same of them all, without exception. The author takes care to put them in such a situation that only one thing is left for them,—to fall down and beat their heads against the floor. With strange, mysterious obstinacy they refuse all the accepted means of salvation. Nicolai Stepanovich, the old professor in *The Tedious Story*, might have attempted to forget himself for a while or to console himself with memories of the past. But memories only irritate him. He was once an eminent scholar: now he cannot work. Once he was able to hold the attention of his audience for two hours on end; now he cannot do it even for a quarter of an hour. He used to have friends and comrades, he used to love his pupils and assistants, his wife and children; now he cannot concern himself with anyone. If people do arouse any feelings at all within him, then they are only feelings of hatred, malice and envy. He has to confess it to himself with the truthfulness which came to him—he knows not why nor whence in place of the old diplomatic skill, possessed by all clever and normal men, whereby he saw and said only that which makes for decent human relations and healthy states of mind. Now everything which he sees or thinks only serves to poison, in himself and others, the few joys which adorn human life. With a certainty which he never attained on the best days and hours of his old theoretical research, he feels that he is become a criminal, having committed no crime. All that he was engaged in before was good, necessary, and useful. He tells you of his past, and you can see that he was always right and ready at any moment of the day or the night to answer the severest judge who should examine not only his actions, but his thoughts as well. Now not only would an outsider condemn him, he condemns himself. He confesses openly that he is all compact of envy and hatred.

'The best and most sacred right of kings,' he says, 'is the right to pardon. And I have always felt myself a king so long as I used this right prodigally. I never judged, I was compassionate, I pardoned every one right and left. . . . But now I am king no more. There's something going on in me which belongs only to slaves. Day and night evil thoughts roam about in my head, and feelings which I never knew before have made their home in my soul. I hate and despise; I'm exasperated, disturbed, and afraid. I've become strict beyond measure, exacting, unkind and suspicious. . . . What does it all mean? If my new thoughts and feelings come from a change of my convictions, where could the change come from? Has the world grown worse and I better, or was I blind and indifferent before? But if the change is due to the general decline of my physical and mental powers—I am sick and losing weight every day—then I am in a pitiable position. It means that my new thoughts are abnormal and unhealthy, that I must be ashamed of them and consider them valueless. . . .'

The question is asked by the old professor on the point of death, and in his person by Chekhov himself. Which is better, to be a king, or an old, envious, malicious 'toad,' as he calls himself elsewhere? There is no denying the originality of the question. In the words above you feel the price which Chekhov had to pay for his originality, and with how great joy he would have exchanged all his original thoughts—at the moment when his 'new' point of view had become clear to him—for the most ordinary, banal capacity for benevolence. He has no doubt felt that his way of thinking is pitiable, shameful and disgusting. His moods revolt him no less than his appearance, which he describes in the following lines: ' . . . I am a man of sixty-two, with a bald head, false teeth and an incurable tic. My name is as brilliant and prepossessing, as I myself am dull and ugly. My head and hands tremble from weakness; my neck, like that of one of Turgenev's heroines, resembles the handle of a counter-bass; my chest is hollow and my back narrow. When I speak or read my mouth twists, and when I smile my whole face is covered with senile, deathly wrinkles.' Unpleasant face, unpleasant moods! Let the most sweet nature and compassionate person but give a side-glance at such a monster, and despite himself a cruel thought would awaken in him: that he should lose no time in killing, in utterly destroying this pitiful and disgusting vermin, or if the laws forbid recourse to such strong measures, at least in hiding him as far as possible from human eyes, in some prison or hospital or asylum. These are measures of suppression sanctioned, I believe, not only by legislation, but by eternal morality as well. But here you encounter resistance of a particular kind. Physical strength to struggle with the warders, executioners, attendants, moralists—the old professor has none; a little child could knock him down. Persuasion and prayer, he knows well, will avail him nothing. So he strikes out in despair: he begins to cry over all the world in a terrible, wild, heartrending voice about some rights of his: '. . . I have a passionate and hysterical desire to stretch out my hands and moan aloud. I want to cry out that fate has doomed me, a famous man, to death; that in some six months here in the auditorium another will be master. I want to cry out that I am poisoned; that new ideas that I did not know before have poisoned the last days of my life, and sting my brain incessantly like mosquitoes. At that moment my position seems so terrible to me that I want all my students to be terrified, to jump from their seats and rush panic-stricken to the door, shrieking in despair.' The professor's arguments will hardly move any one. Indeed I do not know if there is any argument in those words. But this awful, inhuman moan. . . . Imagine the picture: a bald, ugly old man, with trembling hands, and twisted mouth, and skinny neck, eyes mad with fear, wallowing like a beast on the ground and wailing, wailing, wailing. . . . What does he want? He had lived a long and interesting life; now he had only to round it off nicely, with all possible calm, quietly and solemnly to take leave of this earthly existence. Instead he rends himself, and flings himself about, calls almost the whole universe to judgment, and clutches convulsively at the few days left to him. And Chekhov—what did Chekhov do? Instead of passing by on the other side, he supports the prodigious monster, devotes pages and pages to the 'experiences of his soul,' and gradually brings the reader to a point at which, instead of a natural and lawful sense of indignation, unprofitable and dangerous sympathies for the decomposing, decaying creature are awakened in his heart. But every one knows that it is impossible to *help* the professor; and if it is impossible to help, then it follows we must forget. That is as plain as *a b c*. What use or what meaning could there be in the endless picturing—daubing, as Tolstoy would say—of the intolerable pains of the agony which inevitably leads to death?

If the professor's 'new' thoughts and feelings shone bright with beauty, nobility or heroism, the case would be different. The reader could learn something from it. But Chekhov's story shows that these qualities belonged to his hero's old thoughts. Now that his illness has begun, there has sprung up within him a revulsion from everything which even remotely resembles a lofty feeling. When his pupil Katy turns to him for advice what she should do, the famous scholar, the friend of Pirogov, Kavelin and Nekrassov, who had taught so many generations of young men, does not know what to answer. Absurdly he chooses from his memory a whole series of pleasant-sounding words; but they have lost all meaning for him. What answer shall he give? he asks himself. 'It is easy to say, Work, or divide your property among the poor, or know yourself, and because it is easy, I do not know what to answer.' Katy, still young, healthy and beautiful, has by Chekhov's offices fallen like the professor into a trap from which no human power can deliver her. From the moment that she knew hopelessness, she had won all the author's sympathy. While a person is settled to some work, while he has a future of some kind before him, Chekhov is utterly indifferent to him. If he does describe him, then he usually does it hastily and in a tone of scornful irony. But when he is entangled, and so entangled that he cannot be disentangled by any means, then Chekhov begins to wake up. Colour, energy, creative force, inspiration make their appearance. Therein perhaps lies the secret of his political indifferentism. Notwithstanding all his distrust of projects for a brighter future, Chekhov like Dostoevsky was evidently not wholly convinced that social reforms and social science were important. However difficult the social question may be, still it may be solved. Some day, perhaps people will so arrange themselves on the earth as to live and die without suffering: further than that ideal humanity cannot go. Perhaps the authors of stout volumes on Progress do guess and foresee something. But just for that reason their work is alien to Chekhov. At first by instinct, then consciously, he was attracted to problems which are by essence insoluble like that presented in *The Tedious Story*: there you have helplessness, sickness, the prospect of inevitable death, and no hope whatever to change the situation by a hair. This infatuation, whether conscious or instinctive, clearly runs counter to the demands of common sense and normal will. But there is nothing else to expect from Chekhov, an overstrained man. Every one knows, or has heard, of hopelessness. On every side, before our very eyes, are happening terrible and intolerable tragedies, and if every doomed man were to raise such an awful alarm about his destruction as Nicolai Stepanovich, life would become an inferno; Nicolai Stepanovich must not cry his sufferings aloud over the world, but be careful to trouble people as little as possible. And Chekhov should have assisted this reputable endeavour by every means in his power. As though there were not thousands of tedious stories in the world—they cannot be counted! And above all stories of the kind that Chekhov tells should be hidden with special care from human eyes. We have here to do with the decomposition of a living organism. What should we say to a man who would prevent corpses from being buried, and would dig decaying bodies from the grave, even though it were on the ground, or rather on the pretext, that they were the bodies of his intimate friends, even famous men of reputation and genius? Such an occupation would rouse in a normal and healthy mind nothing but disgust and terror. Once upon a time, according to popular superstition, sorcerers, necromancers and wizards kept company with the dead, and found a certain pleasure or even a real satisfaction in that ghastly occupation. But they generally hid themselves away from mankind in forests and caves, or betook themselves to deserts where they might in isolation surrender themselves to their unnatural inclinations; and if their deeds were eventually brought to light, healthy men requited them with the stake, the gallows, and the rack. The worst kind of that which is called evil, as a rule, had for its source and origin an interest and taste for carrion. Man forgave every crime—cruelty, violence, murder; but he never forgave the unmotived love of death and the seeking of its secret. In this matter modern times, being free from prejudices, have advanced little from the Middle Ages. Perhaps the only difference is that we, engaged in practical affairs, have lost the natural *flair* for good and evil. Theoretically we are even convinced that in our time there are not and cannot be wizards and necromancers. Our confidence and carelessness in this reached such a point, that almost everybody saw even in Dostoevsky only an artist and a publicist, and seriously discussed with him whether the Russian peasant needed to be flogged and whether we ought to lay hands on Constantinople.

Mihailovsky alone vaguely conjectured what it all might be when he called the author of *The Brothers Karamazov* a 'treasure-digger.' I say he 'dimly conjectured' because I think that the deceased critic made the remark partly in allegory, even in joke. But none of Dostoevsky's other critics made, even by accident, a truer slip of the pen. Chekhov, too, was a 'treasure-digger,' a sorcerer, a necromancer, an adept in the black art; and this explains his singular infatuation for death, decay and hopelessness.

Chekhov was not of course the only writer to make death the subject of his works. But not the theme is important but the manner of its treatment. Chekhov understands that, 'In all the thoughts, feelings, and ideas,' he says, '[which] I form about anything, there is wanting the something universal which could bind all these together in one whole. Each feeling and each thought lives detached in me, and in all my opinions about science, the theatre, literature, and my pupils, and in all the little pictures which my imagination paints, not even the most cunning analyst will discover what is called the general idea, or the god of the living man. And if this is not there, then nothing is there. In poverty such as this, a serious infirmity, fear of death, influence of circumstances and people would have been enough to overthrow and shatter all that I formerly considered as my conception of the world, and all wherein I saw the meaning and joy of my life. . . .' In these words one of the 'newest' of Chekhov's ideas finds expression, one by which the whole of his subsequent creation is defined. It is expressed in a modest, apologetic form: a man confesses that he is unable to subordinate his thoughts to a higher idea, and in that inability he sees his weakness. This was enough to avert from him to some extent the thunders of criticism and the judgment of public opinion. We readily forgive the repentant sinner! But it is an unprofitable clemency: to expiate one's guilt, it is not enough to confess it. What was the good of Chekhov's putting on sackcloth and ashes and publicly confessing his guilt, if he was inwardly unchanged? If, while his words acknowledged the general idea as god (without a capital, indeed), he did nothing whatever for it? In words he burns incense to god, in deed he curses him. Before his disease a conception of the world brought him happiness, now it had shattered into fragments. Is it not natural to ask whether the conception actually did ever bring him happiness? Perhaps the happiness had its own independent origin, and the conception was invited only as a general to a wedding, for outward show, and never played any essential part. Chekhov tells us circumstantially what joys the professor found in his scientific work, his lectures to the students, his family, and in a good dinner. In all these were present together the conception of the world and the idea, and they did not take away from, but as it were embellished life; so that it seemed that he was working for the ideal, as well as creating a family and dining. But now, when for the same ideal's sake he has to remain inactive, to suffer, to remain awake of nights, to swallow with effort food that has become loathsome to him—the conception of the world is shattered into fragments! And it amounts to this, that a conception with a dinner is right, and a dinner without a conception equally right—this needs no argument—and a conception *an und für sich* is of no value whatever. Here is the essence of the words quoted from Chekhov. He confesses with horror the presence within him of that 'new' idea. It seems to him that he alone of all men is so weak and insignificant, that the others . . . well, they need only ideals and conceptions. And so it is surely, if we may believe what people write in books, Chekhov plagues, tortures and worries himself in every possible way, but he can alter nothing; nay worse, conceptions and ideas, towards which a great many people behave quite carelessly—after all, these innocent things do not merit any other attitude—in Chekhov become the objects of bitter, inexorable, and merciless hatred. He cannot free himself at one single stroke from the power of ideas: therefore he begins a long, slow and stubborn war. I would call it a guerrilla war, against the tyrant who had enslaved him. The whole history and the separate episodes of his struggle are of absorbing interest, because the most conspicuous representatives of literature have hitherto been convinced that ideas have a magical power. What are the majority of writers doing but constructing conceptions of the world—and believing that they are engaged in a work of extraordinary importance and sanctity? Chekhov offended very many literary men. If his punishment was comparatively slight, that was because he was very cautious, and waged war with the air of bringing tribute to the enemy, and secondly, because to talent much is forgiven.

IV

The content of *The Tedious Story* thus reduces to the fact that the professor, expressing his 'new' thoughts, in essence declares that he finds it impossible to acknowledge the power of the 'idea' over himself, or conscientiously to fulfill that which men consider the supreme purpose, and in the service whereof they see the mission, the sacred mission of man. 'God be my judge, I haven't courage enough to act according to my conscience,' such is the only answer which Chekhov finds in his soul to all demands for a 'conception.' This attitude towards 'conceptions' becomes second nature with Chekhov. A conception makes demands; a man acknowledges the justice of these demands and methodically satisfies none of them. Moreover, the justice of the demands meets with less and less acknowledgment from him. In *The Tedious Story* the idea still judges the man and tortures him with the mercilessness peculiar to all things inanimate. Exactly like a splinter stuck into a living body, the idea, alien and hostile, mercilessly performs its high mission, until at length the man firmly resolves to draw the splinter out of his flesh, however painful that difficult operation may be. In *Ivanov* the rôle of the idea is already changed. There not the idea persecutes Chekhov, but Chekhov the idea, and with the subtlest division and contempt. The voice of the living nature rises above the artificial habits of civilisation. True, the struggle still continues, if you will. with alternating fortunes. But the old humility is no more. More and more Chekhov emancipates himself from old prejudices and goes—he himself could hardly say whither, were he asked. But he prefers to remain without an answer, rather than to accept any of the traditional answers. 'I know quite well I have no more than six months to live; and it would seem that now I ought to be mainly occupied with questions of the darkness beyond the grave, and the visions which will visit my sleep in the earth. But somehow my soul is not curious of these questions, though my mind grants every atom of their importance.' In contrast to the habits of the past, reason is once more pushed out of the door with all due respect, while its rights are handed over to the 'soul,' to the dark, vague aspiration which Chekhov by instinct trusts more than the bright, clear consciousness which beforehand determines the beyond, now that he stands before the fatal pale which divides man from the eternal mystery. Is scientific philosophy indignant? Is Chekhov undermining its surest foundations? But he is an overstrained, abnormal man. Certainly you are not bound to listen to him; but once you have decided to do so then you must be prepared for anything. A normal person, even though he be a metaphysician of the extremest ethereal brand, always adjusts his theories to the requirements of the moment; he destroys only to build up from the old material once more. This is the reason why material never fails him. Obedient to the fundamental law of human nature, long since noted and formulated by the wise, he is content to confine himself to the modest part of a seeker after forms. Out of iron, which he finds in nature ready to his hand, he forges a sword or a plough, a lance or a sickle. The idea of creating out of a void hardly even enters his mind. But Chekhov's heroes, persons abnormal *par excellence*, are faced with this abnormal and dreadful necessity. Before them always lies hopelessness, helplessness, the utter impossibility of any action whatsoever. And yet they live on, they do not die.

A strange question, and one of extraordinary moment, here suggests itself. I said that it was foreign to human nature to create out of a void. Yet nature often deprives man of ready material, while at the same time she demands imperatively that he should create. Does this mean that nature contradicts herself, or that she perverts her creatures? Is it not more correct to admit that the conception of perversion is of purely human origin. Perhaps nature is much more economical and wise than our wisdom, and maybe we should discover much more if instead of dividing people into necessary and superfluous, useful and noxious, good and bad, we suppressed the tendency to subjective valuation in ourselves and endeavoured with greater confidence to accept her creations? Otherwise you come immediately to 'the evil gleam,' 'treasure-digging,' sorcery and black magic—and a wall is raised between men which neither logical argument nor even a battery of artillery can break down. I hardly dare hope that this consideration will appear convincing to those who are used to maintaining the norm: and it is probably unnecessary that the notion of the great opposition of good and bad which is alive among men should die away, just as it is unnecessary that children should be born with the experience of men, or that red cheeks and curly hair should vanish from the earth. At any rate it is impossible. The world has many centuries to its reckoning, many nations have lived and died upon the earth, yet as far as we know from the books and traditions that have survived to us, the dispute between good and evil was never hushed. And it always so happened that good was not afraid of the light of day, and good men lived a united, social life; while evil hid itself in darkness, and the wicked always stood alone. Nor could it have been otherwise.

All Chekhov's heroes fear the light. They are lonely. They are ashamed of their hopelessness, and they know that men cannot help them. They go somewhere, perhaps even forward, but they call to no one to follow. All things are taken from them: they must create everything anew. Thence most probably is derived the unconcealed contempt with which they behave to the most precious products of common human creativeness. On whatever subject you begin to talk with a Chekhov hero he has one reply to everything: *Nobody can teach me anything.* You offer him a new conception of the world: already in your very first words he feels that they all reduce to an attempt to lay the old bricks and stones over again, and he turns from you with impatience, and often with rudeness. Chekhov is an extremely cautious writer. He fears and takes into account public opinion. Yet how unconcealed is the aversion he displays to accepted ideas and conceptions of the world. In *The Tedious Story*, he at any rate preserves the tone and attitude of outward obedience. Later he throws aside all precautions, and instead of reproaching himself for his inability to submit to the general idea, openly rebels against it and jeers at it. In *Ivanov* it already is sufficiently expressed; there was reason for the outburst of indignation which this play provoked in its day. Ivanov, I have already said, is a dead man. The only thing the artist can do with him is to bury him decently, that is to praise his past, pity his present, and then, in order to mitigate the cheerless impression produced by death, to invite the general idea to the funeral. He might recall the universal problems of humanity in any one of the many stereotyped forms, and thus the difficult case which seemed insoluble would be removed. Together with Ivanov's death he should portray a bright young life, full of promise, and the impression of death and destruction would lose all its sting and bitterness. Chekhov does just the opposite. Instead of endowing youth and ideals with power over destruction and death, as all philosophical systems and many works of art had done, he ostentatiously makes the good-for-nothing wreck Ivanov the centre of all events. Side by side with Ivanov there are young lives, and the idea is also given her representatives. But the young Sasha, a wonderful and charming girl, who falls utterly in love with the broken hero, not only does not save her lover, but herself perishes under the burden of the impossible task. And the idea? It is enough to recall the figure of Doctor Lvov alone, whom Chekhov entrusted with the responsible rôle of a representative of the all-powerful idea, and you will at once perceive that he considers himself not as subject and vassal, but as the bitterest enemy of the idea. The moment Doctor Lvov opens his mouth, all the characters, as though acting on a previous agreement, vie with each other in their haste to interrupt him in the most insulting way, by jests, threats, and almost by smacks in the face. But the doctor fulfils his duties as a representative of the great power with no less skill and conscientiousness than his predecessors—Starodoum and the other reputable heroes of the old drama. He champions the wronged, seeks to restore rights that have been trodden underfoot, sets himself dead against injustice. Has he stepped beyond the limits of his plenipotentiary powers? Of course not; but where Ivanovs and hopelessness reign there is not and cannot be room for the idea.

They cannot possibly live together. And the eyes of the reader, who is accustomed to think that every kingdom may fall and perish, yet the kingdom of the idea stands firm *in saecula saeculorum*, behold a spectacle unheard of: the idea dethroned by a helpless, broken, good-for-nothing man! What is there that Ivanov does not say? In the very first act he fires off a tremendous tirade, not at a chance corner, but at the incarnate idea—Starodoum-Lvov.

'I have the right to give you advice. Don't you marry a Jewess, or an abnormal, or a blue-stocking. Choose something ordinary, greyish, without any bright colours or superfluous shades. Make it a principle to build your life of *clichés*. The more grey and monotonous the background, the better. My dear man, don't fight thousands single-handed, don't tilt at windmills, don't run your head against the wall. God save you from all kinds of Back-to-the-Landers' advanced doctrines, passionate speeches. . . . Shut yourself tight in your own shell, and do the tiny little work set you by God. . . . It's cosier, honester, and healthier.'

Doctor Lvov, the representative of the all-powerful, sovereign idea feels that his sovereign's majesty is injured, that to suffer such an offence really means to abdicate the throne. Surely Ivanov was a vassal, and so he must remain. How dare he let his tongue advise, how dare he raise his voice when it is his part to listen reverently, and to obey in silent resignation? This is rank rebellion! Lvov attempts to draw himself up to his full height and answer the arrogant rebel with dignity. Nothing comes of it. In a weak, trembling voice he mutters the accustomed words, which but lately had invincible power. But they do not produce their customary effect. Their virtue is departed. Whither? Lvov dares not own it even to himself. But it is no longer a secret to any one. Whatever mean and ugly things Ivanov may have done— Chekhov is not close-fisted in this matter: in his hero's conduct-book are written all manner of offences; almost to the deliberate murder of a woman devoted to him—it is to him and not to Lvov that public opinion bows. Ivanov is the spirit of destruction, rude, violent, pitiless, sticking at nothing: yet the word 'scoundrel,' which the doctor tears out of himself with a painful effort and hurls at him, does not stick to him. He is somehow right, with his own peculiar right, to others inconceivable, yet still, if we may believe Chekhov, incontestable. Sasha, a creature of youth and insight and talent, passes by the honest Starodoum-Lvov unheeding, on her way to render worship to him. The whole play is based on that. It is true, Ivanov in the end shoots himself, and that may, if you like, give you a formal ground for believing that the final victory remained with Lvov. And Chekhov did well to end the drama in this way—it could not be spun out to infinity. It would have been no easy matter to tell the whole of Ivanov's history. Chekhov went on writing for fifteen years after, all the time telling the unfinished story, yet even then he had to break it off without reaching the end. . . .

It would show small understanding of Chekhov to take it into one's head to interpret Ivanov's words to Lvov as meaning that Chekhov, like the Tolstoy of the *War and Peace* period, saw his ideal in the everyday arrangement of life. Chekhov was only fighting against the ideas, and he said to it the most abusive thing that entered his head. For what can be more insulting to the idea than to be forced to listen to the praise of everyday life? But when the opportunity came his way, Chekhov could describe everyday life with equal venom. The story, *The Teacher of Literature*, may serve as an example. The teacher lives entirely by Ivanov's prescription. He has his job and his wife—neither Jewess nor abnormal, nor blue-stocking—and a home that fits like a shell . . . ; but all this does not prevent Chekhov from driving the poor teacher by slow degrees into the usual trap, and bringing him to a condition wherein it is left to him only 'to fall down and weep, and beat his head against the floor.' Chekhov had no 'ideal,' not even the ideal of 'everyday life' which Tolstoy glorified with such inimitable and incomparable mastery in his early works. An ideal presupposes submission, the voluntary denial of one's own right to independence, freedom and power; and demands of this kind, even a hint of such demands, roused in Chekhov all that force off disgust and repulsion of which he alone was capable.

V

Thus the real, the only hero of Chekhov, is the hopeless man. He has absolutely no *action* left for him in life, save to beat his head against the stones. It is not surprising that such a man should be intolerable to his neighbours. Everywhere he brings death and destruction with him. He himself is aware of it, but he has not the power to go apart from men. With all his soul he endeavours to tear himself out of his horrible condition. Above all he is attracted to fresh, young, untouched beings; with their help he hopes to recover his right to life which he has lost. The hope is vain. The beginning of decay always appears, all-conquering, and at the end Chekhov's hero is left to himself alone. He has nothing, he must create everything for himself. And this 'creation out of the void,' or more truly the possibility of this creation, is the only problem which can occupy and inspire Chekhov. When he has stripped his hero of the last shred, when nothing is left for him but to beat his head against the wall, Chekhov begins to feel something like satisfaction, a strange fire lights in his burnt-out eyes, a fire which Mihailovsky did not call 'evil' in vain.

Creation out of the void! Is not this task beyond the limit of human powers, of human *rights*? Mihailovsky obviously had one straight answer to the question. . . . As for Chekhov himself, if the question were put to him in such a deliberately definite form, he would probably be unable to answer, although he was continually engaged in the activity, or more properly, because he was continually so engaged. Without fear of mistake, one may say that the people who answer the question without hesitation in either sense have never come near to it or to any of the so-called ultimate questions of life. Hesitation is a necessary and integral element in the judgment of those men whom Fate has brought near to false problems. How Chekhov's hand trembled while he wrote the concluding lines of his *Tedious Story*! The professor's pupil—the being nearest and dearest to him, but like himself, for all her youth, overstrained and bereft of all hope—has come to Kharkov to seek his advice. The following conversation takes place:

"'Nicolai Stepanich!" she says, growing pale and pressing her hands to her breast. "Nicolai Stepanich! I can't go on like this any longer. For God's sake tell me now, immediately. What shall I do? Tell me, what shall I do?"

"'What can I say? I am beaten. I can say nothing."

"'But tell me, I implore you," she continues, out of breath and trembling all over her body. "I swear to you, I can't go on like this any longer. I haven't the strength."

'She drops into a chair and begins to sob. She throws her head back, wrings her hands, stamps with her feet; her hat falls from her head and dangles by its string, her hair is loosened.

'"Help me, help," she implores. "I can't bear it any more."

'"There's nothing that I can say to you, Katy," I say.

'"Help me," she sobs, seizing my hand and kissing it. "You're my father, my only friend. You're wise and learned, and you've lived long! You were a teacher. Tell me what to do."

'"Upon my conscience, Katy, I do not know."

'I am bewildered and surprised, stirred by her sobbing, and I can hardly stand upright.

'"Let's have some breakfast, Katy," I say with a constrained smile.

'Instantly I add in a sinking voice: "I shall be dead soon, Katy. . ."

'"Only one word, only one word," she weeps and stretches out her hands to me. "What shall I do? . . ."'

But the professor has not the word to give. He turns the conversation to the weather, Kharkov and other indifferent matters. Katy gets up and holds out her hand to him, without looking at him. 'I want to ask her.' he concludes his story, '"So it means you won't be at my funeral?" But she does not look at me; her hand is cold and like a stranger's . . . I escort her to the door in silence. . . . She goes out of my room and walks down the long passage, without looking back. She knows that my eyes are following her, and probably on the landing she will look back. No, she did not look back. The black dress showed for the last time, her steps were stilled. . . . Good-bye, my treasure! . . .'

The only answer which the wise, educated, long-lived Nicolai Stepanovich, a teacher all his life, can give to Katy's question is, 'I don't know.' There is not, in all his great experience of the past, a single method, rule, or suggestion, which might apply, even in the smallest degree, to the wild incongruity of the new conditions of Katy's life and his own. Katy can live thus no longer; neither can he himself continue to endure his disgusting and shameful helplessness. They both, old and young, with their whole hearts desire to support each other; they can between them find no way. To her question: 'What shall I do?' he replied: 'I shall soon be dead.' To his 'I shall soon be dead' she answers with wild sobbing, wringing her hands and absurdly repeating the same words over and over again. It would have been better to have asked no question, not to have begun that frank conversation of souls. But they do not yet understand that. In their old life talk would bring them relief and frank confession, intimacy. But now, after such a meeting they can suffer each other no longer. Katy leaves the old professor, her foster-father, her true father and friend, in the knowledge that he has become a stranger to her. She did not even turn round towards him as she went away. Both felt that nothing remained save to beat their heads against the wall. Therein each acts at his own peril, and there can be no dreaming of a consoling union of souls.

VI

Chekhov knew what conclusions he had reached in *The Tedious Story* and *Ivanov*. Some of his critics also knew, and told him so. I cannot venture to say what was the cause—whether fear of public opinion, or his horror at his own discoveries, or both together—but evidently there came a moment to Chekhov when he decided at all costs to surrender his position and retreat. The fruit of this decision was *Ward No. 6*. In this story the hero of the drama is the same familiar Chekhov character, the doctor. The setting, too, is quite the usual one, though changed to a slight extent. Nothing in particular has occurred in the doctor's life. He happened to come to an out-of-the way place in the provinces, and gradually, by continually avoiding life and people, he reached a condition of utter will-lessness, which he represented to himself as the ideal of human happiness. He is indifferent to everything, beginning with his hospital, where he can hardly ever be found, where under the reign of the drunken brute of an assistant the patients are swindled and neglected.

In the mental ward reigns a porter who is a discharged soldier: he punches his restless patients into shape. The doctor does not care, as though he were living in some distant other world, and does not understand what is going on before his very eyes. He happens to enter his ward and to have a conversation with one of his patients. He listens quietly to him; but his answer is words instead of deeds. He tries to show his lunatic acquaintance that external influences cannot affect us in any way at all. The lunatic does not agree, becomes impertinent, presents objections, in which, as in the thoughts of many lunatics, nonsensical assertions are mixed with very profound remarks. Indeed, there is so little nonsense that from the conversation you would hardly imagine that you have to do with a lunatic. The doctor is delighted with his new friend, but does nothing whatsoever to make him more comfortable. The patient is still under the porter's thumb as he used to be, and the porter gives him a thrashing on the least provocation. The patient, the doctor, the people round, the whole setting of the hospital and the doctor's rooms, are described with wonderful talent. Everything induces you to make absolutely no resistance and to become fatalistically indifferent:—let them get drunk, let them fight, let them thieve, let them be brutal—what does it matter! Evidently it is so predestined by the supreme council of nature. The philosophy of inactivity which the doctor professes is as it were prompted and whispered by the immutable laws of human existence. Apparently there is no force which may tear one from its power. So far everything is more or less in the Chekhov style. But the end is completely different. By the intrigues of his colleague, the doctor himself is taken as a patient into the mental ward. He is deprived of freedom, shut up in a wing of the hospital, and even thrashed, thrashed by the same porter whose behaviour he had taught his lunatic acquaintance to accept, thrashed before his acquaintance's very eyes. The doctor instantly awakens as though out of a dream. A fierce desire to struggle and to protest manifests itself in him. True, at this moment he dies; but the idea is triumphant, still. The critics could consider themselves quite satisfied. Chekhov had openly repented and renounced the theory of non-resistance; and, I believe, *Ward No. 6* met with a sympathetic reception at the time. In passing I would say that the doctor dies very beautifully: in his last moments he sees a herd of deer. . . .

Indeed, the construction of this story leaves no doubt in the mind. Chekhov wished to compromise, and he compromised. He had come to feel how intolerable was hopelessness, how impossible the creation from a void. To beat one's head against the stones, eternally to beat one's head against the stones, is so horrible that it were better to return to idealism. Then the truth of the wonderful Russian saying was proved: Don't forswear the beggar's wallet nor the prison.' Chekhov joined the cherished Russian writers, and began to praise the idea. But not for long. His very next story, *The Duel*, has a different character. Its conclusion is also apparently idealistic, but only in appearance. The principal hero Layevsky is a parasite like all Chekhov's heroes. He does nothing, can do nothing, does not even wish to do anything, lives chiefly at others' expense, runs up debts, seduces women. . . . His condition is intolerable and he is living with another man's wife, whom he has come to loathe as he loathes himself, yet he cannot get rid of her. He is always in straitened circumstances and in debt everywhere: his friends dislike and despise him. His state of mind is always such that he is ready to run no matter where, never looking backwards, only away from the place where he is living now. His illegal wife is in roughly the same position, unless it be even more horrible. Without knowing why, without love, without even being attracted, she gives herself to the first, commonplace man she meets; and then she feels as though she had been covered from head to foot in filth, and the filth had stuck so close to her that not ocean itself could wash her clean. This couple lives in the world, in a remote little place in the Caucasus, and naturally attracts Chekhov's attention. There is no denying the interest of the subject: two persons befouled, who can neither tolerate others nor themselves. . . .

For contrast's sake Chekhov brings Layevsky into collision with the zoologist. Von Koren, who has come to the seaside town on important business—every one recognises its importance—to study the embryology of the medusa. Von Koren, as one may see from his name, is of German origin and therefore deliberately represented as a healthy, normal, clean man, the grandchild of Goncharov's Stolz, the direct opposite of Layevsky, who on his side is nearly related to our old friend Oblomov. But in Goncharov the contrast between Stolz and Oblomov is quite different in nature and meaning to the contrast in Chekhov. The novelist of the 'forties hoped that a *rapprochement* with Western culture would renew and resuscitate Russia. And Oblomov himself is not represented as an utterly hopeless person. He is only lazy, inactive, unenterprising. You have the feeling that were he to awaken he would be a match for a dozen Stolzes. Layevsky is a different affair. He is awake already, he was awakened years ago, but his awakening, did him no good. . . . 'He does not love nature; he has no God; he or his companions had ruined every trustful girl he had known; all his life long he had not planted one single little tree, not grown one blade of grass in his own garden, nor while he lived among the living, had he saved the life of one single fly; but only ruined and destroyed, and lied, and lied. . . .' The good-natured sluggard Oblomov degenerated into a disgusting, terrible animal, while the clean Stolz lived and remained clean in his posterity! But to the new Oblomov he speaks differently. Von Koren calls Layevsky a scoundrel and a rogue, and demands that he should be punished with the utmost severity. To reconcile them is impossible. The more they meet, the deeper, the more merciless, the more implacable is their hatred for each other. It is impossible that they should live together on the earth. It must be one or the other; either the normal Von Koren, or the degenerate decadent Layevsky. Of course, all the external, material force is on Von Koren's side in the struggle. He is always in the right, always victorious, always triumphant—in act no less than in theory. It is curious that Chekhov, the irreconcilable enemy of all kinds of philosophy—not one of his heroes philosophises, or if he does, his philosophising is unsuccessful, ridiculous, weak and unconvincing—makes an exception for Von Koren, a typical representative of the positive, materialistic school. His words breathe vigour and conviction. They have in them even pathos and a maximum of logical sequence. There are many materialist heroes in Chekhov's stories, but in their materialism there is a tinge of veiled idealism, according to the stereotyped prescription of the 'sixties. Such heroes Chekhov ridicules and derides. Idealism of every kind, whether open or concealed, roused feelings of intolerable bitterness in Chekhov. He found it more pleasant to listen to the merciless menaces of a downright materialist than to accept the dry-as-dust consolations of humanising idealism. An invincible power is in the world, crushing and crippling man—this is clear and even palpable. The least indiscretion, and the mightiest and the most insignificant alike fall victims to it. One can only deceive oneself about it so long as one knows of it only by hearsay. But the man who had once been in the iron claws of necessity loses for ever his taste for idealistic self-delusion. No more does he diminish the enemy's power, he will rather exaggerate it. And the pure logical materialism which Von Koren professes gives the most complete expression of our dependence upon the elemental powers of nature. Von Koren's speech has the stroke of a hammer, and each blow strikes not Layevsky but Chekhov himself on his wounds. He gives more and more strength to Von Koren's arm, he puts himself in the way of his blows. For what reason? Decide as you may. Perhaps Chekhov cherished a secret hope that self-inflicted torment might be the one road to a new life? He has not told us so. Perhaps he did not know the reason himself, and perhaps he was afraid to offend the positive idealism which held such undisputed sway over contemporary literature. As yet he dared not lift up his voice against the public opinion of Europe— for we do not ourselves invent our philosophical conceptions; they drift down on the wind from Europe! And, to avoid quarrelling with people, he devised a commonplace, happy ending for his terrible story. At the end of the story Layevsky 'reforms': he marries his mistress; gives up his dissolute life; and begins to devote himself to transcribing documents, in order to pay his debts. Normal people can be perfectly satisfied, since normal people read only the last lines of the fable,—the moral; and the moral of *The Duel* is most wholesome: Layevsky reforms and begins transcribing documents. Of course it may seem that such an ending is more like a gibe at morality; but normal people are not too penetrating psychologists. They are scared of double meanings and, with the 'sincerity' peculiar to themselves, they take every word of the writer for good coin. Good luck to them!

VII

The only philosophy which Chekhov took seriously, and therefore seriously fought, was positivist materialism—just the positivist materialism, the limited materialism which does not pretend to theoretical completeness. With all his soul Chekhov felt the awful dependence of a living being upon the invisible but invincible and ostentatiously soulless laws of nature. And materialism, above all scientific materialism, which is reserved and does not hasten in pursuit of it the final word and eschews logical completeness, wholly reduces to the definition of the external conditions of our existence. The experience of every day, every hour, every minute, convinces us that lonely and weak man brought to face with the laws of nature, must always adapt himself and give way, give way, give way. The old professor could not regain his youth; the overstrained Ivanov could not recover his strength; Layevsky could not wash away the filth with which he was covered—interminable series of implacable, purely materialistic *non possumus*, against which human genius can set nothing but submission or forgetfulness. *Résigne-toi, mon coeur, dors ton sommeil de brute*—we shall find no other words before the pictures which are unfolded in Chekhov's books. The submission is but an outward show; under it lies concealed a hard, malignant hatred of the unknown enemy. Sleep and oblivion are only seeming. Does a man sleep, does he forget, when he calls his sleep, *sommeil de brute*? But how can he change? The tempestuous protests with which *The Tedious Story* is filled, the need to pour forth the pent-up indignation, soon begin to appear useless, and even insulting to human dignity. Chekhov's last rebellious work is *Uncle Vanya*. Like the old professor and like Ivanov, Uncle Vanya raises the alarm and makes an incredible bother about his ruined life. He, too, in a voice not his own, fills the stage with his cries: 'Life is over, life is over,'—as though indeed any of these about him, any one in the whole world, could be responsible for his misfortune. But wailing and lamentation is not sufficient for him. He covers his own mother with insults. Aimlessly, like a lunatic, without need or purpose, he begins shooting at his imaginary enemy, Sonya's pitiable and unhappy father. His is voice is not enough, he turns to the revolver. He is ready to fire all the cannon on earth, to beat every drum, to ring every bell. To him it seems that the whole of mankind, the whole of the universe, is sleeping, that the neighbours must be awakened. He is prepared for any extravagance, having no rational way of escape; for to confess at once that there is no escape is beyond the capacity of any man. Then begins a Chekhov history: 'He cannot reconcile himself, neither can he refuse so to reconcile himself. He can only weep and beat his head against the wall.' Uncle Vanya does it openly, before men's eyes; but how painful to him is the memory of this frank unreserve! When every one has departed after a stupid and painful scene, Uncle Vanya realizes that he should have kept silence, that it is no use to confess certain things to any one, not even to one's nearest friend. A stranger's eyes cannot endure the sight of hopelessness. 'Your life is over— you have yourself to thank for it: you are a human being no more, all human things are alien to you. Your neighbours are no more neighbours to you, but strangers. You have no right either to help others or to expect help from them. Your destiny is—absolute loneliness.' Little by little Chekhov becomes convinced of this truth: *Uncle Vanya* is the last trial of loud public protest, of a vigorous 'declaration of rights.' And even in this drama Uncle Vanya is the only one to rage, although there are among the characters Doctor Astrov and poor Sonya, who might also avail themselves of their right to rage, and even to fire the cannon. But they are silent. They even repeat certain comfortable and angelic words concerning the happy future of mankind; which is to say that their silence is doubly deep, seeing that 'comfortable words' upon the lips of such people are the evidence of their final severance from life: they have left the whole world, and now they admit no one to their presence.

They have fenced themselves with comfortable words, as with the Great Wall of China, from the curiosity and attention of their neighbours. Outwardly they resemble all men, therefore no man dares to touch their inward life.

What is the meaning and significance of this straining inward labour in those whose lives are over? Probably Chekhov would answer this question as Nicolai Stepanovich answered Katy's, with 'I do not know.' He would add nothing. But this life alone, more like to death than life, attracted and engaged him. Therefore his utterance grew softer and slower with every year. Of all our writers Chekhov has the softest voice. All the energy of his heroes is turned inwards. They create nothing visible; worse, they destroy all things visible by their outward passivity and inertia. A 'positive thinker' like Von Koren brands them with terrible words, and the more content is he with himself and his justice, the more energy he puts into his anathemas. 'Scoundrels, villains, degenerates, degraded animals!'—what did Von Koren not devise to fit the Layevskys? The manifestly positive thinker wants to force Layevsky to transcribe documents. The surreptitiously positive thinkers—idealists and metaphysicians—do not use abusive words. Instead they bury Chekhov's nerves alive in their idealistic cemeteries, which are called conceptions of the world. Chekhov himself abstains from the 'solution of the question' with a persistency to which most of the critics probably wished a better fate, and he continues his long stories of men and the life of men, who have nothing to lose, as though the only interest in life were this nightmare suspension between life and death. What does it teach us of life or death? Again we must answer: 'I do not know,'—those words which arouse the greatest aversion in positive thinkers, but appear in some mysterious way to be the permanent elements in the ideas of Chekhov's people. This is the reason why the philosophy of materialism, though so hostile, is yet so near to them. It contains no answer which can compel man to cheerful submission. It bruises and destroys him, but it does not call itself rational; it does not demand gratitude; it does not demand anything, since it has neither soul nor speech. A man may acknowledge it and hate it. If he manages to get square with it—he is right; if he fails—*vae victis*. How comfortably sounds the voice of the unconcealed ruthlessness of inanimate, impersonal, indifferent nature, compared with the hypocritical and cloying melodies of idealistic, humanistic conceptions of the world! Then again—and this is the chiefest thing of all—men can struggle with nature still! And in the struggle with nature every weapon is lawful. In the struggle with nature man always remains man, and, therefore, right, whatever means he tries for his salvation, even if he were to refuse to accept the fundamental principle of the world's being—the indestructibility of matter and energy, the law of inertia and the rest—since who will dispute that the most colossal dead force must be subservient to man? But a conception of the world is an utterly different affair! Before uttering a word it puts forward an irreducible demand: man must serve the idea. And this demand is considered not merely as something understood, but as of extraordinary sublimity. Is it strange then that in the choice between idealism and materialism Chekhov inclined to the latter— the strong but honest adversary? With idealism a man can struggle only by contempt and Chekhov's works leave nothing to be desired in this respect. . . . But how shall a man struggle with materialism? And can it be overcome? Perhaps Chekhov's method may seem strange to my reader, nevertheless it is clear that he came to the conclusion that there was only one way to struggle, to which the prophets of old turned themselves: to beat one's head against the wall. Without thunder or cannon or alarm, in loneliness and silence, remote from their fellows and their fellows' fellows, to gather all the forces of despair for an absurd attempt long since condemned by science. Have you any right to expect from Chekhov an approval of scientific methods? Science has robbed him of everything: he is condemned to create from the void, to an activity of which a normal man, using normal means, is utterly incapable. To achieve the impossible one must first leave the road of routine. However obstinately we may pursue our scientific quests, they will not lead us to the elixir of life. Science began with casting away the longing for human omnipotence as in principle unattainable: her methods are such that success along certain of her paths preclude even seeking along others. In other words scientific method is defined by the character of the problems which she puts to herself. Indeed, not one of her problems can be solved by beating one's head against the wall. But this method, old-fashioned though it is—I repeat, it was known to the prophets and used by them—promised more to Chekhov and his nerves than all inductions and deductions (which were not invented by science, but have existed since the beginning of the world). This prompts a man with some mysterious instinct, and appears upon the scene whenever the need of it arises. Science condemns it. But that is nothing strange: it condemns science.

VIII

Now perhaps the further development and direction of Chekhov's creation will be intelligible, and that peculiar and unique blend in him of sober materialism and fanatical stubbornness in seeking new paths, always round about and hazardous. Like Hamlet, he would dig beneath his opponent a mine one yard deeper, so that he may at one moment blow engineer and engine into the air. His patience and fortitude in this hard, underground toil are amazing and to many intolerable. Everywhere is darkness, not a ray, not a spark, but Chekhov goes forward, slowly, hardly, hardly moving. . . . An inexperienced or impatient eye will perhaps observe no movement at all. It may be Chekhov himself does not know for certain whether he is moving forward or marking time. To calculate beforehand is impossible. Impossible even to hope. Man has entered that stage of his existence wherein the cheerful and foreseeing mind refuses its service. It is impossible for him to present to himself a clear and distinct notion of what is going on. Everything takes on a tinge of fantastical absurdity. One believes and disbelieves—everything. In *The Black Monk* Chekhov tells of a new reality, and in a tone which suggests that he is himself at a loss to say where the reality ends and the phantasmagoria begins. The black monk leads the young scholar into some mysterious remoteness, where the best dreams of mankind shall be realised. The people about call the monk a hallucination and fight him with medicines—drugs, better foods and milk. Kovrin himself does not know who is right. When he is speaking to the monk, it seems to him that the monk is right; when he sees before him his weeping wife and the serious, anxious faces of the doctors, he confesses that he is under the influence of fixed ideas, which lead him straight to lunacy. Finally, the black monk is victorious. Kovrin has not the power to support the banality which surrounds him; he breaks with his wife and her relations, who appear like inquisitors in his eyes, and goes away somewhere—but in our sight he arrives nowhere. At the end of the story he dies in order to give the author the right to make an end. This is always the case: when the author does not know what to do with his hero he kills him. Sooner or later in all probability this habit will be abandoned. In the future, probably, writers will convince themselves and the public that any kind of artificial completion is absolutely superfluous. The matter is exhausted—stop the tale short, even though it be on a half-word. Chekhov did so sometimes, but only sometimes. In most cases he preferred to satisfy the traditional demands and to supply his readers with an end. This habit is not so unimportant as at first sight it may seem. Consider even *The Black Monk*. The death of the hero is as it were an indication that abnormality must, in Chekhov's opinion, necessarily lead through an absurd life to an absurd death: but this was hardly Chekhov's firm conviction. It is clear that he expected something from abnormality, and therefore gave no deep attention to men who had left the common track. True, he came to no firm or definite conclusions, for all the tense effort of his creation. He became so firmly convinced that there was no issue from the entangled labyrinth, that the labyrinth with its infinite wanderings, its perpetual hesitations and strayings, its uncaused griefs and joys uncaused

—in brief, all things which normal men so fear and shun—became the very essence of his life. Of this and this alone must a man tell. Not of our invention is normal life, nor abnormal. Why then should the first alone be considered as the real reality?

The Sea-Gull must be considered one of the most characteristic, and therefore one of the most remarkable of Chekhov's works. Therein the artist's true attitude to life received its most complete expression. Here all the characters are either blind, and afraid to move from their seats in case they lose the way home, or half-mad, struggling and tossing about to no end nor purpose. Arkadzina the famous actress clings with her teeth to her seventy thousand roubles, her fame, and her last lover. Tregovin the famous writer writes day in, day out: he writes and writes, knowing neither end nor aim. People read his works and praise them, but he is not his own master; like Marko, the ferryman in the tale, he labours on without taking his hand from the oar, carrying passengers from one bank to the other. The boat, the passengers, and the river too, bore him to death. But how can he get rid of them? He might give the oars over to the first-comer: the solution is simple, but after it, as in the tale, he must go to heaven. Not Tregovin alone, but all the people in Chekhov's books who are no longer young remind one of Marko the ferryman. It is plain that they dislike their work, but, exactly as though they were hypnotised, they cannot break away from the influence of the alien power. The monotonous, even dismal, rhythm of life has lulled their consciousness and will to sleep. Everywhere Chekhov underlines this strange and mysterious trait of human life. His people always speak, always think, always do one and the same thing. One builds houses according to a plan made once for all (*My Life*); another goes on his round of visits from morn to night, collecting roubles (*Yonitch*); a third is always buying up houses (*Three Years*). Even the language of his characters is deliberately monotonous. They are all monotonous, to the point of stupidity, and they are all afraid to break the monotony, as though it were the source of extraordinary joys. Read Tregovin's monologue:

'. . . Let us talk. . . . Let us talk of my beautiful life. . . . What shall I begin with? [Musing a little.] . . . There are such things as fixed ideas, when a person thinks day and night, for instance, of the moon, always of the moon. I too have my moon. Day and night I am at the mercy of one besetting idea: "I must write, I must write, I must." I have hardly finished one story than, for some reason or other, I must write a second, then a third, and after the third, a fourth. I write incessantly, post-haste. I cannot do otherwise. Where then, I ask you, is beauty and serenity? What a monstrous life it is! I am sitting with you now, I am excited, but meanwhile every second I remember that an unfinished story is waiting for me. I see a cloud, like a grand piano. It smells of heliotrope. I say to myself: a sickly smell, a half-mourning colour. . . . I must not forget to use these words when describing a summer evening. I catch up myself and you on every phrase, on every word, and hurry to lock all these words and phrases into my literary storehouse. Perhaps they will be useful. When I finish work I run to the theatre, or go off fishing: at last I shall rest, forget myself. But no! a heavy ball of iron is dragging on my fetters,—a new subject, which draws me to the desk, and I must make haste to write and write again. And so on for ever, for ever. I have no rest from myself, and I feel that I am eating away my own life. I feel that the honey which I give to others has been made of the pollen of my most precious flowers, that I have plucked the flowers themselves and trampled them down to the roots. Surely, I am mad. Do my neighbours and friends treat me as a sane person? "What are you writing? What have you got ready for us?" The same thing, the same thing eternally, and it seems to me that the attention, the praise, the enthusiasm of my friends is all a fraud. I am being robbed like a sick man, and sometimes I am afraid that they will creep up to me and seize me, and put me away in an asylum.'

But why these torments? Throw up the oars and begin a new life. *Impossible*. While no answer comes down from heaven, Tregovin will not throw up the oars, will not begin a new life. In Chekhov's work, only young, very young and inexperienced people speak of a new life. They are always dreaming of happiness, regeneration, light, joy. They fly headlong into the flame, and are burned like silly butterflies. In *The Sea-Gull*, Nina Zaryechnaya and Trepliev, in other works other heroes, men and women alike—all are seeking for something, yearning for something, but not one of them does that which he desires. Each one lives in isolation; each is wholly absorbed in his life, and is indifferent to the lives of others. And the strange fate of Chekhov's heroes is that they strain to the last limit of their inward powers, but there are no visible results at all. They are all pitiable. The woman takes snuff, dresses slovenly, wears her hair loose, is uninteresting. The man is irritable, grumbling, takes to drink, bores every one about him. They act, they speak—always out of season. They cannot, I would even say they do not want to, adapt the outer world to themselves. Matter and energy unite according to their own laws—people live according to their own, as though matter and energy had no existence at all. In this Chekhov's intellectuals do not differ from illiterate peasants and the half-educated bourgeois. Life in the manor is the same as in the valley farm, the same as in the village. Not one believes that by changing his outward conditions he would change his fate as well. Everywhere reigns an unconscious but deep and ineradicable conviction that our will must be directed towards ends which have nothing in common with the organised life of mankind. Worse still, the organisation appears to be the enemy of the will and of man. One must spoil, devour, destroy, ruin. To think out things quietly, to anticipate the future—that is impossible. One must beat one's head, beat one's head eternally against the wall. And to what purpose? Is there any purpose at all? Is it a beginning or an end? Is it possible to see in it the warrant of a new and inhuman creation, a creation out of the void? 'I do not know' was the old professor's answer to Katy. 'I do not know' was Chekhov's answer to the sobs of those tormented unto death. With these words, and only these, can an essay upon Chekhov end. *Résigne-toi, mon coeur, dors ton sommeil de brute.*

FRANCIS FERGUSSON

The Cherry Orchard:
A Theater-Poem of the Suffering of Change

The Plot of *The Cherry Orchard*

The Cherry Orchard is often accused of having no plot whatever, and it is true that the story gives little indication of the play's content or meaning; nothing happens, as the Broadway reviewers so often point out. Nor does it have a thesis, though many attempts have been made to attribute a thesis to it, to make it into a Marxian tract, or into a nostalgic defense of the old regime. The play does not have much of a plot in either of these accepted meanings of the word, for it is not addressed to the rationalizing mind but to the poetic and histrionic sensibility. It is an imitation of an action in the strictest sense, and it is plotted according to the first meaning of this word which I have distinguished in other contexts: the incidents are selected and arranged to define an action in a certain mode; a complete action, with a beginning, middle, and end in time. Its freedom from the mechanical order of the thesis or the intrigue is the sign of the perfection of Chekhov's realistic art. And its apparently casual incidents are actually composed with most elaborate and conscious skill to reveal the underlying life, and the natural, objective form of the play as a whole.

In *Ghosts*, . . . the action is distorted by the stereotyped requirements of the thesis and the intrigue. That is partly a matter of the mode of action

From *Chekhov's Great Plays*. © 1981 by New York University Press.

which Ibsen was trying to show; a quest "of ethical motivation" which requires some sort of intellectual framework, and yet can have no final meaning in the purely literal terms of Ibsen's theater. *The Cherry Orchard*, on the other hand, is a drama "of pathetic motivation," a theater-poem of the suffering of change; and this mode of action and awareness is much closer to the skeptical basis of modem realism, and to the histrionic basis of all realism. Direct perception before predication is always true, says Aristotle; and the extraordinary feat of Chekhov is to predicate nothing. This he achieves by means of his plot: he selects only those incidents, those moments in his characters' lives, between their rationalized efforts, when they sense their situation and destiny most directly. So he contrives to show the action of the play as a whole—the unsuccessful attempt to cling to the cherry orchard—in many diverse reflectors and without propounding any thesis about it.

The slight narrative thread which ties these incidents and characters together for the inquiring mind, is quickly recounted. The family that owns the old estate named after its famous orchard—Lyubov', her brother Gayev, and her daughters Varya and Anya—is all but bankrupt, and the question is how to prevent the bailiffs from selling the estate to pay their debts. Lopakhin, whose family were formerly serfs on the estate, is now rapidly growing rich as a businessman, and he offers a very sensible plan: chop down the orchard, divide the property into small lots, and sell them off to make a residential suburb for the growing industrial town nearby. Thus the cash value of the estate could be not only preserved, but increased. But this would not save what Lyubov' and her brother find valuable in the old estate; they cannot consent to the destruction of the orchard. But they cannot find, or earn, or borrow the money to pay their debts either; and in due course the estate is sold at auction to Lopakhin himself, who will make a very good thing of it. His workmen are hacking at the old trees before the family is out of the house.

The play may be briefly described as a realistic ensemble pathos: the characters all suffer the passing of the estate in different ways, thus adumbrating this change at a deeper and more generally significant level than that of any individual's experience. The action which they all share by analogy, and which informs the suffering of the destined change of the cherry orchard, is "to save the cherry orchard": that is, each character sees some value in it—economic, sentimental, cultural—which he wishes to keep. By means of his plot, Chekhov always focuses attention on the general action: his crowded stage, full of the characters I have mentioned as well as half a dozen hangers-on, is like an implicit discussion of the fatality which concerns them all; but Chekhov does not believe in their ideas, and the interplay he shows among his dramatic personae is not so much the play of thought as the alternation of the characters' perceptions of their situation, as the moods shift and the time for decision comes and goes.

Though the action which Chekhov chooses to show onstage is "pathetic," i.e., suffering and perception, it is complete: the cherry orchard is constituted before our eyes, and then dissolved. The first act is a prologue: it is the occasion of Lyubov"s return from Paris to try to resume her old life. Through her eyes and those of her daughter Anya, as well as from the complementary perspectives of Lopakhin and Trofimov, we see the estate as it were in the round, in its many possible meanings. The second act corresponds to the agon; it is in this act that we become aware of the conflicting values of all the characters, and of the efforts they make (offstage) to save each one *his* orchard. The third act corresponds to the pathos and peripety of the traditional tragic form. The occasion is a rather hysterical party which Lyubov' gives while her estate is being sold at auction in the nearby town; it ends with Lopakhin's announcement, in pride and the bitterness of guilt, that he was the purchaser. The last act is the epiphany: we see the action, now completed, in a new and ironic light. The occasion is the departure of the family: the windows are boarded up, the furniture piled in the corners, and the bags packed. All the characters feel, and the audience sees in a thousand ways, that the wish to save the orchard has amounted in fact to destroying it; the gathering of its denizens to separation; the homecoming to departure. What this "means" we are not told. But the action is completed, and the poem of the suffering of change concludes in a new and final perception, and a rich chord of feeling.

The structure of each act is based upon a more or less ceremonious social occasion. In his use of the social ceremony—arrivals, departures, anniversaries, parties—Chekhov is akin to James. His purpose is the same: to focus attention on an action which all share by analogy, instead of upon the reasoned purpose of any individual, as Ibsen does in his drama of ethical motivation. Chekhov uses the social occasion also to reveal the individual at moments when he is least enclosed in his private rationalization and most open to disinterested insights. The Chekhovian ensembles may appear superficially to be mere pointless stalemates—too like family gatherings and arbitrary meetings which we know offstage. So they are. But in his miraculous arrangement the very discomfort of many presences is made to reveal fundamental aspects of the human situation.

That Chekhov's art of plotting is extremely conscious and deliberate is clear the moment one considers the distinction between the stories of his characters as we learn about them, and the moments of their lives which he chose to show directly onstage. Lopakhin, for example, is a man of action like one of the new capitalists in Gor'kiy's plays. Chekhov knew all about him, and could have shown us an exciting episode from his career if he had not chosen to see him only when he was forced to pause and pathetically sense his own motives in a wider context which qualifies their importance. Lyubov' has been dragged about Europe for years by her ne'er-do-well lover, and her life might have yielded several sure-fire erotic intrigues like those of the commercial theater. But Chekhov, like all the great artists of modern times, rejected these standard motivations as both stale and false. The actress Arkadina, in *The Seagull*, remarks, as she closes a novel of Maupassant's, "Well, among the French that may be, but here with us there's nothing of the kind, we've no set program." In the context the irony of her remark is deep: she is herself a purest product of the commercial theater, and at that very time she is engaged in a love affair of the kind she objects to in Maupassant. But Chekhov, with his subtle art of plotting, has caught her in a situation, and at a brief moment of clarity and pause, when the falsity of her career is clear to all, even herself.

Thus Chekhov, by his art of plot-making, defines an action in the opposite mode to that of *Ghosts*. Ibsen defines a desperate quest for reasons and for ultimate, intelligible moral values. This action falls naturally into the form of the agon, and at the end of the play Ibsen is at a loss to develop the final pathos, or bring it to an end with an accepted perception. But the pathetic is the very mode of action and awareness which seems to Chekhov closest to the reality of the human situation, and by means of his plot he shows, even in characters who are not in themselves unusually passive, the suffering and the perception of change. The "moment" of human experience which *The Cherry Orchard* presents thus corresponds to that of the Sopho-clean chorus, and of the evenings in the *Purgatorio*. *Ghosts* is a fighting play, armed for its sharp encounter with the rationalizing mind, its poetry concealed by its reasons. Chekhov's poetry, like Ibsen's, is behind the natu-ralistic surfaces; but the form of the play as a whole is "nothing but" poetry in the widest sense: the coherence of the concrete elements of the composi-tion. Hence the curious vulnerability of Chekhov on the contemporary stage: he does not argue, he merely presents; and though his audiences even on Broadway are touched by the time they reach the last act, they are at a loss to say what it is all about.

It is this reticent objectivity of Chekhov also which makes him so diffi-cult to analyze in words: he appeals exclusively to the histrionic sensibility where the little poetry of modern realism is to be found. Nevertheless, the effort of analysis must be made if one is to understand this art at all; and if the reader will bear with me, he is asked to consider one element, that of the scene, in the composition of the second act.

ACT II: The Scene as a Basic Element in the Composition

Jean Cocteau writes, in his preface to *Les Mariés de la Tour Eiffel*: "The action of my play is in images (*imagée*) while the text is not: I attempt to substitute a 'poetry of the theater' for 'poetry in the theater.' Poetry in the theater is a piece of lace which is impossible to see at a distance. Poetry of the theater would be coarse lace; a lace of ropes, a ship at sea. *Les Mariés* should have the frightening look of a drop of poetry under the microscope. The *scenes* are integrated like the *words* of a poem."

This description applies very exactly to *The Cherry Orchard*: the larger elements of the composition—the scenes or episodes, the setting, and the developing story—are composed in such a way as to make a poetry of the theater; but the "text" as we read it literally, is not. Chekhov's method, as Stark Young puts it in the preface to his translation of *The Seagull*, "is to take actual material such as we find in life and manage it in such a way that the inner meanings are made to appear. On the surface the life in his plays is natural, possible, and at times in effect even casual."

Young's translations of Chekhov's plays, together with his beautifully accurate notes, explanations, and interpretations, have made the text of Chekhov at last available for the English-speaking stage, and for any reader who will bring to his reading a little patience and imagination. Young shows us what Chekhov means in detail: by the particular words his characters use; by their rhythms of speech; by their gestures, pauses, and bits of stage business. In short, he makes the text transparent, enabling us to see through it to the music of action, the underlying poetry of the composition as a whole— and this is as much as to say that any study of Chekhov (lacking as we do adequate and available productions) must be based upon Young's work. At this point I propose to take this work for granted; to assume the translucent text; and to consider the role of the setting in the poetic or musical order of Act II.

The second act, as I have said, corresponds to the agon of the traditional plot scheme: it is here that we see most clearly the divisive purposes of the characters, the contrasts between their views of the cherry orchard itself. But the center of interest is not in these individual conflicts, nor in the contrasting versions for their own sake, but in the common fatality which they reveal: the passing of the old estate. The setting, as we come to know it behind the casual surfaces of the text, is one of the chief elements in this poem of change: if Act II were a lyric, instead of an act of a play, the setting would be a crucial word appearing in a succession of rich contexts which endow it with a developing meaning.

Chekhov describes the setting in the following realistic terms. "A field.

An old chapel, long abandoned, with crooked walls, near it a well, big stones that apparently were once tombstones, and an old bench. A road to the estate of Gayev can be seen. On one side poplars rise, casting their shadows, the cherry orchard begins there. In the distance a row of telegraph poles; and far, far away, faintly traced on the horizon, is a large town, visible only in the clearest weather. The sun will soon be down."

To make this set out of a cyclorama, flats, cut-out silhouettes, and lighting effects would be difficult, without producing that unbelievable but literally intended—and in any case indigestible—scene which modern realism demands; and here Chekhov is uncomfortably bound by the convention of his time. The best strategy in production is that adopted by Robert Edmond Jones in his setting for *The Seagull*: to pay lip service only to the convention of photographic realism, and make the trees, the chapel, and all the other elements as simple as possible. The less closely the setting is defined by the carpenter, the freer it is to play the role Chekhov for it: a role which changes and develops in relation to the story. Shakespeare did not have this problem; he could present his setting in different ways at different moments in a few lines of verse:

> Alack! the night comes on, and the bleak winds
> Do sorely ruffle; for many miles about
> There's scarce a bush.

Chekhov, as we shall see, gives his setting life and flexibility in spite of the visible elements onstage, not by means of the poetry of words but by means of his characters' changing sense of it.

When the curtain rises we see the setting simply as the country at the sentimental hour of sunset. Yepikhodov is playing his guitar and other hangers-on of the estate are loafing, as is their habit, before supper. The dialogue which starts after a brief pause focuses attention upon individuals in the group: Sharlotta, the governess, boasting of her culture and complaining that no one understands her; the silly maid Dunyasha, who is infatuated with Yasha, Lyubov"s valet. The scene, as reflected by these characters, is a satirical period-piece like the "Stag at Eve" or "The Maiden's Prayer"; and when the group falls silent and begins to drift away (having heard Lyubov', Gayev, and Lopakhin approaching along the path) Chekhov expects us to smile at the sentimental clichés which the place and the hour have produced.

But Lyubov"s party brings with it a very different atmosphere: of irritation, frustration, and fear. It is here we learn that Lopakhin cannot persuade Lyubov' and Gayev to put their affairs in order; that Gayev has been making futile gestures toward getting a job and borrowing money; that

Lyubov' is worried about the estate, about her daughters, and about her lover, who has now fallen ill in Paris. Lopakhin in a huff, offers to leave; but Lyubov' will not let him go—"It's more cheerful with you here," she says; and this group in its turn falls silent. In the distance we hear the music of the Jewish orchestra—when Chekhov wishes us to raise our eyes from the people in the foreground to their wider setting, he often uses music as a signal and an inducement. This time the musical entrance of the setting into our consciousness is more urgent and sinister than it was before: we see not so much the peace of evening as the silhouette of the dynamic industrial town on the horizon, and the approach of darkness. After a little more desultory conversation, there is another pause, this time without music, and the foreboding aspect of the scene in silence is more intense.

In this silence Firs, the ancient servant, hurries on with Gayev's coat, to protect him from the evening chill, and we briefly see the scene through Firs's eyes. He remembers the estate before the emancipation of the serfs, when it was the scene of a way of life which made sense to him; and now we become aware of the frail relics of this life: the old gravestones and the chapel "fallen out of the perpendicular."

In sharpest contrast with this vision come the young voices of Anya, Varya, and Trofimov, who are approaching along the path. The middle-aged and the old in the foreground are pathetically grateful for this note of youth, of strength, and of hope; and presently they are listening happily (though without agreement or belief) to Trofimov's aspirations, his creed of social progress, and his conviction that their generation is no longer important to the life of Russia. When the group falls silent again, they are all disposed to contentment with the moment; and when Yepikhodov's guitar is heard, and we look up, we feel the country and the evening under the aspect of hope— as offering freedom from the responsibilities and conflicts of the estate itself:

YEPIKHODOV *passes by at the back, playing his guitar.*

LYUBOV' *lost in thought*: Yepikhodov is coming—
ANYA *lost in thought*: Yepikhodov is coming.
GAYEV: The sun has set, ladies and gentlemen.
TROFIMOV: Yes.
GAYEV *not loud and as if he were declaiming*: Oh, Nature, wonderful, you gleam with eternal radiance, beautiful and indifferent, you, whom we call Mother, combine in yourself both life and death, you give life and take it away.
VARYA *beseechingly*: Uncle!

Gayev's false, rhetorical note ends the harmony, brings us back to the present and to the awareness of change on the horizon, and produces a sort of empty stalemate—a silent pause with worry and fear in it.

> *All sit absorbed in their thoughts. There is only the silence. Firs is heard muttering to himself softly. Suddenly a distant sound is heard, as if from the sky, like the sound of a snapped string, dying away, mournful.*

This mysterious sound is used like Yepikhodov's strumming to remind us of the wider scene, but (though distant) it is sharp, almost a warning signal, and all the characters listen and peer toward the dim edges of the horizon. In their attitudes and guesses Chekhov reflects, in rapid succession, the contradictory aspects of the scene which have been developed at more length before us:

LYUBOV': What's that?
LOPAKHIN: I don't know. Somewhere far off in a mine shaft a
    bucket fell. But somewhere very far off.
GAYEV: And it may be some bird—like a heron.
TROFIMOV: Or an owl—
LYUBOV' *shivering*: It's unpleasant, somehow. *A pause.*
FIRS: Before the disaster it was like that. The owl hooted and the
    samovar hummed without stopping, both.
GAYEV: Before what disaster?
FIRS: Before the emancipation.
    A pause.
LYUBOV': You know, my friends, let's go. . . .

Lyubov' feels the need to retreat, but the retreat is turned into flight when "the wayfarer" suddenly appears on the path asking for money. Lyubov' in her bewilderment, her sympathy, and her bad conscience, gives him gold. The party breaks up, each in his own way thwarted and demoralized.

Anya and Trofimov are left onstage; and, to conclude his theatrical poem of the suffering of change, Chekhov reflects the setting in them:

ANYA *a pause*: It's wonderful here today!
TROFIMOV: Yes, the weather is marvelous.
ANYA: What have you done to me, Petya, why don't I love the
    cherry orchard any longer the way I used to? I loved it too
    tenderly; it seemed to me there was not a better place on earth
    than our orchard.

TROFIMOV: All Russia is our garden. The earth is immense
and beautiful. . . . .

The sun has set, the moon is rising with its chill and its ancient animal excite-
ment, and the estate is dissolved in the darkness as Nineveh is dissolved in a
pile of rubble with vegetation creeping over it. Chekhov wishes to show the
cherry orchard as "gone"; but for this purpose he employs not only the literal
time-scheme (sunset to moonrise) but, as reflectors, Anya and Trofimov, for
whom the present in any form is already gone and only the bodiless future is
real. Anya's young love for Trofimov's intellectual enthusiasm (like Juliet's
"all as boundless as the sea") has freed her from her actual childhood home,
made her feel "at home in the world" anywhere. Trofimov's abstract aspirations give him a chillier and more artificial, but equally complete, detach-
ment not only from the estate itself (he disapproves of it on theoretical
grounds) but from Anya (he thinks it would be vulgar to be in love with her).
We hear the worried Varya calling for Anya in the distance; Anya and
Trofimov run down to the river to discuss the socialistic *Paradiso Terrestre*;
and with these complementary images of the human scene, and this subtle
chord of feeling, Chekhov ends the act.

The "scene" is only one element in the composition of Act II, but it
illustrates the nature of Chekhov's poetry of the theater. It is very clear, I
think, that Chekhov is not trying to present us with a rationalization of social
change *à la* Marx, or even with a subtler rationalization *à la* Shaw. On the
other hand, he is not seeking, like Wagner, to seduce us into one passion. He
shows us a moment of change in society, and he shows us a "pathos"; but the
elements of his composition are always taken as objectively real. He offers us
various rationalizations, various images, and various feelings, which cannot
be reduced either to one emotion or to one idea. they indicate an action and
a scene which is "there" before the rational formulations, or the emotionally
charged attitudes, of any of the characters.

The surrounding scene of *The Cherry Orchard* corresponds to the
significant stage of human life which Sophocles' choruses reveal, and to the
empty wilderness beyond Ibsen's little parlor. We miss, in Chekhov's scene,
any fixed points of human significance, and that is why, compared with
Sophocles, he seems limited and partial—a bit too pathetic even for our
bewildered times. But, precisely because he subtly and elaborately develops
the moments of pathos with their sad insights, he sees much more in the little
scene of modern realism than Ibsen does. Ibsen's snowpeaks strike us as
rather hysterical; but the "stage of Europe" which we divine behind the
cherry orchard is confirmed by a thousand impressions derived from other
sources. We may recognize its main elements in a cocktail party in

Connecticut or Westchester: someone's lawn full of voluble people; a dry white clapboard church (instead of an Orthodox chapel) just visible across a field; time passing, and the muffled roar of a four-lane highway under the hill—or we may be reminded of it in the final section of *The Wasteland*, with its twittering voices, its old gravestones and deserted chapel, and its dim crowd on the horizon foreboding change. It is because Chekhov says so little that he reveals so much, providing a concrete basis for many conflicting rationalizations of contemporary social change: by accepting the immediacy and unintelligibility of modern realism so completely, he in some ways transcends its limitations, and prepares the way for subsequent developments in the modern theater.

CHEKHOV'S HISTRIONIC ART: AN END AND A BEGINNING

Purgatorio, CANTO VIII—

> Era già l'ora che volge il disio
> > ai naviganti e intenerisce il core,
> > lo dì ch'han detto ai dolci amici addio;
> e che lo nuovo peregrin d'amore
> > punge, se ode squilla di lontano,
> > che paia il giorno pianger che si more.

The poetry of modern realistic drama is to be found in those inarticulate moments when the human creature is shown responding directly to his immediate situation. Such are the many moments—composed, interrelated, echoing each other—when the waiting and loafing characters in Act II get a fresh sense (one after the other, and each in his own way) of their situation on the doomed estate. It is because of the exactitude with which Chekhov perceives and imitates these tiny responses, that he can make them echo each other, and convey, when taken together, a single action with the scope, the general significance or suggestiveness, of poetry. Chekhov, like other great dramatists, has what might be called an ear for action, comparable to the trained musician's ear for musical sound.

The action which Chekhov thus imitates in his second act (that of lending ear, in a moment of freedom from practical pressures, to impending change) echoes, in its turn, a number of other poets: Laforgue's "poetry of waiting-rooms" comes to mind, as well as other works stemming from the period of hush before the First World War. The poets are to some extent talking about the same thing, and their works, like voices in a continuing colloquy, help to explain each other: hence the justification and the purpose of seeking comparisons. The eighth canto of the *Purgatorio* is widely separated from *The Cherry Orchard* in space and time, but these two poems unmistakably echo and confirm each other. Thinking of them together, one can begin to place Chekhov's curiously nonverbal dramaturgy and understand the purpose and the value of his reduction of the art to histrionic terms, as well as the more obvious limitations which he thereby accepts. For Dante accepts similar limitations at this point but locates the mode of action he shows here at a certain point in his vast scheme.

The explicit coordinates whereby Dante places the action of Canto VIII might alone suffice to give one a clue to the comparison with *The Cherry Orchard*: we are in the Valley of Negligent Rulers who, lacking light, unwillingly suffer their irresponsibility, just as Lyubov' and Gayev do. The *antepurgatorio* is behind us, and Purgatory proper, with its hoped-for work, thought, and moral effort, is somewhere ahead, beyond the night which is now approaching. It is the end of the day; and as we wait, watch, and listen, evening moves slowly over our heads, from sunset to darkness to moonrise. Looking more closely at this canto, one can see that Dante the Pilgrim and the Negligent Rulers he meets are listening and looking as Chekhov's characters are in Act II: the action is the same; in both, a childish and uninstructed responsiveness, an unpremeditated obedience to what is actual, informs the suffering of change. Dante the author, for his elaborate and completely conscious reasons, works here with the primitive histrionic sensibility; he composes with elements sensuously or sympathetically, but not rationally or verbally, defined. The rhythms, the pauses, and the sound effects he employs are strikingly similar to Chekhov's. And so he shows himself—Dante "the new Pilgrim"—meeting this mode of awareness for the first time: as delicately and ignorantly as Gayev when he feels all of a sudden the extent of evening, and before he falsifies this perception with his embarrassing apostrophe to Nature.

If Dante allows himself as artist and as protagonist only the primitive sensibility of the child, the naïf, the natural saint, at this point in the ascent, it is because, like Chekhov, he is presenting a threshold or moment of change in human experience. He wants to show the unbounded potentialities of the psyche before or between the moments when it is morally and intellectually realized. In Canto VIII the pilgrim is both a child and a child who is changing; later moments of transition are different. Here he is virtually (but for the Grace of God) lost; all the dangers are present. Yet he remains uncommitted and therefore open to finding himself again and more truly. In all of this the parallel to Chekhov is close. But because Dante sees this moment as a moment only in the ascent, Canto VIII is also composed in ways in which Act II of *The Cherry Orchard* is not—ways which the reader of the *Purgatorio* will not understand until he looks back from the top of the mountain. Then he will see the homesickness which informs Canto VIII in a new light, and all of the concrete elements, the snake in the grass, the winged figures that roost at the edge of the valley like night-hawks, will be intelligible to the mind and, without losing their concreteness, take their place in a more general frame. Dante's fiction is laid in the scene beyond the grave, where every human action has its relation to ultimate reality, even though that relation becomes explicit only gradually. But Chekhov's characters are seen in the flesh and in their very secular emotional entanglements: in the contemporary world as anyone can see it—nothing visible beyond the earth's horizon, with its signs of social change. The fatality of the *Zeitgeist* is the ultimate reality in the theater of modern realism; the anagoge is lacking. And though Ibsen and Chekhov are aware of both history and moral effort, they do not know what to make of them—perhaps they reveal only illusory perspectives, "masquerades which time resumes." If Chekhov echoes Dante, it is not because of what he ultimately understood but because of the accuracy with which he saw and imitated that moment of action.

If one thinks of the generation to which Anya and Trofimov were supposed to belong, it is clear that the new motives and reasons which they were to find, after their inspired evening together, were not such as to turn all Russia, or all the world, into a garden. The potentialities which Chekhov presented at that moment of change were not to be realized in the wars and revolutions which followed: what actually followed was rather that separation and destruction, that scattering and destinationless trekking, which he also sensed as possible. But, in the cultivation of the dramatic art after Chekhov, renewals, the realization of hidden potentialities, did follow. In Chekhov's histrionic art, the "desire is turned back" to its very root, to the immediate response, to the movements of the psyche before they are limited, defined, and realized in reasoned purpose. Thus Chekhov revealed hidden potentialities, if not in the life of the time, at least in ways of seeing and showing human life; if not in society, at least in the dramatic art. The first and most generally recognized result of these labors was to bring modem realism to its final perfection in the productions of the Moscow Art Theater and in those who learned from it. But the end of modern realism was also a return to very ancient sources; and in our time the fertilizing effect of Chekhov's humble objectivity may be traced in a number of dramatic forms which cannot be called modem realism at all.

The acting technique of the Moscow Art Theater is so closely connected, in its final development, with Chekhov's dramaturgy, that it would be hard to say which gave the more important clues. Stanislavskiy and

Nemirovich-Danchenko from one point of view, and Chekhov from another, approached the same conception: both were searching for an attitude and a method that would be less hidebound, truer to experience, than the cliché-responses of the commercial theater. The Moscow Art Theater taught the performer to make that direct and total response which is the root of poetry in the widest sense: they cultivated the histrionic sensibility in order to free the actor to realize, in his art, the situations and actions which the playwright had imagined. Chekhov's plays demand this accuracy and imaginative freedom from the performer; and the Moscow Art Theater's productions of his works were a demonstration of the perfection, the reticent poetry, of modern realism. Modem realism of this kind is still alive in the work of many artists who have been more or less directly influenced either by Chekhov or by the Moscow Art Theater. In our country, for instance, there is Clifford Odets; in France, Vildrac and Bernard, and the realistic cinema, of which *Symphonie Pastorale* is an example.

But this cultivation of the histrionic sensibility, bringing modern realism to its end and its perfection, also provided fresh access to many other dramatic forms. The Moscow technique, when properly developed and critically understood, enables the producer and performer to find the life in any theatrical form; before the revolution the Moscow Art Theater had thus revivified *Hamlet*, *Carmen*, the interludes of Cervantes, neoclassic comedies of several kinds, and many other works which were not realistic in the modern sense at all. A closely related acting technique underlay Reinhardt's virtuosity; and Copeau, in the Vieux Colombier, used it to renew not only the art of acting but, by that means, the art of playwriting also. . . .

After periods when great drama is written, great performers usually appear to carry on the life of the theater for a few more generations. Such were the Siddonses and Macreadys who kept the great Shakespearian roles alive after Shakespeare's theater was gone, and such, at a further stage of degeneration, were the mimes of the Commedia dell'Arte, improving on the themes of Terence and Plautus when the theater had lost most of its meaning. The progress of modern realism from Ibsen to Chekhov looks in some respects like a withering and degeneration of this kind: Chekhov does not demand the intellectual scope, the ultimate meanings, which Ibsen demanded, and to some critics Chekhov does not look like a real dramatist but merely an overdeveloped mime, a stage virtuoso. But the theater of modern realism did not afford what Ibsen demanded, and Chekhov is much the more perfect master of its little scene. If Chekhov drastically reduced the dramatic art, he did so in full consciousness, and in obedience both to artistic scruples and to a strict sense of reality. He reduced the dramatic art to its ancient root, from which new growths are possible.

RUFUS W. MATHEWSON, JR.

Chekhov's Legacy:
Icebergs and Epiphanies

When a person expends the least possible amount of energy on a certain act, that is grace.

Chekhov in a letter to Gorky

Chekhov's gift to the world has been variously received: each reader can create his own Chekhov; critics and scholars have been slow to recover a more objective version of his legacy to us; writers have intuited the essential Chekhov with miraculous success. His imprint can be found on a range of writers from Katherine Mansfield and Sherwood Anderson through John O'Hara and Isaac Babel to Flannery O'Connor, Yurii Kazakov and Grace Paley. In the dominant mode in short fiction since 1900—the casual telling of a nuclear experience in an ordinary life, rendered with immediate and telling detail—Chekhov now appears to us as chief legislator or licenser of a new and distinct way of writing. The first to do it, he made it possible for later writers to do what they have done, not necessarily by way of direct influence, but by setting a happy precedent that has released the creative energies of others by whatever untraceable routes.

I would separate the Chekhovian short form from another which may

From *Chekhov and Our Age: Responses to Chekhov by American Writers and Scholars.* © 1984 by Cornell University Center for International Studies.

have begun in modern times with Kafka. In it a magical metamorphosis—man to bug, say—replaces a vision which resembles the world we think we live in, with another, derived from abnormal mental states, or from hypotheses—the "What if . . .?" buried in most of Borges's fictions. Fantasy's monkey-link is inserted in the chain of reality, suspending natural law, or linear time or causal process at one crucial point. This kind of writing has coexisted with the Chekhovian kind for a number of decades, and if, as many have noted, the attenuated and formulaic New Yorker story represents the final stage of the older form, it may be that the Kafkan mode is gaining ascendancy over modern tastes. If so, we must accept Pynchon's albino alligators as permanent successors to Hemingway's bulls and buffaloes and all those fish of various sizes and shapes. Whether or not the Chekhovian era is receding into the past, it has been visible to many as a distinctive part of modern literature. Too often, however, it is discussed without a precise or complete sense of its first legislator's contribution. Toward rectifying this, I propose to set Chekhov against two writers—Hemingway of the *Forty-Nine Stories* and Joyce of *Dubliners*—who were at the center of the Chekhovian era, and seem to form a web of connections between him and later writers, including some, perhaps, who have contributed to this collection. Affinity is all I will try to show, not a plotted CompLit diagram of influences, for which there is not yet enough supporting evidence. The transmission process, we can only guess, was a series of intuitive apprehensions, at times and places we often do not know. Still, it is instructive, I think, to discover that qualities in the prose of later writers, some of which have been perpetuated as critical commonplaces—"iceberg" and "epiphany," to name two—are clearly visible in Chekhov's work.

A number of present-day scholars in the Soviet Union and elsewhere are accomplishing the critical recovery of Chekhov on a one-story-at-a-time basis, but this process has been slowed by a set of institutionalized misreadings which have endured with astonishing vitality. The standard political misreading—that Chekhov was some kind of subliminal Bolshevik, unknowingly forecasting the 1905 Revolution—is to be expected from the Soviet Union, but there are other sources. Not long ago the Old Vic ended a sensitive playing of *Three Sisters* with this final scene: when the sisters gather on the apron to utter their harmonized complaint, the military band which has been playing offstage, for the regiment's departure, switches to the "Internationale," and a stage-wide picture of the Kremlin is flashed through the transparent drop onto the back wall of the stage. The actors utter the lines as written but contradict their meaning by their actions: the sisters turn, one at a time, and walk off, their heads held high in a full spot—presumably into the Bolshevik dawn. This political atrocity may be allowed to stand for all efforts to shape Chekhov to fit any set of abstractions, political or otherwise.

A family of misreadings can be grouped under the heading "The Voice of Twilight Russia," a designation that speaks for itself. These misreaders fail to see the formal intricacy of the Chekhov story, and because they do not know how to read it, they fail to respond to its moral power. *This* Chekhov writes stories without beginnings or endings or plotted action, stories that convey a "mood," and then fade, or "droop," as one of them has said, into a shrug, a sigh or a yawn. Chekhov, himself, is seen as a gentle, observant shoulder-shrugging doctor who told his countrymen, in Gorky's words, "You live badly, my friends, it is shameful to live like that."

The serious writers who have read Chekhov carefully and might claim descent from him, have avoided both the programmatic and the sentimental misreadings. They have sensed in their own ways that Chekhov possessed one of the finest and toughest sensibilities in literature, that even when the central event in a story is a choice *not* made or an action *not* taken, the contending forces in the story are as tightly knit as in a well-made sonnet, and the *denouement* is reached with an Aristotelian rigor. They have learned too that there is a high incidence of violence, both psychic and physical (in one story an infant is murdered in boiling water), and that though there is pity, it is astringent, earned, and appropriate.

The most precise misreadings are often the most instructive, calling attention to the essential qualities of a story by overlooking them. Such has been the case with Chekhov's "Enemies" (1887), one of his finest stories, though in one important sense an uncharacteristic one. The misreadings of it point to a difficulty the reader or critic may have with any major writer of this school, the failure to detect the psychological clues or moral signals buried under the surface of the random and the everyday—what the Stanislavsky troupe called the "sub-text." But in the case of "Enemies" and its misreaders, what is normally implicit—the moral action of the story—is brought to the surface and made perfectly explicit. And still the point is missed.

No retelling of this startling story can reproduce the miracle of the telling, and all it shows us of Chekhov's vision of experience. But one must try. A stranger seeking help rings a doctor's doorbell just moments after the doctor's only son has died of diphtheria. Stupefied by grief, the doctor forgets the stranger seconds after he has received him, and walks slowly through his house. He mechanically lifts his feet higher than need be over the thresholds between rooms, this gesture telling us all we need to know about the strength of his feelings, and blankness of his mind. The stillness of the house tells of the furious activity just ended, which is felt in the glaring light, and in the disarray of medical gear scattered over the furniture and the floor. His wife lies motionless on a bed; the dead boy's eyes have begun to recede into his skull. The doctor returns to the stranger at the door who implores him to drive a considerable distance to attend his wife who has had a heart attack. The doctor protests, then numbly gives in.

The story is about grief—here caught at the moment of its onset. We know this because Chekhov, quite uncharacteristically, intrudes in his story to tell us so in a long paragraph about the mysterious beauty of that emotion, which can be told, he says, only in the language of music. He shows us—and tells us—something else about grief: it is a totally self-absorbing emotion; in its grip, moral crimes may be committed. In the working out of the story, Chekhov is at pains to make the stranger less attractive than the doctor. He is rich, pampered, affected. His house is richly and modishly furnished—a shiny new cello stands provocatively in the corner. To top off these clues, which tend to disparage the stranger, we learn that his wife has feigned her illness in order to run off with her husband's best friend. His grief, though very real, is edged with farce. Then, each locked in his separate misery, the two men rage at each other, overwhelming one another with the vilest insults they can muster. But the story is not allowed to end as the ironic presentation of a moral standoff. The doctor, we are made to realize, is in the wrong and will remain so because he will never forgive his "enemy," will refuse forever to recognize the other man's suffering. Grief has issued in injustice. How do we know? Chekhov enters his story once more and tells us so.

> Time will pass and Kirikov's sorrow, too, but this conviction, unjust and unworthy of the human heart, will not pass, it will remain in the doctor's mind until the grave.

Even when the untold story is clearly told, the misreadings burgeon. When V. Ermilov, a Soviet commentator of the Stalin era, laid his Marxist grid on the story, he discovered that the doctor represents the progressive forces of history and chided Chekhov for not realizing it. When Ronald Hingley, Chekhov's English biographer, perfectly misled by the false clues, discovers only that the doctor is by far the more attractive figure, the programmatic and the subjective have come from opposite starting points to the same false conclusion, and this with *all* signals flying in the story. And when a Chekhov story tells itself—relies, that is, on "the power of the tacit"—the critical errors multiply.

Chekhov once described implicit narration this way: "People are eating dinner—just eating dinner—and at that moment their happiness is taking shape and their lives are being smashed. . . ." This sense of the play between surface and depth does indeed remind us of Hemingway's "iceberg" story, with the largest fraction of it invisible under the surface, and of Joyce's mysteriously wrought "epiphanies," brought on by a "random" external event but bringing into view the essence of a character's inner condition. We are touching upon a strategic principle common to all three writers, and to this mode of writing, in general. We hear John Cheever noting its presence in Chekhov in a recent interview:

> I love Chekhov very much. He *was* an innovator—stories that seemed to the unknowing to have no endings but had instead a whole new inner structure.

This is the kind of writer's perception that spread the Chekhovian message from one to another over the decades. In possession of this insight, Cheever becomes an initiate and is, one would like to think, forever armed against the critical misreadings.

We can assume, Carlos Baker tells us, that Hemingway read Chekhov with the other Russians when he went to school at Sylvia Beach's Paris bookstore, but in the absence of any explicit reference to that experience, we cannot know what happened to him when he did. We are confined to the study of likenesses and to the assertion of affinities.

With Joyce the problem is more difficult. We are confronted with a flat denial—a denial, I would add, that taxes credulity. Many critics have noted the likenesses. Gilbert Phelps has written: "Many of the tales in James Joyce's *Dubliners*, notably 'The Dead,' are closer to Chekhov in tone, feeling and shape than the most painstaking English imitations." Magalaner and Kain, speculating on the likelihood of influence, have drawn up a list of the Chekhov stories Joyce may have read. Ellmann, too, notes the similarities—"the closest parallels to Joyce's stories are Chekhov's"—but it is he who cites Joyce's statement that he had not read Chekhov before he wrote *Dubliners*. For now, his must remain the last word. We confront, rather, a mysterious affinity, as tangible and as inexplicable as that between Dickens and Gogol. Affinity, then, is our subject, and if we proceed from the lesser to the greater degree, we should begin with Hemingway.

If we think of "Enemies" as the quintessential Chekhov story laid bare, there are other properties to be found, in addition to the buried story, which are common to the entire genre. There is, for example, a deliberate toughness of attitude toward routinized patterns of feeling and the language that expressed them—we recall Hemingway's hatred of the literary "padding" which obscured a true view of things, or Joyce's ruthless way with the pieties of his paralyzed Dublin.

This habit of iconoclasm, no doubt, accounts for the hostility and incomprehension which characterized the initial reception of all three writers, and allows us to assume that Chekhov's deliberate spelling out of his exact meaning in "Enemies" was a tactical attempt to forestall predictable misunderstandings of his unconventional view of grief.

The effort to desentimentalize carries its own risks, most visible, perhaps, in Hemingway when toughness may turn into that cruelty which is the other face of sentimentality. He takes this chance with his men at war, his has-been fighters of men or of bulls, his failed hunters—when a puerile *machismo* may be validated by demonstrations of insensitivity. Chekhov has been accused of cruelty through the years, though seldom of sentimentality, and one suspects that his lapses into either are fewer than Hemingway's. Both writers walk the thin line between these pitfalls in their stories about childhood.

Concentration on the biological stages of human life is a hallmark of the Chekhovian story, often marked by the painful passage from one stage to another. Earlier short forms in the nineteenth century—the tale, the *conte*, the *povest'*—had tended to resemble novels, reduced in scale but retaining the leisurely exposition, the extended time span, and the scaffolding of prologue and epilogue. The process of a life could be measured by a chain of many small changes, as in Tolstoy's prose. Chekhov's compression of the form required tighter focus on a single profound episode if the whole curve of a character's life was to be illuminated. These pivotal incidents were more readily to be found in the moments of transition in biological and cultural growth and decay as one crossed from one to another of the ages of man. Children in collision with the adult world, passing or not passing the barriers of initiation, became a natural point of concentration for the whole laconic mode, with all the risks of false emotion which Dickens discovered in his treatment of children's suffering. Chekhov wrote some two dozen stories between 1884 and 1888 in which children find themselves in brutal conflict with the world they are growing up into. They are lied to, fed vodka, bullied, mocked, seduced and starved. They witness infidelity, forced marriage, violence of all kinds, death and suicide. In almost all of these stories the climax, or the moment of maximum shock and pain, is marked by the onset of delirium, and by the invariable signalling phrase, "trembling from head to foot." In the denouement, even when there is a measure of relief for the child, we do not doubt that a scar will remain.

The age of the child is always precisely given. The youngest ("Grisha") is two years, eight months old (he is fed vodka, made delirious by the shock, and given caster oil by an uncomprehending mother). The oldest may be Volodya, in late adolescence. He is failing in the *gymnasium*, is humiliated by his social-climbing mother, and then is seduced by a married woman who mocks him for his poor performance and calls him an "ugly duckling." He blows his brains out in the genteel pension where he and his mother live. In these stories, occasionally there is succor, the rising sun ends a night of terror, or a fatherly figure (though seldom the father) provides comfort; or, very rarely, the culture itself offers a soothing formula, as in the incantatory rhythms of a card game ("In the Coach House"). Far more often the culture seems to be the victimizer, presented simply as the heedless way of the adult world, into which the child is initiated in a painful, destructive manner. The child passes through a series of bruising, deforming experiences before he arrives desensitized (after a moment of cruel awareness) and acculturated to the world of his seniors.

This profoundly pessimistic view of the human situation is well put in an aphorism from Chekhov's notebooks: "With the insects the butterfly comes out of the caterpillar; with mankind, it is the other way around: the caterpillar comes out of the butterfly" (XII, 263). The metamorphosis is a moral one: growing up, in this sense, is a kind of growing down. One may speak of the descent from childhood. Such a metamorphosis, he notes in a letter, is undergone by members of the intelligentsia as they pass into maturity:

> While they are still university students they are an honorable, good people, our hope, the future of Russia; but when they . . . turn into adults our hope and the future of Russia go up in smoke, and in the filter are left nothing but doctors, owners of dachas, insatiable officials, thieving engineers (XVIII, 88).

They are somehow encased in professional boxes, social categories, and moral attitudes.

In the state of childhood, first of man's ages, the human animal is sensitive, morally alive. As he grows up these qualities are blunted, neutralized, or killed. We can be quite sure of this because in all these stories we experience the world as the young person does, through his sensations, his impressions and his feelings.

After "The Steppe" in 1888, Chekhov never again made a child the central sensibility in his stories. He concentrated on the later ages of man, writing most often about life gone wrong in the middle years; or, less often, life evaluated in retrospect, against the onset of death.

Entirely missing from the work of the masked and reticent Chekhov is the autobiographical foundation of the ten Nick Adams stories, which treat the bruising passage from childhood into adolescence and adulthood. Not all these transitions leave bruises or scars. Nick learns about the pleasures of sex, unlike Volodya who learns the opposite and dies of his new knowledge. But they do rest on a foundation of the biological-cultural ages of man and of the traumas of growth, presenting a sequence of initiation experiences from childhood to full maturity. Nick goes away to war, as a man must, and then has to deal with the memory of its horror. In a number of stories we see him, in effect, "trembling from head to foot," as the psyche wobbles under the onslaught of what he called "it," most notably, perhaps, in "Big, Two-Hearted River," where undefined terror lies under the surface of natural beauty, precisely as it does for Chekhov's nine-year-old in "The Steppe."

In "Fathers and Sons," Nick recalls in the presence of his young son episodes of his own initiation into hunting and sex, and the simultaneous estrangement from his father. (He had been unable then to stand the smell of his father's undershirt.) Presumably, the same process is under way, linking the generations through the common experience of separation, as Nick understands, since the son must undergo these rites on his own. With few exceptions, Chekhov ignores the moment when the parent confronts his responsibility for the generation following on his own.

In the stories of Nick's own early childhood, the similarities with Chekhov are greater. They are told through the child's consciousness, with a minimum of visible narrative apparatus. In "Indian Camp," which may stand for several stories, Nick crosses the lake with his father, the doctor, who will perform a bloody, all-night Caesarian operation on an Indian woman. When the delivery is over, Nick's father asks if he wants to watch him sew up the incision. But "Nick did not watch. His curiosity had been gone for a long time." It's there, the trembling, but given in a lower key than Chekhov's. The terror of the delivery is topped by the discovery of the Indian father's suicide—he has sliced his own throat. (The two incisions comment on each other, of course: one issuing in life, the other in death.) And then there is a measure of solace. The father extends an aura of protection, and Nick finds temporary comfort in being a child: "In the early morning on the lake sitting in the stern of the boat with his father rowing"—so runs the final sentence— "he felt quite sure that he would never die" (193). But we know the scars are there; we have seen the wounds inflicted.

The child of Chekhov's "In the Coach-House" watches mysterious events as a kind of shadow play behind the lighted windows across the court-yard where he is playing cards with his grandmother and the janitor. The child slowly realizes that a suicide has taken place. This horror is heightened by the folkloric tales the adults tell about a suicide's corpse-as-carrion, a response of the culture which domesticates the event for them, but renders it more awful for the child who has never heard of this belief before. His terror reaches its peak when he views the laid-out body through the windows. The grandfather's kindly presence offers some solace, as does the culture, which intervenes in another guise. He finally falls asleep that night to the soothing cadences of the peasants' card game. *"Byu i navalivayu"* (I trump you and play again)" (VI, 236), a rhythmically repeated phrase, is the last thing he hears. When he wakes with the sun, the horror has been dispelled, but the scars—we do not doubt—are there.

Both Chekhov and Hemingway risked the pitfalls of false feeling by ending stories with children who are left stripped and desolate by brutal adults. In Hemingway's "My Old Man," after the child learns from callous strangers that his father had died in disgrace, the story ends, "Seems like when they get started they don't leave a guy nothing" (303). In Chekhov's "A Domestic Trifle," after a child has had his deepest confidence betrayed by his mother's suspicious lover ("a big, serious man, he had nothing to do with boys") the story ends: "He trembled, stammered and wept," and learned that there are "things which have no name in children's language" (V, 176). There is no sign of succor in either story. That pain and pity are kept intact, free of cruelty or sentimentality in both stories, is the best measure of the writers' achievement.

Hemingway is more laconic than Chekhov. The proportion of the untold to the told is greater: his iceberg rides a little lower in the water. It is a matter of degree, however. Both seek the same effect: the removal of all interpretive screens which blur the reader's *direct* apprehension of the reported-on experience, and yet without sacrifice of formal symmetry, dramatic design, or moral disclosure. Chekhov advised young writers

> to divide their manuscripts in two and throw away the first half. . . . Beginners usually try, as they say, "to lead into the story," and they write that superfluous first half. One ought to write so that the reader is able to understand what is going on from the course of the story and from the characters' conversation or actions, without explanations from the author.

Elsewhere, he said that the story's first and last paragraphs should be thrown away: "It is here," he told Bunin, "that we writers of fiction do more lying than anywhere else." And we must recall that the aim of Chekhov's art is "the absolute and honest truth" (XIII, 262).

When Scott Fitzgerald advised internal cuts in an early version of *The Sun Also Rises*, Hemingway threw away the first fifteen pages, realizing that the background biographies of his characters could be brought in by way of the action. This was not a mere editorial decision, as Carlos Baker points out, but was intended to "provide a further test of Ernest's aesthetic theory in those years," the theory of the direct and simple transcription of things as they are, "the essence of active experience," relying on the same "immense power of the tacit" that John Berryman discovered in Stephen Crane, Maupassant and Chekhov.

We are concerned with more than the suppression of the kind of information found in conventional beginnings and endings, the prologues and epilogues often favored by Turgenev, James and Conrad. Various kinds of narrative scaffolding are discarded—above all, the need for an authorial presence to perform the acrobatics of introducing character, setting and himself. Chekhov most often opens with an impersonal communique, like the lead into a news story telling who (often giving his age), what, when and where, with a brief notation on the protagonists' spiritual condition, and sometimes an atmospheric detail—like the tea smelling of fish in "Peasants"—which suggests the taste or moral flavor of the entire story. Hemingway gives us less. His stories sometimes begin in the middle of a conversation or a monologue, or with statements which appear to be answers to unasked questions: "That night we lay on the floor in the room and I listened to the silkworms eating" (461), ("Now I Lay Me"). Hemingway's sawed-off endings bear a close comparison with Chekhov's, which project a kind of dotted line in the direction of future events that, we realize, need no explanation.

Cutting so much out or pushing it under the surface, calling our attention to the story beneath the story in a very muted way, both writers ask the reader to work harder. "When I write," Chekhov once said, "I rely on my reader fully, assuming that he himself will add the subjective elements that are lacking . . ." (XV, 51). By responding in the right way, the reader collaborates in the experience of the story, as an actor interprets the text of a play, or a musician a score. A good "performance" by the reader will depend on his ability to detect the pattern of the charged details, the emotional coloration or moral tonality in the bare description of places, things, people. The reader/performer of a Hemingway story must be alert to all kinds of clues, sometimes to no more than hidden bits of information. If we missed or didn't understand the phrase "let the air in" (373) in "Hills Like White Elephants," we would not know that the story was about abortion, or if we failed to note the gender of the pronoun referring to the lover the girl is running away to join, we could not know that "sea change" in the story of that name concerns a shift from a heterosexual to a homosexual attachment. If there were nothing else to say about these stories, it would seem that concealment had become a mere game with the reader and had usurped the narrative. A sharp eye for the single detail would replace the finely tuned sensibility, responding to a pattern of signals, that Chekhov always requires if his stories are to be fully experienced.

In "The Steppe" and "Big, Two-Hearted River," when they both are at their best, they are also closest together. Both are concerned with capturing in language the exact contour of their worlds—primarily the natural worlds—rendered through the evidence of the senses (Chekhov wrote in a letter while he was working on "The Steppe" that it was going well: he had caught the "smell of hay" XIV, 14), captured as an *impression* on the mind of the observers, an impression formed partly by the emotion with which it is received, which in turn is transmitted back to and invested in the object. We know the beauty and the terror of the landscape, and we know when we have approached or crossed the boundary between them, because Chekhov's child and Hemingway's vulnerable adult have apprehended them that way. These major emotions are felt through a perfectly wrought texture of the random, the trivial, the everyday—in Chekhov's story the chance encounters of a routine journey across the steppe, in Hemingway's the minutely recorded details of the rituals and circumstances of fishing in a particular river. If they had been contemporaries, neither, I am sure, would have misread the full human disclosure in the other's story. They had seen the world similarly, and recorded it in similar ways.

They were not contemporaries, of course, and I have been content to celebrate likenesses—to establish affinity, not influence. Still, the possibility of a common ancestry is worth noting. Flaubert's hard, exact surfaces, with meanings latent in the "observed" details, or Tolstoy's focus on the perceptual play between mind and object, are likely models for both Chekhov and Hemingway. Maupassant must be mentioned here, too, as occupying a central position in the formation of the modern short story. In the case of these two stories a fourth, and unexpected source, proposes itself—Henry David Thoreau.

F.O. Mattheissen points out in *American Renaissance* that Thoreau was the first American to try to capture the actual look, feel and sound of things in prose, as Hemingway was later to do. "Thoreau's convictions about the nature of art," he writes, "look forward to Hemingway's,"—and we could add, to Chekhov's. Carlos Baker notes the other aspect of this kind of perception, the pursuit of the implicit meaning beneath the "observed" object.

> Under the surface of both Thoreau and Hemingway one finds an objective consciousness of what Thoreau himself called "dusky knowledge," a sense of the connotations of things existing in and below the denoted shapes and colors.

And it was Chekhov, in between the two, who helped to make this two-level perception, derived perhaps from transcendentalism, into a principle of fictional order.

II

Hemingway placed *Dubliners* on a list of works he most admired. If influence were the goal of this inquiry, one would proceed from Chekhov through Joyce to Hemingway, but Joyce's denial that he had read Chekhov removes the middle term of the sequence and destroys the hope of continuity. By going from Hemingway to Joyce we shift on the scale of affinities from the easily demonstrable to the uncanny, as others have sensed. Common ancestry remains a possibility. The writers Joyce most admired were Flaubert and Tolstoy. Of the latter he said, "Tolstoy is a magnificent writer. He is never dull, never stupid, never pedantic, never theatrical. He is head and shoulders over the others." Tolstoy's presence behind all these writers may well result from his mastery of the physical universe, and of the play he discloses between it and the minds of his characters. Or, we may speculate, Chekhov and those who succeeded him have found a model for the short story in the discrete episodes of the great novels, where a single character moves from one stage of understanding of the world to another, the new stage reached in the form of an epiphany of thought and feeling, a new crystallization of consciousness. Thus the single emotional step Anna Karenina takes toward Vronsky and away from Karenin during the train ride from Moscow to Saint Petersburg (marked at the end by her sudden discovery of her husband's protruding ears) might be seen as a self-contained short story, sketching in miniature the entire curve of Anna's development.

Abrupt beginnings and abbreviated endings, a minimum of exposition, and an implicit treatment of crisis and defeat under the surface of ordinary life, are the marks of the Chekhovian mode in Joyce's Dublin cycle. If Chekhov's several hundred stories were grouped according to the kinds of crisis explored, it would be found that these fourteen by Joyce would take their places under many of the same headings. Under "entrapment," for example, we would place stories by both in which the character begins in a trap and generates a plan, or entertains a desire, or responds to an invitation, to escape—with the denouement marking the failure of the intention, through inaction, self-deception, or some fault of will or understanding. Indeed, "paralysis," Joyce's governing motif, may be said to have been Chekhov's as well, matched by the term *poshlost*, that harsh, provincial vulgarity which deadens the heart and mind in the same way. Each system of moral inertia has its "enforcers": consider the self-appointed trio of judges who "examine" Dr. Ragin in "Ward No. 6," deciding that his disgust with his own and the town's life are signs of insanity, and lock him up with the lunatics; or the bully-boy brother of Polly Doran in "The Boarding House," who lets any man who might dishonor his sister know that he'd "bloody well put his teeth down his throat, so he would." In other stories, the power of custom, habit, or routine defeats the fragile longings in a more impersonal way.

Joyce is more systematic than Chekhov in his concern with the ages of man, with the primacy of the biological life cycle, with intimations of mortality, with the destructive passage of time and the final onset of death and oblivion. It is the governing scheme of *Dubliners*, shaping the sequence of stories into an aesthetic whole; it plots the same curve any Chekhov character may be placed on, defining his situation and controlling his vision of it if he is able to perceive it. Joyce's stories are arranged more or less exactly along this parabola: three stories about misused children, "Sisters," "An Encounter," "Araby," are followed by three stories about men on either side of thirty. The line of the curve becomes less distinct in stories about love gone wrong, or rancid family life, and in two excursions into public life: politics in "Ivy Day in the Committee Room" and the church in "Grace." Both bespeak the decay of once vital institutions. The note of personal mortality is struck in several stories toward the end of the collection—Maria's old age in "Clay," the question of responsibility for the death of Mrs. Sinico, and James Duffy's sense of his own death-in-life in "A Painful Case"; until we are given the full perspective in "The Dead," as Gabriel, in sudden tenderness and understanding, settles for the little he is, or has become, against the presence of death made universal by the falling snow.

Counterparts for all these subjects can be found in Chekhov's stories. Those about children center on the same painful collision between generations. Stories about the middle years also hinge on the discovery of blight in a mislived or unlived life, of love gone wrong, in any number of ways, of help refused when it might save a life, of pain passed on.

Death-in-life, that premature surrender of the conscience or the heart, is a frequent theme. In "The Name-Day Party," the stillborn child stands as an exact emblem of the death of the marriage. In "A Dreary Story," the aging professor dies emotionally, and knows it, while he remains biologically alive in that dreary hotel room in Kharkov. The walking dead of "Vierochka," "The Man in A Case," "Ionich," "About Love" and many other stories destroy the lives of those who turn to them for help, as Joyce's James Duffy destroys the life of Mrs. Sinico. Oblivion—Gusev's corpse attacked by a shark ("Gusev"), the archbishop's person erased from living memory after his funeral ("The Archbishop")—is as certain as that promised to Gabriel Conroy at the end of Joyce's sequence.

Joyce's "The Sisters," when set against Chekhov's stories about childhood, heightens the sense of detailed correspondences between the two writers. Both tell their stories through the thoughts and feelings of a child— Chekhov most often through an adult who hovers over the child's mind, reporting only on *his* experience, but translating it into adult language; Joyce in this story (and in "Araby" and "An Encounter") letting the boy do the telling, a strategy calling for a slightly implausible maturity from the narrator. As in Chekhov, child and adult live on different planes, judge by different norms. Old Cotter, the voice of the adult culture, opposes the boy's relationship with the dying priest—children's minds "are so impressionable" (11). Old Cotter is right, and when we learn what the boy's impressions have been, we realize that the two generations are in competition over the value and meaning of the experience.

Through his talks with Father Flynn, the child has been exposed to history, to exotic languages and distant places, and to the ancient and intricate mysteries of the Church. When he learns of the priest's responsibilities toward the Eucharist, he wonders "how anybody had ever found in himself the courage to undertake them" (13), thus evoking momentarily the vitality and commitment of the Church—qualities that have ebbed out of this semi-paralyzed, snuff-covered priest whose faltering hand once dropped the chalice during Mass.

The boy has also been exposed to sin and to death. He has known awe, wonder, a guilty pleasure in his sense of the nearness of evil, and an underlying feeling of dread. His rich and bewildering experience has been marked for him by strange new words—"paralysis," "gnomon," "simony" (9), but adult understanding of the priest's life is recorded in a litany of dead language. The stereotyped Irish vocabulary of death is introduced early by Father Flynn, whom the boy recalls as saying "I'm not long for this world" (9). The same note is sounded after the priest dies: " 'God have mercy on his soul,' said my aunt piously" (10). After the viewing of the body (the boy is observant but confused: "I could not gather my thoughts") the aunt and the sisters take control of the narrative, blanketing his own perceptions with a web of language made from the clichés of Irish death. Laced through their matter-of-fact account of his passing—the laying out and washing of the corpse, the obituary notice in *The Freeman's General*, the payment of insurance—are expressions like "Ah, Well, he's gone to a better world" (15), "You couldn't tell when the breath went out of him" (15), "No one would think he'd make such a beautiful corpse" (15). When death has been wrapped up in all its ritual sentiments, Eliza presents her banal report on his life: his delinquency (the dropping of the chalice), his slow decline, and the final hint of madness.

The boy is subdued, afraid of making a noise, and he withdraws from the scene except as objective observer, though we do not doubt that the same active sensibility is there. We have been prepared for his reticence with adults: we know that he is silent and unresponsive when he is "under observation" in their oppressive presence. We know that he is there to observe and absorb, but his (and, of course, Joyce's) reticence about his feelings means we cannot locate that Chekhovian moment of "trembling" if, in fact, it occurs. Or it may be that the relief he has felt at Father Flynn's death signals his ultimate acquiescence in the adult's prosaic version of the events. If so, his freedom is short-lived; his entrapment has begun. In any case, the process of acculturation is very Chekhovian. The clichéd language, the mundane account of the priest's life, drain the experience of its wonder and its menace, performing both functions of this process as we noted it in two Chekhov stories: it dulls the pain and fear, and at the same time dispels the mystery which the boy's fresh and open sensibility has responded to. It may be, though we are not told it, that it serves the further office of beginning to still his curiosity. A kind of wound may have been inflicted by insensitive, though not cruel, "enforcers" of the culture of deadened feelings.

In stories of the middle years, the brute power of inertia crushes the longings of characters at critical moments of their lives. The action is, in effect, inaction, but the rise and fall of tension is marked by the fate of the aspiration, from its genesis to its defeat. Such stories are built upon the life-history of an illusion. Sometimes the inertial force emanates from the domestic nest. In "A Little Cloud," Little Chandler's imagined literary career in London, stimulated by the visit of his successful friend, Gallaher, and set afloat on more booze than he is used to, is blasted out of existence by the baby screaming in his arms and the return of his reproachful wife. In Chekhov's "The Teacher of Literature," the happy marriage slowly sours. There are the cats in the bed, and the bacterial dairy cultures in the basement. The teacher never gets around to reading Lessing, and he plays cards in the club—a sure sign in Chekhov's system of signals of the death of the heart. In his final rage against his condition he acknowledges his defeat by it.

Just as often, the longing to be married gives rise to the illusion that one can or will attain felicity that way. In Chekhov's superb "A Woman's Kingdom," when the young woman factory-owner determines to break out of her situation and marry beneath her station, a small army of "enforcers"—servants, dependents and employees—crushes her impulse toward liberation and drives her back to her solitary eminence, with, one suspects, her capacity to hope in ruins. At the end the upwelling of bitter feeling and the knowledge of her condition that accompanies it, show forth to her (and to us) the quiddity, the "whatness," of her situation.

Joyce's Eveline, in the story of that name, feels the powerful tug of her dreary, routinized life when she refuses at the last minute to board the ship for Argentina with her fiance and falls back into the squalid existence we have just seen her about to abandon. No "enforcers" are needed; the stagnant culture has been internalized.

In other stories built on the longing to marry, we may note the likeness between the two writers' use of the epiphany. In Chekhov's "The Kiss," when the local gentry invite the officers of a passing artillery regiment to an evening party, we attend, in the company of the unprepossessing Ryabovich. Ill at ease with his correct but distant hosts, he wanders through the manor house and, in a darkened room, is kissed by an unknown woman. This "touch" in the dark generates a daydream in the course of summer maneuvers, that he will return, marry the woman, and attain the dignity and status of other men. The story's course is plotted by two other symbolic "touches." When he expresses his vision in all its fullness to his battery-mates, he is astonished to discover that it takes only a few seconds to tell, and, when one of them responds uncomprehendingly with a vulgar anecdote, in effect puncturing the illusion, Ryabovich regrets having exposed it, but less able than the reader to grasp what has happened—he manages to keep it intact for a while longer. When the regiment returns to the same village at the end of the summer, and while he awaits the invitation to return to the same manor house and to his "love," he walks along the familiar riverbank. Time's processes are in the air: he notes how the vegetation has changed from early to late summer. When he walks out on a bathing pier over the river, the third "touch" occurs: he puts his hand on a cold, wet towel and precipitates a complex change in his consciousness. The illusion of married felicity shatters, we are told and we are shown, by the action of ripples on the river's surface which break up the moon's reflection on the water. The strong current reminds him of nature's endlessly recurrent cycles: the water rushing beneath his feet may well be the same he saw on his first visit, returning after it had gone to sea, risen to the clouds by evaporation, and fallen again as rain. Yet the proper analogy for Ryabovich is not with nature's perpetual cycles, but with the vegetation dying in the movement of the seasons. He has glimpsed the span of his own life, and sensed his own mortal horizon; he has been deprived of his illusion, and—we may assume again—of his capacity to hope. He has grasped the "whatness" of his situation by also grasping the "whereness" of his place in the span of mortality. (Among the various intimations of this awareness, it is likely that Joyce would have singled out as the most telling detail the most incidental one—the cold, wet towel—although the snow of "The Dead" is only one indication that he could use nature to the same effect.) When the invitation finally arrives, he starts up for a moment, and then falls back on his bed, in total defeat. Presumably, the new knowledge he has acquired has blighted his life.

Lenehan, in Joyce's "Two Gallants," is thirty-one but dresses much younger—the face under the jaunty yachting cap had "a ravaged look." Like Ryabovich, he senses his own insignificance, but he lives in a meaner world of touts and tarts and police informers. And he lives on the edge of this barroom society, in the margins of other people's lives, as toady, cadger, jester, and general parasite—above all, as a parasite on others' experience.

In emphasis and proportion Joyce's story differs from Chekhov's, but the basic situation bears close comparison. In the long opening and closing sections, Lenehan is living his marginal life, hurrying along in the gutter beside his big, beefy friend, who is on his way to a squalid assignation with a "slavey" girl. The central section, the interlude of revelation, corresponds to the end of "The Kiss." Through the surface of false and vulgar feeling—Lenehan's dance of hypocrisy—the permanent and the genuine begin to appear:

> Corley occasionally turned to smile at some of the passing girls
> but Lenehan's gaze was fixed on the large faint moon circled with
> a double halo. He watched earnestly the passing of the grey web
> of twilight across its face (52).

A few minutes later he experiences the Chekhovian "touch" (although it is an auditory one), when he hears a street harpist playing "Silent, O Moyle." "The notes of the air," we are told, "throbbed deep and full" (54). After Corley has left for his rendezvous, the notes take possession of Lenehan, and "control his movements. His softly padded feet played the melody while his fingers swept a scale of variations idly along the railings after each group of notes" (56). The music has taken temporary possession of his mind as well, precipitating an assessment of his situation, and of his aspirations. As he eats his meal of peas and ginger beer, and thinks of Corley's adventure with the slavey, he felt "keenly his own poverty of purse and spirit" (57). His longings for change are modest enough. As he thinks of his age—thirty-one, a critical age in both writers' stories—and of his precarious existence, he longs for a steady job, and, like Ryabovich, for a wife and a nest. "If he could only come across some good simpleminded girl with a little of the ready" (58). This small moment of authenticity, of limited self-scrutiny and flickering aspirations, is brought to an end by a second "touch," not unlike the cold towel in "The Kiss." Again it is auditory, but this time it is language, reproduced for us as indirect discourse. He meets some of his friends on the street and they talk:

> One said that he had seen Mac an hour before on Westmoreland
> Street. At this Lenehan said that he had been with Mac the night

before in Egan's. The young man who had seen Mac in West-
moreland Street asked was it true that Mac had won a bit over a
billiard match. Lenehan did not know he said that Holahan had
stood them drinks in Egan's (58).

This patch of "dead air," with its clammy banality and its leaden irrelevan-
cies (we never know who Mac is, or care), accomplishes several things. It puts
an end to Lenehan's self-examination, both the candid look at his own situation and his modest program for the good life; and it reintegrates him into
his inauthentic existence as hanger-on. In effect, he walks back freely, even
eagerly—"his mind became active again"—into his trap, his Chekhovian
"case," when he hurries to share the details of Corley's nasty exploitation of
his slavey. Escape is shut off for good, as it was for Ryabovich. Each is
returned to his half life, though with one difference: Ryabovich knows it;
Lenehan does not.

The mechanism of revelation Chekhov and Joyce shared is used differently in these two stories. In "The Kiss," the first random "touch" precipitates the aspiration and the illusion; the final one punctures them both and
brings understanding and with it despair. In "Two Gallants" the first
"touch"—the music—brings understanding, then aspiration, then confusion;
and the second—the conversation—restores Lenehan to his "real" but inauthentic life, eclipsing the moment of revelation in the middle of the story.
Seen schematically, these stories appear very nearly opposite. But neither
pattern is the exclusive property of one or the other; both writers worked
many variations on both. The affinity between them is to be found in the
precise and deliberate preparation for the full disclosure, the cocking early in
the story of the gun that goes off at the end.
     There is a technical difference in the triggering effect the two writers
use in these stories: Chekhov's is a three-part process, and Joyce's two-part.
I do not mean to draw a general distinction between them on these grounds.
In Joyce's "Araby," the entire story may be seen as suspended between two
"touches": the stimulating sight of Mangan's sister—"Her dress swung as she
moved her body and the soft rope of her hair tossed from side to side" (30)—
and the deadening effect of the shop-girl's flirtatious chatter at the bazaar
which precipitates his final anguish and anger. But between these two there
is another premonitory signal which works in the same way as Ryabovich's
exposure of his aspiration to his fellow-officers. He does not fully understand
its meaning but it points the way toward the final puncturing of his illusion.
In "Araby," when the uncle returns the boy hears him in the hall "talking to
himself" and also hears "the hall-stand rocking when it received the weight

of his overcoat." "I could interpret these signs," he says. He knows that his uncle is drunk and is not surprised that the trip to the bazaar has been forgotten. But he cannot understand its full meaning, that his uncle's indifference to the boy's longing signals a reversal of direction in the fate of that longing, toward its final exposure as an illusion. These few examples do not, of course, exhaust the possibilities for discovering the similarities between the ways the two writers organize their stories.

At the same time it would be misleading to force the two writers into too close a relationship, especially in the light of Joyce's denial that he knew Chekhov. After all, *Ulysses*, which is to follow, puts all of observed Dublin at the service of myth; Chekhov continues and concludes his career with the plays which extend and refine his literature of observation to some ultimate point. This difference of direction is already visible in the stories, particularly in the resonance of symbols. Chekhov's are locally generated, taken from the data within the story, and unattached to any larger body of mythology, or to any thesis about the past or future of Russia. The total corpus of his work may be seen as a *Comedie humaine russe*, as some have said, but if his characters sometimes talk indistinctly about progress, it is always beyond the mortal horizon of the speaker, and is more accurately seen as an index of character than as prophetic utterance. Chekhov may have hoped to shame his countrymen into self-examination, but we do not suspect him of wishing to "forge" his nation's "uncreated conscience."

In *Dubliners* Joyce's symbols often invoke—through a song, a detail from folklore, an historical reference—a body of Irish legend and myth which bespeaks a more vital past. Dublin's paralysis, we assume, represents the end of a long decline. Rather than chart the upturn he seemed to promise at the end of *Portrait of the Artist*, Joyce has preferred in *Ulysses* to enlarge the Irish mythological background of his human Dublin, to encompass Shakespeare, the Bible, Homer and much more.

I have sought the grounds of affinity only in the short story about the behavior and failings of ordinary people in contemporary life, and in the techniques used to show forth the essence of these lives.

If there were space enough and time, I would conclude this sketch of literary likenesses by bringing together for a close comparative look: Chekhov's "Steppe," Hemingway's "Big, Two-Hearted River," and Joyce's "The Dead," three stories representing a kind of joint apotheosis of this mode. A longer study would search out in each the tight-knit order under the random rattle of daily life, the freighted details which carry the inner story, the disclosure of depth through the suggested and the unsaid, and the statement of human possibilities within the larger limits that contain them.

There is more to be said, of course, on every aspect of a topic like this.

In the hope that one contributes by being suggestive, I have assumed that a sketch of affinities falls somewhere between the catalogue of misreadings and the precise map of influences, that it is a necessary preliminary to the full-length study of the properties of the Chekhovian mode, of its full literary pedigree, and of the actual routes by which it entered modern literature and moved around within it.

Still in an attitude of suggestiveness, I have placed Hemingway and Joyce in the middle position between Chekhov and later writers—Flannery O'Connor, for a likely example. We do not know how or where she absorbed it, but we can find the Chekhovian imprint throughout her "Everything that Rises Must Converge." It is even certified by an upsidedown misreading. Irving Howe's programmatic misrepresentation of the story is instructive, too, because he has beep misled by a typical Chekhovian false clue: he seems to have failed to note that the holder of the most advanced social views in the story is meant to be seen as the least admirable human being.

I have had to assume that the Chekhovian legacy was passed on by a series of acts of intuitive possession by working writers, neither helped nor hindered by the criticial commentary. This network of transmission is largely invisible, but here, in her reading of Chekhov's "Gusev," I think we have caught Virginia Woolf in the act:

> Some Russian soldiers lie ill on board a ship which is taking them back to Russia. We are given a few scraps of their talk and some of their thoughts; then one of them dies and is carried away; the talk goes on among the others for a time until Gusev himself dies, and looking "like a carrot or a radish" is thrown overboard. The emphasis is laid upon such unexpected places that at first it seems as if there were no emphasis at all; and then as the eyes accustom themselves to twilight and discern the shapes of things in a room we see how complete the story is, how profound, and how truly in obedience to his vision Chekhov has chosen this, that, and the other and placed them together to compose something new.

HOWARD MOSS

Three Sisters

"Loneliness is a terrible thing, Andrei."

In *Three Sisters*, the inability to act becomes the action of the play. How to make stasis dramatic is its problem and Chekhov solves it by a gradual deepening of insight rather than by the play of event. The grandeur of great gestures and magnificent speeches remains a Shakespearian possibility—a diminishing one. Most often, we get to know people through the accretion of small details—minute responses, tiny actions, little gauze screens being lifted in the day-to-day pressure of relationships. In most plays, action builds toward a major crisis. In *Three Sisters*, it might be compared to the drip of a faucet in a water basin; a continuous process wears away the enamel of facade.

Many stories are being told simultaneously: the stories of the four Prozorov orphans—three girls, one boy, grown up in varying degrees—living in one of those Chekhovian provincial towns that have the literal detail of a newspaper story but keep drifting off into song. There is the old drunken doctor, Chebutykin, once in love with the Prozorovs' mother, there is a slew of battery officers stationed in the town—one of them, Vershinin, a married man, falls in love with the already married middle-sister, Masha; another

From *Chekhov and Our Age: Responses to Chekhov by American Writers and Scholars*. © 1984 by Cornell University Center for International Studies.

proposes to the youngest, Irena; and still a third, Soliony, also declares his love for her. There is Olga, the oldest sister, and Kulighin, Masha's awkward school-teacher husband, and there is Natasha, the small town girl who sets her heart on Andrei, the brother. It is Natasha's and Andrei's marriage that provides the catalyst of change. Each of these characters might be conceived as a voice entering the score at intervals to announce or to develop its subject, to join and part in various combinations: duets, trios, and so on. *Three Sisters* is the most musical of all of Chekhov's plays in construction, the one that depends most heavily on the repetition of motifs. And it uses music throughout: marching bands, hummed tunes, "the faint sound of an accordion coming from the street," a guitar, a piano, the human voice raised in song.

Yet too much can be made of the "music" of the play at the expense of its command of narrative style. Private confrontation and social conflict are handled with equal authority, and a symbolism still amateur in *The Seagull*, written five years earlier, has matured and gone underground to permeate the texture of the work. No dead bird is brought onstage weighted with meaning. No ideas are embalmed in objects. What we have instead is a kind of geometric structure, one angle of each story fitting into the triangular figure of another, and, overlaying that, a subtle web of connected images and words. Seemingly artless, it is made of steel. In a letter to his sister, Chekhov complained, "I find it very difficult to write *Three Sisters*, much more difficult than any of my other plays." One can well believe it.

Because immobility is the subject—no other play catches hold of the notion so definitively with the exception of *Hamlet*—secondary characters carry the burden of narration forward. Natasha and Andrei establish the main line of construction; their marriage is the network to which everything else attaches. Yet Andrei never spins the wheels of action. That task is left to Natasha, a character originally outside the immediate family, and to another stranger to the domestic circle, Soliony. One a provincial social climber, the other a neurotic captain, each takes on, in time, an ultimate coloration: Natasha, the devouring wife, Soliony, the lethal friend.

Natasha's motives are obvious enough to be disarming—disarming in its literal sense: to deprive one of weapons. No one need *suspect* her of the worst; her lies are so transparent that every civilized resource is called upon to deal with the transparency rather than the lie.

Soliony lacks accessible motivation but is easily recognizable as a true creature from life. Panicky and literal, he is repellent—one of the few repellent characters Chekhov ever created. If Soliony is shy, shyness is dangerous. Instinct, not insight leads him to the weak spot in other people. A deeply wounded man who has turned into a weapon, he is a member of a species:

the seducer-duelist, a 19th century stock character Chekhov manages to twist into a perverse original.

When Irena rejects him, he says he will kill anyone who wins her; and in the name of affection, he makes good his threat. Ironically, Irena's half-hearted relationship to Tuzenbach becomes the fatal rivalry of the play; Tuzenbach has won Irena's hand but not her heart. Moreover, Soliony is introduced into the Prozorov circle by Tuzenbach, who therefore begins the chain of events leading to his own death.

Nothing redeems Soliony except the barbarity of his manner, a symptom of an alienation deep enough, perhaps, to evoke pity. A person who cannot feel pleasure and destroys everyone else's, his touchy uneasiness is irrational, the punishment it exacts inexhaustible. Unwilling to be mollified by life's niceties or won over by its distractions, he is a definite negative force in a play in which a lack of energy is crucial. Natasha turned inside-out, a killer without her affectations and pieties, he is, if never likeable, at least not a liar. He tells us several times that, even to him, the scent he uses fails to disguise the smell of a dead man. That stench rises from a whole gallery of literary soldiers. No matter how heroic a military man may be, he is, functionally, a murderer. Soliony reminds us of that easily forgotten fact: He is the gunman of the play.

And the gunshot in *Three Sisters* is fired offstage—a shot heard before in *Ivanov*, *The Seagull*, and *The Wood Demon*. In *Uncle Vanya*, the shots occur *on*stage; half-farcical, they are not without psychological danger. Vanya shoots out of humiliation; his failure to hit anything only deepens it. The offstage gunshot in *Three Sisters* does more than end Tuzenbach's life and destroy Irena's marriage. A final fact, it leaves in its wake a slowly emerging revelation, the dark edge of an outline: the black side of Irena.

In the scene just preceding the shot, Tuzenbach makes a crucial request. Irena has described herself earlier as a locked piano to which she has lost the key.

> TUZENBACH: I was awake all night. Not that there's anything to be afraid of in my life, nothing's threatening . . . Only the thought of that lost key torments me and keeps me awake. Say something to me . . . (A pause) Say something!
> IRENA: What? What am I to say? What?
> TUZENBACH: Anything.

Tuzenbach, about to fight a duel with Soliony, needs Irena's reassurance. Forced to obscure a fact while trying to express an emotion, he says, ". . . nothing's threatening . . ." He is telling a lie, and unaware of his true situation, Irena can hardly be blamed for not understanding its desperate-ness. And there is something odd about Tuzenbach's request in the first place: he already knows Irena doesn't love him and is hoping against hope for a last reprieve. The inability to bare or face emotional realities—a favorite Chekhovian notion—is only partly in question here; here there is something worse: to feel the demand but not the attraction. For even if Irena under-stood Tuzenbach's request, her response, if honest, would have to be equiv-ocal. They are both guilty; he for demanding love where he knows it doesn't exist; she for not loving. He is asking too much; she is offering too little.

Tuzenbach's request echoes almost exactly the one Katya makes to the Professor at the end of "A Dreary Story," where it is met with the same failure:

> "Help me, help me!" she begs. "I can't stand any more."
> "There's nothing I can say, Katya."
> I am at a loss, embarrassed, moved by her sobbing, and I can hardly stand.
> "Let's have lunch, Katya," I say with a forced smile. "And stop that crying." "I shall soon be dead, Katya," I at once add in a low voice.
> "Just say one word, just one word!" she cries, holding out her hands.

Katya seems as impervious to the Professor's death sentence as he is to her despair. Each is too full of his own suffering. The characters in *Three Sisters*, like Katya and the Professor, do not hear each other's pleas, partly out of selfishness—other people's troubles are boring—partly out of self-protec-tion. If they *did* hear them, what could they do?

Needs, revealed but never satisfied, drive Chekhov's characters toward two kinds of action: the deranged—Vanya's hysterical outbursts, Treplev's suicide—or flight. They desert each other—as Katya deserts the Professor half a page after the dialogue above, and as Trigorin abandons Nina in *The Seagull*. Nothing could be more Chekhovian than the last sentence of "A Dreary Story." The Professor, watching Katya go, wonders if she'll turn around and look back at him for the last time. She doesn't. Then he says to himself, "Goodbye, my treasure."'—end of story. But those three words are endlessly and ambiguously illuminating. Does he love Katya? Is she his trea-sure because this is the last feeling he will ever have? Is this final desertion the one symptom of his being human? Is there a tiny sarcastic twinge to "treasure"? In regard to people, every credible truth is only partial.

The inability to respond evokes responses: coldness, hatred, contempt.

Loneliness can be viewed as humiliation and misfortune as insult. What cannot be given is interpreted as being withheld. The wrong people always love each other—bad luck or the telltale sign of a fundamental incapacity to love. The typical Chekhovian character longs for what he can neither express nor have, and each unrequited wish is one more dream in a universal nightmare. If the great treachery lies in the disparity between what we feel and what we say, between what we want and what we get, do we have—through an unconscious perversity—a vested interest in disparity itself? Proust, the ultimate dissecter of jealousy, thought so, and it is odd to think that Chekhov, working with such different material and in such a different way, may have come to a similar conclusion. The truth is that what is interesting about love is how it doesn't work out, and Proust and Chekhov saw that truth and that interest from different angles. Surprisingly, like Proust in *Remembrance of Things Past*, who provides us with not one example of a happy marriage in over 4,000 pages, Chekhov offers us none either.

And both Proust and Chekhov concern themselves with a social class that is about to be overwhelmed by forces rising from below. In Proust, the class distinctions are clear; we know exactly who is noble, and who is middle-class. We have to, because the impingement of one upon the other is one of the themes of the novel. That certainly eludes us in Chekhov's case. Olga, Masha, and Irena belong to a social class that has no counterpart in America. We see them as a kind of provincial nobility (partly because we have got to them so often through English accents) whereas they represent the lowest rung of a rural aristocracy, a sort of down-at-the-heels upper middle-class living in the country; squires going to seed, a gentry saddled with land that no longer interests them, fitful leftovers unable to cope with the unfamiliar and the new. Chekhov's plays suffer from classlessness in translation, and more than classlessness in certain productions: maids become heroines and stable boys stars. The main difficulty is: One can hardly imagine Irena in Kansas, say, stretching her hands toward an imaginary New York. She would have already been there, traveling by jet. And, in *The Seagull*, would anyone have the faintest notion of just what *kind* of bank Madame Arkadina kept her much-discussed securities in?

But power, as a source, is general no matter the specific version, and both Natasha and Soliony are interested in it. Each is allowed to inherit a particular world: domestic tyranny in Natasha's case, the completed fantasy of the romantic egoist in Soliony's: the destruction of the rival lover. The passivity of the others gives them permission, it invites them in.

An embittered fact-monger, Soliony is unable to respond to any shade of irony. And though Irena is too young to know it, to be literal and humorless—qualities equally at home in the romantic and the dullard—can be as poisonous as deception or ingrained meanness. Worldliness is never an issue in *Three Sisters* though it might well be. Vershinin brings a breath of it in the door with him with his arrival, but it is the weary urbanity of a disappointed middle-aged man. A lack of worldliness in people forced to live in the world is always a potential source of suffering. Those people doomed to love late and to be ultimately denied it: like Masha and Vershinin, arrive at it by way of lost opportunities and through a web of feeling. In *Three Sisters*, we get two warped version of it: Natasha's grasping selfishness and the doctor's cynicism. They are the merest echoes of the real thing. What we have in its place is innocence on the one hand and frustration on the other. There is no wise man in the play for the others to turn to; there is no mother and father for children who remain children, though they walk about as if they were adults, to run to for comfort and advice. In Chekhov's view, even worldliness, we suspect, would be another inadequate means of dealing with life, as powerless as innocence to fend off its evils, and, because it comes in the guise of wisdom, perhaps the most deceptive of all.

It is not always clear in various editions of the play that these revelations occur over a period of five years. We watch Irena, in fact, change from a young girl into a woman. The time scheme is relatively long, the roles are enigmatically written and need to be played with the finest gradations in order to develop their true flavors and poisons. If Natasha is immediately recognizable as evil, or Soliony as the threat of the play, a great deal is lost in characterization and suspense. Irena's cry of "Moscow! . . . Moscow!" at the end of the second act should be a note in a scale, not a final sounding. She has not realized, she is *beginning* to realize that what she hopes for will remain a dream.

Compared to *The Seagull* and *Uncle Vanya*, a technical advance occurs in *Three Sisters* that may account for a greater sounding of the depths. Chekhov's mastery of the techniques of playwriting may be measured by his use of the gun; it is farther offstage here than before—not in the next room but at the edge of town, which suggests that it might, finally, be dispensed with, as it is in *The Cherry Orchard*, where the only sound we hear, ultimately, is an axe cutting down trees. As he went on, Chekhov let go of the trigger, his one concession to the merciless demands of the stage. The gunshot in *Three Sisters*, unlike the shot in *Vanya*, is terminal. But Tuzenbach's death has further implications; it is partly the result of, and the price paid for, Irena's lack of love. Something suicidal colors Tuzenbach's death, and we pick it up in his last big speech:

> TUZENBACH: . . . Really, I feel quite elated. I feel as if I were
> seeing those fir trees and maples and birches for the first time in

my life. They all seem to be looking at me with a sort of inquis-
itive look and waiting for something. What beautiful trees—and
how beautiful, when you think of it, life ought to be with trees
like these!

(Shouts of 'Ah-oo! Heigh-ho' are heard.)

I must go, it's time. . . . Look at that dead tree, it's all dried up,
but it's still swaying in the wind along with the others. And in the
same way, it seems to me that, if I die, I shall still have a share in
life somehow or other. Goodbye, my dear . . . (Kisses her hands.)
Your papers, the ones you gave me, are on my desk, under the
calendar.

Tuzenbach never had much of "a share in life"; he has always been a
"dried-up (tree) . . . swaying in the wind . . ." If Irena had been able to love
him, would he have tried to talk to Soliony or to Dr. Chebutykin, in some
way mediated the pointlessness of this ending? A pointlessness equally vivid,
one suspects, whether he had married Irena or not.

The key to Irena's heart, that locked piano, is lost. Neither Tuzenbach
nor Soliony ever had it. So their duel, though in deadly earnest, turns out to
be an ironic, even a ludicrous footnote. Who holds the key to Irena's heart?
Someone offstage—like the gun—whom she hopes to meet in Moscow. "The
right one" is how she describes him, the unmeetable ideal who dominates the
fantasies of schoolgirls. The doctor may comfort himself with bogus philosophy and claim that nothing matters but the others tend to confirm not his
thesis but its perverse corollary. By the indecisiveness of their actions, by
their inability to deal head-on with what is central to their lives, they make,
in the end, what matters futile. They unwittingly prove Dr. Chebutykin's
false notion: what *does* Tuzenbach's death matter? Would Irena be any more
lonely with him than without him? Would he have been content living with
someone who doesn't love him, he who needs love to make himself feel love-
able? Would Irena have joined him in "work"—her idealized version of it—
and not be working alone? At what? Reality intrudes upon a pipedream, but
even the reality is dreamlike. The Baron's sacrifice does little for the cause of
either work or love.

Of the three sisters, Olga is the least interesting: nothing romantic
attaches to her. She is neither unhappily married or unhappily *un*married. A
person of feeling who has suppressed or never felt the pull of the irrational,

she is the substitute mother or the spinster-mother—a recognizable type for whom the traditional role is the aunt, boringly earnest but secretly admirable. She represents a standard of behavior unwillingly, almost painfully, for her nerves are not equal to the moral battles in which she must take part, yet those very nerves are the barometric instruments that register ethical weather. Two sets of values are in conflict in *Three Sisters*, as well as two social classes, and nothing makes those values clearer than Olga's and Natasha's confrontation over Anfisa, the 80-year-old nurse. To Olga, Anfisa deserves the respect accorded the old and the faithful. Natasha uses Anfisa as another means of enforcing a pecking order whose main function is to make her status visible. She demands that Anfisa stand up in her presence like a soldier at attention. In this clash of feelings and wills, Olga doesn't defend Anfisa as she should in true opposition, in attack. She is too stunned, too hurt. She says, ". . . everything went black." Natasha, out to win, wins in spite of what would ordinarily be a great drawback—her affair with Poptopopov. Even her open-faced adultery, commented upon by the doctor in the third act, doesn't undercut her position. People prefer to ignore her rather than precipitate a series of crises whose logical end could only be an attack on Andrei. And Andrei cannot be attacked. Affection, pity, and, most of all, necessity are his three shields. Natasha has found the perfect nest to despoil. Andrei was always too weak, too self-centered, in spite of his shyness, to guard his sisters' interests. Now he is not only weak; he is torn.

But Olga is too morally good to let Natasha's rudeness to Anfisa pass without protest—as so many other instances have passed: Natasha's request for Irena's room, made both to Irena and Andrei, for instance, which is met with a kind of cowed acquiescence. It is a demand so basically impossible that no immediate way of dealing with it comes to hand. Natasha apologizes to Olga but it is an apology without understanding, without heart. Actually, it is motivated by Natasha's fear that she has revealed too much, gone too far. Finally, Olga removes Anfisa from the household. There is a tiny suite for her at the school where Olga becomes headmistress, a place where Anfisa may stay for the rest of her life. It is easier—and wiser, too—to get out than to go on fighting a battle already lost. But whether the existence of that suite sways Olga in her decision to *become* a headmistress is left hanging.

Though Natasha and Soliony are the movers and the shakers of the play, another neurotic character, invisible throughout, is a spur to its conflicts: Vershinin's suicidal fishwife of a mate, whom he fears, comes to detest, and yet who controls his life. He is weak, too, unable to make a clean break with his own misery. Chekhov points up one of the strangest true facts of emotional life: nothing binds people closer together than mutual unhappiness. And that is why Chekhov is sometimes so funny. The very horrors of people's lives—short of poverty and disease—are also the most ludicrous things about them. Vanya with a gun! How sad! Yet everyone laughs. The absurd and the tragic are uncomfortably close. Like the figure of the clown, and the wit in black humor, Chekhov teeters on a seesaw. Even a suggestion of the excessive would be ruinous. One gunshot too many, one sob prolonged a second longer than necessary and we have crossed over to the other side. Chekhov, to be played properly, has to be played on a hairline.

Vershinin's mirror-image is Masha, the most interesting of the three sisters, an interest dramatically mysterious because we know so little about her. But we know she is a woman of temperament, a woman capable of passion and that in itself distinguishes her from Olga, to whom something of the old maid clings, just as something of the ingenue mars Irena. Masha wears black throughout the play, reminding us of her namesake, Masha Shamrayev, in *The Seagull*, who also always wears black because she is "in mourning for my life." (It may be of some interest to note that, in the same play, Madame Arkadina's first name is Irena.)

Masha is the onlooker who comments or withholds comment, often to devastating effect. She is the one freespeaker of the play. She tells us the truth about Natasha from the beginning, if only by implication; as a matter of fact, she tells us the truth about everything, even herself, blurting out the facts to her unwilling listeners, Olga and Irena, who don't want to hear of her love for Vershinin, don't want to be involved in a family betrayal. If adultery is a black mark against the detested Natasha, what must one make of it with the beloved Masha? The categories begin to blur, the certainties become uncertain. Like a lot of truth tellers, Masha is morally impeccable in regard to honesty but something of a menace; she puts people in impossible positions. She is the romantic heart of the play just as Irena is the romantic lead. Unlike Irena, Masha is a lover disillusioned by life, not deluded by it. She married her schoolmaster when she was a young student and bitterly learns that the man who struck her as superior is at heart a fool. The reigning intelligence of the play is Masha's. It might have been the doctor's if intelligence were not so dangerous a gift for a man who has taught himself to be disingenuous.

Masha is still something of an impulsive child, a far different thing from being an adolescent like Irena, or living a self-imposed second childhood like the doctor, whose drunken dream is to make second childhood permanent. Masha isn't interested in intelligence per se and the doctor can't afford to be. If he ever let himself know what he knows, it would destroy him. And so he protects himself by a kind of slow-motion destruction, infinitely easier to handle. He keeps telling us how impossible it is to bear reality in a play in which everyone else keeps saying how impossible it is to know what reality is.

In spite of a loveless marriage (from *her* point of view), Masha has Kulighin, who, for all his absurdity, has something everyone else lacks: a true position. Too emasculated to oppose Masha's affair with Vershinin, he nevertheless loves her, sticks by her, and would be desperate without her. A stuffed shirt, a mollycoddle, a bower and a scraper, his ridiculousness masks the genuine feelings of a boy—he loves out of dependency but who else is able to love in *Three Sisters*? Masha, yes, but her love is romantic; Irena, no, *because* her love is romantic. Kulighin ends up with something: he may wander about the stage calling for Masha who never seems to be there, but he has the *right* to call her, and knows she will go home with him in the end. She has nowhere else to go.

The three marriages in the play—Masha-Kulighin, Vershinin and his offstage wife and Natasha-Andrei—are all unhappy. Strangely, Masha and Kulighin do not have children, and no mention is ever made of their childlessness. A matter of no significance, it seems, yet it becomes important in regard to Natasha for it is through the cardinal bourgeois virtue of motherhood that she manipulates the household. Masha provides no counterweight. A subterranean notion percolates at the lowest level of *Three Sisters*—moral righteousness as the chief disguise of self-interest. Power is consolidated under the smokescreen of moral urgency. The Dreyfus Affair, the Reichstag fire, and Watergate are extensions of the same basic principle. Natasha's emotions are as false as her values. Under the camouflage of maternal love, she gains possession of Irena's room and has the maskers dismissed. Whatever *she* may think, it is clear to us that what motivates her action is not her love for her children but her love for herself.

And something similar may be said of Soliony. The duel, though illegal, was a process by which men of Soliony's day still settled matters of honor too refined or too personal for the courts. But it was also a vehicle for machismo pride hidden in the trappings of a gentleman's code. Emotional illness has never found a better front than ethical smugness.

In contrast to the Prozorovs as we first see them, and in spite of her malevolence, Natasha is creating a true family, one with a real mother, father, and children, where only a semblance of family life had existed before. The ghosts of family attachments haunt the wanderers crossing the threshholds of rooms, as if they were searching for a phrase impossible to recall, or had fixed their eyes on an invisible figure. The word "orphan" rings its bell. And Natasha, carrying the energetic serum of the new, has only one goal: to possess a material world. Starting out as a girl who doesn't even know how to dress, she ends up as an unwitting domestic servant of change, dusting a corner here, tearing down a cobweb there. Not one of these acts has a generous motive. She is only a force for progress by being lower-class and on the move. She thinks of herself as the mistress of a house that had for too long been in disorder without her. And in a certain sense, that view is not irrational. Two questions that can never be answered are asked *sotto voce* in the play: What would have happened to everyone if Andrei hadn't married Natasha? And: What will Andrei's and Natasha's children be like?

But even Natasha is up against something too subtle to control. Conquerors have their opposites—losers. But Natasha is working not in a house of losers but of survivors. Something too lively makes Chekhov's characters, even the desperate ones, convincing candidates for yet another day of hopes and dreams. One feels their mortality less than their indestructibility. Everyone casts the shadow of age ahead; it is hard to think of anyone dying in a Chekhov play who isn't actually killed during the action. Some predisposition to live, some strain of the *type* transfixes the individual into permanent amber, so that, unheroic as they may be, we think of them somewhat in the way we think of Shakespearian heroes. They may languish in life but they refuse to die in art, and with a peculiar insistence—an irony only good plays manage to achieve because it is only on the stage that the human figure is always wholly represented and representative. When we speak of "Masha" or "Vanya," we are already talking about the future. One of the side-effects of masterpieces is to make their characters as immortal as the works in which they appear. And so Natasha is stuck among her gallery-mates forever, always *about* to take over the house.

And she is about to do so by exploiting bourgeois morality for ugly ends—an old story. But the subject is the key to Chekhov's method here: the business of unmasking. The soldiers' uniforms hide the same boring civilians underneath. It is important for Tuzenbach literally to take off his clothes and become a civilian "so plain" that Olga cries when she first sees him. Natasha's sash is a tiny repetition of this motif when she reverses roles and comments on Irena's belt in the last act, a bit of signalling uncharacteristic of Chekhov, who rarely stoops to a device so crude. It is already clear that the outsider of Act I has become the dominating power of the household.

Unfulfilled wishes allow for seemingly random duets that enrich the texture of the play by showing us major characters in minor relationships—psychological side pockets of a sort that cast desperate or ironic lights. Olga and Kulighin, for instance, in their discussion of marriage defend it as an institution and as a source of happiness. Yet Olga is a spinster and Kulighin a cuckold. Both schoolteachers, they are drawn together by their profession and by a kind of innocent idealism that overrides fact and disappointment. Theirs might have been the only happy marriage in the play, and Kulighin says he often thinks if he hadn't married Masha, he would have married Olga. In the face of adultery, alcoholism, compulsive gambling, irrational rage, and attempted suicide, Olga still believes in the "finer things," in the vision of human goodness.

Similarly, Irena and Dr. Chebutykin are connected by a thread of sympathy and habit—the oldest and the youngest in one another's arms, each equally deluded, alcohol fuzzing the facts for the doctor, and the determined unawareness of youth providing Irena with a temporary protective barrier. These uneasy alliances are touching because they rise out of needs that bear little relation to their satisfactions. It is precisely Kulighin's marriage to Masha that makes Olga more deeply aware she is a spinster; it is Chebutykin's drinking and his smashing of her mother's clock that will finally curdle Irena's affection for him. And this kind of delicate interplay between the loving and the hateful aspects of relationships is re-enforced often by the action of the play itself. It is Chebutykin, for example, who is the Baron's second at the duel in which Irena is deprived of her husband-to-be, her one chance of making a bid for another life. Trusted by the Baron, Chebutykin has some reason for hoping the Baron is killed—namely, to protect the continuation of his relationship to Irena. If that is true, there is a further irony: the doctor doesn't realize that he has already put that relationship in serious jeopardy. And then there are relationships by omission: Andrei's outpourings to the deaf servant Ferapont, Masha's never addressing a single word to Natasha throughout the entire course of the play. Masha—like her creator—makes the inarticulate eloquent.

The random duets are complemented by a series of trios: two are obvious: Masha-Kulighin-Vershinin and Irena-Tuzenbach-Soliony. But a third is not: Chebutykin's ambiguous relationship to Irena provides her with an underground suitor; his is one of those fatherly-grandfatherly roles whose sexual, affectionate, and narcissistic aspects are impossible to unravel, and he places himself in position as a member of a male trio: Tuzenbach-Soliony-Chebutykin. The doctor has a claim on Irena; he was her protector in the past; she is his lifeline now. It is through the subtle shifts of Irena's relationship to Chebutykin that we watch Irena grow from an unknowing girl into a woman who is beginning to see the truth. Chebutykin is onstage, but by being a kind of subliminal lover, he brings to mind, or to the back of the mind, three *off*stage characters essential to the conflicts of the play: Vershinin's wife; Natasha's lover, Protopopov; and the sisters' mother, each an invisible figure in a triangle. If Chebutykin was once in love with the Prozorovs' mother, he was part of an unacknowledged trio: the mother of the sisters, their father, and himself. The mother's image is kept alive in Irena, who resembles her. These offstage-onstage love affairs—one of which we see, one of which we watch being covered up, and one of which we merely hear about—complicate the action and re-enforce the play's design of interlocking triangles.

Irena is part of two other triangles, one onstage, one off. Our study in ingenuousness, an ingenuousness that will become educated before our eyes, she is joined to Second Lieutenant Fedotik and Rode by the enthusiasms and innocence of youth. If the play were a ballet, at some point they would have a divertissement to themselves. They isolate Chebutykin in a particular way: the contrast between their trio and the doctor makes time physically visible. And then Irena might be considered part of yet another triangle; her dreamed-of "someone" whom she hopes to meet in Moscow is as much of a threat to her happiness with Tuzenbach as Soliony is. It is he, in her mind, who holds the key to the locked piano. Overall, we have our fixed image of a trio, our superimposed stereotype: the three sisters themselves.

The themes of *Three Sisters*, the gulf between dream and action, between hope and disappointment, have finer variations. Even accepting the "real" is thwarted. Irena's compromise in marrying the Baron proves to be impossible. Having given up Moscow, Irena is not even allowed, so to speak, its drearier suburbs. She has met the fate that awaited her all along. Her cry of "work, work," echoed by Tuzenbach, is a hopeless cry. The issue is real, the solution false: what could a dreamy schoolgirl and a philosophical Baron contribute to a brickworks?

But something more than simple evasiveness frustrates the actors in *Three Sisters*. There is a grand plan working out its design, moving the players beyond their ability to act. And the military here perform a special function. When the battery is moved to Poland—its rumored destination was Siberia—the soldiers and officers reverse positions with the sisters who can never get to Moscow, the dreamland of easy solutions. The sisters are psychologically "stationed" in the house by a force as ineluctable as that which sends the soldiers on their way. The dispatchment of soldiers is an event inevitable in time. And illusion gathers strength in ratio to time: the longer an idea is believed the more powerful it becomes "If we only knew," the sisters say at the end. "If we could only know . . ." Know what? Something already known—time moves people without their moving: the soldiers are forced to go, the sisters to stay. The object the doctor breaks in his drunkenness is a clock, and for good reason. Time's pervasiveness—its importance—is stressed many times in the play: the announcement of what time the maskers are to arrive; the hour set for the duel (at one point, the doctor takes out his hunting watch to verify it); the fifteen minutes Natasha allows herself on the sleigh ride with her lover; the no longer available date on which Andrei's papers have to be signed; the very first scene, in fact, which is both an anniversary and a name day. As the minutes tick themselves off, action is always being performed, even by omission. Deluded into thinking time is eternal, events infinitely postponable, the sisters keep hoping problems will solve themselves, somehow, in time. They do, but not as a requital to hope. Birth and death, introduced in the anniversary-name day occasion of the first scene, are more sharply contrasted and connected in the last. Natasha's newest baby is wheeled back and forth in a carriage, a bit of counterpoint to Tuzenbach's death. In between, we have, simply, age—the eighty years of Anfisa's life.

Time sounds a recurrent note in *Three Sisters*; place is more subtly emphasized. The idea of a journey hovers in the air and charges the atmosphere—the journey never taken, the journey never to *be* taken. The repeated sounding of "Moscow!" is more than the never-to-be-reached Eldorado of the work or its lost Eden; it is a symbol of distance itself, that past or future in space from which the characters are forever barred. On this score, the play peculiarly divides itself on sexual grounds: the men want to stay, the women to go. Memory lures them, in opposite directions, and Masha's halting bit of verse clues us in. What cannot be remembered takes on importance; it begins to have the force of a prediction in the same way that the unconscious, unable to bring significant material to the surface, determines future behavior. What does her verse mean? Where has she heard it? She says nothing for the first fifteen minutes of the play, she hums a little tune, remembers a line of verse she can't quite place. She has given up the piano. Enraged beyond speech, she feels—when we first see her—that any communication would be a betrayal. What Masha remembers most vividly, and whose betrayal she cannot forgive, is herself. Even music and poetry, because they evoke memory, are forms of conspiracy: they reveal the sensibility she has forfeited for the stupidity of the world she lives in.

The women want to go; more than that, they want to go *back*. Back to a life they once lived (they think), certainly not the one they are living. As for a brave new world, there are no explorers in *Three Sisters*, no wanderers ready to set forth for the unknown. The word "Siberia" runs its little chill through the kitchen. The play is nostalgic, for one set of people would do anything *not* to be removed from where they are (a form of self-miring in present as if it *were* the past), and one set would do anything, short of what is necessary, to *be* removed. The setting is . . . where? A country town. But it is the least realistic of Chekhov's plays, or at least what is realistic about it always suggests the allusive, one image connecting with or piling up on a similar one. Masha gives up the piano; Irena is a locked piano; Andrei plays the violin. Vershinin receives letters; Kulighin has his notebooks; Andrei is translating an English novel. A whistled phrase is a signal from Vershinin to

Masha or vice versa; the doctor bangs on the floor—his little Morse code. Irena gives her room up for a baby; Olga gives it up for an old woman, Anfisa. These networks are fine meshes thrown over the realistic surface of the play. The webs of character obscure—and enrich—the scaffold of action. And what is allusive about the play suggests the thematically symbolic. Where do people move? From room to room. (Is that why the first thing we see is a room within a room?) But two crucial moves, Irena and Olga doubling up in one bedroom, and Anfisa moving out, are overshadowed by the movement, the literal displacement, of the soldiers going to two possible destinations: Poland (where we are still within the limits of the civilized and the credible) and Siberia (where we move into the realm of fear and fantasy).

The sense of danger, a hairsbreadth away from the cozy, becomes actual in the fire of Act 3. People can really be forced out of their houses, they can be *made to move* by events beyond their power to predict or to control. The fire presents us with a true Apocalypse, its victims huddled downstairs, lost souls wandering about, crying, the rescuers, inside and out, trying to keep the contagion from spreading. Blankets, beds, food are commandeered. Still the shadow of the flames races up the walls. We are in a disaster area, a battlefield. We are also in Olga's and Irena's bedroom. The disaster outside is the general counterpart of the specific horrors within. They have one thing in common: dislocation. For the burning houses are no longer truly houses, any more than the room is now either Olga's *or* Irena's. Natasha has invaded the place of privacy, the source of identity, and we get to know that because it is *after* this scene that Olga moves out to become headmistress and *during* it that Irena decides to marry the Baron and Masha to sleep with Vershinin. And these three decisions prepare us for a fourth: the removal of Anfisa from the household. That is not as simple a decision as it first appears, for Anfisa is the basic—and the last—link with whatever living tradition ties the sisters to their childhoods. The issue of Anfisa is the scale that balances the strengths and weaknesses of Olga and Natasha, the turning point of the act and the breaking point of the play. In a psychological terror scene the fate of the Prozorovs is decided. Natasha's taking over of the house is played against the bigger landscape of the fire destroying the adjacent houses. But the small wreck and the large are equally devastating.

Each sister is given an opportunity for moral or emotional expansion and is finally enclosed in the limited world of the possible. Each outlasts a wish and is forced to go on living a life without any particular pleasure or savor. The sway of compulsion is important to the play because compulsion suggests what must be limited: to be compelled is the opposite of being able to make a free choice. And there are enough examples of the irrational in the air to make the fearful and the uncontrollable real: Vershinin's wife's suicide

attempts, Andrei's gambling, the doctor's alcoholism, Natasha's temper. And
Soliony, our capital case, because he brings about what we are most afraid of:
death. The departed, the unloved, the disappointed—all these are pale imitations of true oblivion. Soliony is the darkest cloud of all.

Three Sisters is enigmatic—it would be hard to say just how the last
speeches should be played—sadly, bitterly?—as a kind of cosmic, ridiculous
joke? Realistically?—as if in the face of hopelessness it were possible to
conceive a Utopia? Only *Hamlet* offers so many unresolved possibilities.
Could the doctor have saved Tuzenbach in the last act? Does he let him die
to ensure his own continuing relationship to Irena? Is there a homosexual
undercurrent in the relationship between Soliony and Tuzenbach? It was
suggested in the Olivier-Bates version of the play. Is the trio of Irena's
suitors—the doctor, Soliony, and Tuzenbach—an ironic, or merely an instru-
mental little mirror-play of the sisters themselves, trio for trio? Is Vershinin's
vision of the world to come just another more cosmic version of the
never-to-be-attained Moscow of Irena's dreams? There are overtones and
undertows. More clearly than in any of Chekhov's other plays, fantasy
imbues consciousness with a strength similar to the power of dreams in the
unconscious. The play teeters on an ambiguity: if coming to terms with
reality is a sign of psychological maturity, philosophy offers a contrary alter-
native: in letting go of an ideal, the sisters may be depriving themselves—or
are being deprived—of the one thing that makes life worth living.

These positive-negative aspects of the play are not easily resolved.
Ambivalence enriches the action but fogs the ending. The problems *Three
Sisters* raises have been presented to us with a complexity that allows for no
easy solutions. Yet the curtain has to come down, the audience depart. And
Chekhov, almost up to the last moment, keeps adding complications. In spite
of its faultless construction, or because of it, the play is full of surprises.
Andrei's moving and unexpected speech about Natasha's vulgarity, for
instance. He knows how awful she is, and yet he loves her, and can't understand why—an unusual, and far from simpleminded, admission.

The sisters long to accomplish the opposite of what they achieve, to
become the contrary of what they are. Masha is most honest about this and
most hopeless; she cannot console herself with the optimistic platitudes of
Irena or shore herself up with the resigned Puritanism of Olga. Irena is
about to rush off to her brick factory and Olga to her schoolroom. Masha
lives with and within herself—a black person in a black dress, beautiful,
loving, without joy. *Three Sisters*, in spite of its ambiguously worded
life-may-be-better-in-the-future ending, might properly be subtitled,
"Three Ways of Learning to Live without Hope." It is a drama of induced
stupors and wounds and its tagged-on hopefulness is the one thing about it

that doesn't ring true. People use each other in the play sentimentally, desperately, and, finally, fatally, and there is no reason to assume that, given the choice, they will ever do anything else.

What we hear in *Three Sisters* are the twin peals of longing and departure. They are amplified by human ineptitude, human error, human weakness. And behind them we hear the clangings of the extreme: the childish, the monstrous, the insane. The Brahmsian overcast of sadness that darkens the action—little outbursts of joy and gaiety always too soon stifled or abandoned—helps to make what is essentially a terrible indictment of life bearable. Sadness is at least not hopelessness. A play of girlhood, it is a play of loss, but not only feminine loss, though that strikes the deepest note. The drums and fifes offstage, the batteries that occasionally go off, the gambling house and the office—male institutions and trimmings—are shadowy and have nothing of the power and the immediacy of preparations for a meal, the giving of gifts, the temperature of a nursery—the force of the domestic, whether frustrated and virginal, or fulfilled and turning sour. A play about women—men are strangely absent even in the moment of their presence—its author clearly saw what lay at its most profound level: helplessness, a real, social, or contrived trait associated with, and sometimes promulgated by, women. Social class and the accident of sex work hand in hand to defeat desire and ambition. Watchers watching life go by, a stately frieze longing for the activity of movement, that is the central image of *Three Sisters*. Not so much "If we had only known . . ." as "If we could only *move* . . ." Temperament, breeding, upbringing fix the sisters to separate stakes. They go on, hoping for the best, getting the worst, which is, in their case, to stay exactly as they were.

MARTIN ESSLIN

Chekhov and the Modern Drama

Anton Chekhov was one of the major influences in the emergence of a wholly new approach to the subject matter, structure, and technique of dramatic writing at the end of the nineteenth century. It can be argued that he, in fact, occupies a key position at the point of transition between a millennial convention of "traditional" and the emergence of "modern" drama.

What was it that the "modern" drama replaced? What was it that the multifarious types of traditional dramatic fiction, however different they might appear, had fundamentally in common—from Greek tragedy and comedy to the well-made play of the nineteenth century; what were the characteristics that all these shared that were so decisively displaced by the new elements of the "modern"?

It was not what had so long been regarded as the hallmarks of the truly correct and classical form of drama: the Aristotelian unities of time, place, and action. After all, medieval drama, the Elizabethans, and the Romantics had superseded those by constructing rambling, epic plot-lines. But Greek drama and the French classical tradition, the medieval mystery plays and the Spanish theatre of the "siglo d'oro," Shakespeare and commedia dell'arte, Restoration comedy and the well-made play, do have a number of characteristics in common. Foremost among them is the assumption that the audience must be explicitly and clearly told what the principal characters' state of mind

From *A Chekhov Companion*. © 1985 by Toby W. Clyman.

is at any given moment in the play, whether through the monologues of Shakespeare and the Elizabethans that are directly addressed to the audience, or the use of confidants in French classical drama, or, indeed through "asides" uttered in the presence of other characters who, by convention, were assumed to remain unaware of them.

Even more important perhaps was another basic assumption that underlay all language used in drama: that what a character said was not only what he or she meant to say, but that he or she was expressing it as clearly and eloquently as possible. Dramatic speech was deeply influenced by, and obeyed the rules of, the classical tradition of rhetoric as practiced and formulated by Demosthenes, Cicero, and Quintilian, and as it was taught in the schools from the time of Socrates to the nineteenth century and beyond (in the United States, in public speaking courses in some colleges and universities to this day).

Similar ideas of a clear, transparent structure (derived from the rhetorical rules of statement of theme, development, and conclusion) also governed the construction of the plot from exposition through complication and reversal to a definite and conclusive ending.

That the theatre should attempt to present a picture of the world as it really is never occurred to the theoreticians or practitioners of pre-modern drama. The theatre was an art—and art was artifice, quite apart from the practical impossibility of creating a true facsimile of human life under the technological conditions of a stage in the open air, or lit by candles, with painted scenery, or no scenery at all. The theatre could only present the essential aspects of the human condition, compressed and idealised, according to a firmly established set of conventions (just as, for example, painting eliminated pubic hair in nudes and showed crowds of people in neatly stylised groupings).

It was the great change in the technology of theatre (with gas and later electrical lighting, hydraulic stage machinery, and so on) which, combined with the rise of the scientific world view, led to the idea that the stage could not only reproduce an accurate image of "real life," but should also become like an instrument of scientific inquiry into human behaviour, a laboratory in which the laws governing the interaction of human beings and social classes could be studied.

Yet Zola who first formulated the theoretical concept of the theatre of Naturalism and Ibsen who was the first to gain gradual acceptance for it—through scandal and the violent partisanship of radicals—found it very difficult to liberate themselves from some of the old conventions. Although Ibsen did away with the soliloquy and the "aside," although he tried to create, in his socially oriented drama, stage environments of the greatest possible realism—rooms with the fourth wall removed—structurally, he tended to adhere to the convention of the well-made play. Ibsen's analytical plots developed toward a climax with the relentless logic and compressed time-scale of French classical drama. Even so, his failure to let his characters explain themselves to the audience mystified even intelligent playgoers. As Clement Scott, in reviewing a performance of *Rosmersholm* in 1891, put it:

> The old theory of playwriting was to make your story or your study as simple as possible. The hitherto accepted plan of a writer for the stage was to leave no possible shadow of doubt concerning his characterisation. But Ibsen loves to mystify. He is as enigmatic as the Sphynx. Those who earnestly desire to do him justice and to understand him keep on saying to themselves, "Granted all these people are egotists, or atheists, or agnostics, or emancipated, or what not, still I can't understand why he does this or she does that."

It was Chekhov who took the decisive step beyond Ibsen. He not only renounced the convention of characters who constantly explain themselves to the audience, but he also discarded the last remnants of the plot structure of the well-made play. As a natural scientist and physician, Chekhov rebelled against the artificiality of the conventional dramatic structure. As early as 1881, when he was embarking on his first full-length play, which he discarded (the untitled manuscript, usually referred to as *Platonov*) after it had been rejected by Ermolova, he formulated his ideas as follows:

> In real life people do not spend every minute in shooting each other, hanging themselves or declaring their love for each other. They don't devote all their time to trying to say witty things. Rather they are engaged in eating, drinking, flirting and talking about trivialities—and that is what should be happening on stage. One ought to write a play in which people come and go, eat, talk about the weather and play cards. Life should be exactly as it is, and people exactly as they are. On stage everything should be just as complicated and just as simple as in life. People eat their meals, and in the meantime their fortune is made or their life ruined.

It took Chekhov some fifteen years before he himself succeeded in bringing this theoretical program to full practical realisation and fruition with *The Seagull*. For it was not easy to work out all the implications of the endeavour to present real "slices of life" on the stage. It meant, for one, that the action on stage would have to get as near as possible to "real elapsed time," that is, that an hour on stage would have to correspond to an hour of "real life." How could one tell a story with a scope larger than that of one-acts (such as Chekhov's own *The Proposal* and *The Bear*) by adhering to this principle? The solution that emerged was to present a number of significant episodes showing the characters and their situation in detail and in as near to "real time" as possible in widely separated segments extracted from the flow of time (usually four acts)—so that the events of months and years became visible by implication through the way in which the situation in each vignette differed from the previous one. Thus, the relentless forward pressure of the traditional dramatic form was replaced by a method of narration in which it was the *discontinuity* of the images that told the story, by implying what had happened in the gaps between episodes.

Even more decisive, however, was the demand that the characters should not be shown in unnaturally "dramatic" and climactic situations but pursuing the trivial occupations of real life—eating, drinking, making small talk, or just sitting around reading the newspaper. The state of mind of the characters, the emotional tensions between them, the subterranean streams of attraction and repulsion, love and hate, now frequently had to be indicated indirectly, so that the audience would be able to apprehend them by inference. In other words, the playwright had to supply the signs from which the spectators, having been turned into equivalents of Sherlock Holmes, would deduce the meaning of seemingly trivial exchanges, and, indeed, the meaning of silences, words that remained unspoken. This, after all, is what happens in real life: we meet people and from the cut of their clothes, the accents of their speech, the tone of voice with which they address remarks to us about the weather, we have to deduce their character or their intentions toward us. In our small ways each of us has to be a semiotician decoding the signs supplied to us by our fellow human beings and the environment.

Another consequence of this program for a new drama was the abandonment of the central figure—the hero—of the drama. There are no subsidiary characters in real life, no Rosencrantzes and Guildensterns whose presence in the play is merely dictated by the requirements of the plot and who therefore remain uncharacterised. In the traditional drama such characters were emotionally expendable. It was the hero or heroine alone with whom the spectator was meant to identify, from whose point of view he or she was supposed to experience the action, living through, vicariously, the emotions felt by such central characters. The new drama required a far more detached, clinical attitude that would allow the audience to look at all the characters with the same cool objectivity.

Characters viewed objectively, from the outside rather than through identification, tend to appear comic. If we identified ourselves with the man who slips on a banana peel we would feel his pain; if we viewed him from the outside we could laugh at his misfortune. The characters in Chekhov's mature plays, in which he succeeded in putting his program into practice, are thus essentially comic characters, even if what happens to them (frustration in love, loss of an estate, inability to move to Moscow) is sad or even tragic. Thus, Chekhov's program for a new approach to drama implied the emergence of tragicomedy as the dominant genre.

Chekhov's conflict with Stanislavskii about the production of his plays centered around this demand for a cool, sharp objectivity that would preserve the essentially comedic form of the tragic events, while Stanislavskii wanted to milk the tragic elements to produce an elegiac and as Chekhov felt "larmoyant" effect.

The demand for absolute truth, full conformity with the randomness and triviality of "real life," from which Chekhov started out, was clearly inspired by the same positivist, scientific ideas that had led Zola to proclaim the program of Naturalism. But, paradoxically, the resolve to reproduce the casualness and triviality of ordinary life led to a higher rather than a lesser degree of "artificiality." For, if meaning was to emerge from the depiction of people pursuing commonplace activities, if the spectator was to be enabled to deduce significance from the multitude of signifiers offered by decoding what they revealed, every move, every word, every object had to be carefully planned and designed as a bearer of such meaning. In other words, as real randomness would be totally meaningless, it was merely the *appearance* of randomness and triviality that had to be evoked by creating a structure of which every element contributed to the production of meaning. This type of drama thus required a far greater degree of skill in weaving an intricate texture of great complexity which could, nevertheless, add up to the intended effect and meaning.

This also was the reason why Chekhov so strenuously objected to Stanislavskii's overloading his productions with a clutter of details not indicated in the text. The proliferation of off-stage sound effects and other naturalistic detail brought in for the sake of mere "reality" smothered the structure of the signifiers Chekhov had carefully written into his scripts.

The dense texture of signifying detail within each segment of seemingly "real time" and the building of a sense of larger time-spans through a discontinuous four-act structure require a very high degree of control over the expressive means at the disposal of the playwright, a sense of rhythm and orchestration that would unify the seemingly casual and disconnected elements and transform the text into a texture as complex as that of the counterpoint of an orchestral score. Thus, the program that started from a rejection of "the poetic" on stage paradoxically led to a new kind of more complex poetry. Chekhov himself, in his acrimonious discussions with Stanislavskii, repeatedly insisted that the theatre was an art, striving to produce the appearance of reality, but it was never to be confused with reality.

On the other hand, the cold, objective nature of this art makes it impossible for the playwright to take sides or to offer solutions to the problems posed in his or her work:

> You are right to demand that an author take a conscious stock of what he is doing, but you are confusing two concepts: answering the questions and formulating them correctly. Only the latter is required of an author. It is the duty of the court to formulate the questions correctly, but it is up to each member of the jury to answer them according to his own preference.

Chekhov's drama thus rejects all moralising, just as it eschews the neat solutions that were required by the playwrights of traditional drama. With him "open form" entered the theatre.

It took a long time for Chekhov's revolutionary innovations to be recognised, let alone generally accepted outside Russia, where the successful production of his plays by Stanislavskii's and Nemirovich-Danchenko's Moscow Art Theatre (however much Chekhov himself disagreed with them) had established him as a major playwright.

In Russia Gorkii was deeply influenced by Chekhov's technique, although his plays were far more partisan and explicitly political than Chekhov's. But it was only after the discomfiture of the revolutionary avant-garde and the introduction of socialist realism as the leading aesthetic doctrine in the Soviet Union in the 1930s that the Moscow Art Theatre was elevated into the model for Soviet drama, and Chekhov became the official model, at least as far as the superficial and external aspects of his "realistic" technique were concerned. In spirit the stereotype of the contemporary Russian "realistic" play, with its openly propagandistic message, is far removed from Chekhov.

Western Europeans found it difficult at first to understand Chekhov's intentions. Early performances of *Uncle Vania* in Berlin (1904) and Munich (1913), *The Seagull* in Berlin (1907), Glasgow (1909), and Munich (1911) and *The Cherry Orchard* in London (1911) remained without lasting echo. There was one major exception: Bernard Shaw was so deeply impressed that he modeled his own *Heartbreak House* (1919) on *The Cherry Orchard*. He clearly saw the parallel between the death of the Russian upper classes and the inevitable decline of English society.

After World War I, tours by the Moscow Art Theatre to Germany, France, and the United States spread the Russian playwright's fame. In France the Pitoeff family, exiled from Russia, consolidated his reputation, but there too they only gained general acceptance for him after World War II.

It was in England that Chekhov first achieved recognition as a classic and one of the great innovators of drama. A production of *The Cherry Orchard* by J. B. Fagan (with the young John Gielgud as Trofimov) at the Oxford Playhouse in January 1925 was so successful that the play was transferred to London and ran there for several months. Yet the real breakthrough for Chekhov came with a series of productions of his late plays by the Russian emigré director Theodore Komisarjevsky at the small Barnes Theatre in London in 1926. By the end of the 1930s Chekhov had become a recognised classic in the English theatre. Since then Shakespeare, Ibsen, and Chekhov have been regarded as the standard classics of the English repertoire. No British actor or actress can lay claim to major status without having successfully portrayed the principal parts created by these playwrights.

The reasons for Chekhov's spectacular rise to the status of a classic in Britain are complex. The fact that pre-revolutionary Russia and England were both societies in which the upper classes spent a great deal of their time in country houses populated by a large cast of family members and guests may well have something to do with it. In these plays theatre audiences in England recognised their own way of life. Similarly, Chekhov's use of "subtext" has its affinities with the English penchant for "understatement." English audiences may thus have been more skilled than those of other countries in the art of decoding subtle nuances of utterance. The fact remains that actors like Gielgud, Laurence Olivier, Peggy Ashcroft, Ralph Richardson, Michael Redgrave, and Alec Guinness made Chekhov their own and that he has remained one of the most performed standard authors over a period of 50 years.

That an author so favoured by major actors would have an influence on the writing of plays in Britain was inevitable. Among the many direct, if shallow, imitators of the Chekhovian style are playwrights like N. C. Hunter (1908–1971) whose *Waters of the Moon* (1951) scored a big success by providing fat parts for "Chekhovian" actors; Enid Bagnold (1889–1981); or Terence Rattigan (1911–1977) who used Chekhovian techniques in plays like *The Browning Version* (1948) and *Separate Tables* (1954).

In the United States Chekhov's influence spread indirectly through the success of Stanislavskii's approach to the technique of acting, not least through the efforts of Chekhov's nephew Michael Alexandrovich Chekhov (1891–1955) who had emigrated to England in 1927 and moved to America in 1939. Undoubtedly playwrights like Tennessee Williams, Arthur Miller,

William Inge, or Clifford Odets absorbed at least some of Chekhov's ideas about the "subtext" and the emotional overtones of seemingly trivial conversation.

Yet to look for the direct influence of Chekhov on individual playwrights is perhaps futile. His real influence, though mainly indirect, goes far deeper and is far more pervasive. For he was one of the major innovators who changed the basic assumptions upon which the drama of our time (and "drama" nowadays includes the dramatic material of the cinema, television and radio) is founded.

Many influences, often of a seemingly contradictory nature, have shaped present approaches to drama. George Buechner (1813–1837), also a physician and natural scientist, but almost certainly unknown to Chekhov as he was only being rediscovered at the turn of the century, in many ways anticipated the technique of discontinuous plot development and the use of a type of dialogue that was both documentary and poetically orchestrated. The Naturalists—Ibsen, Strindberg, Gerhart Hauptmann, Arthur Schnitzler —eliminated the conventions of the soliloquy and aside; Frank Wedekind was a pioneer of dialogue in which people talked past each other, neither listening nor answering their interlocutor's points; the German Expressionists, following the lead of Strindberg in the last phase of his career, shifted the plane of the action from the external world to the inner life of the leading character so that the stage became a projection of his or her fantasies and hallucinations; Bertolt Brecht rebelled against the theatre as a house of illusions, the tight construction of continuous plot-lines and developed his own, discontinuous "epic" technique of storytelling; Antonin Artaud tried to devalue the word as an element of drama; and the "Absurdist" playwrights of the 1950s and 1960s (Samuel Beckett, Jean Genet, Arthur Adamov, Eugene Ionesco) created a non-illusionistic theatre of concrete stage metaphors.

Many of these tendencies seem to be in direct contradiction to Chekhov's program of a theatre that would faithfully reproduce the appearance of real life, its casualness and its seeming triviality. Yet, paradoxically, his example and his practice contributed a great deal to developments that, at first sight, may seem very far removed from his ideas and intentions.

Above all, Chekhov, more than any other innovator of drama, established the concept of an "open" form. By putting the onus of decoding the events on the stage on the spectators, by requiring them to draw their own conclusions as to the meaning as well as the ultimate message of the play, and by avoiding to send them home with a neatly packaged series of events in their minds, Chekhov anticipated Brecht's "Verfremdungseffekt" (which he may well himself have inherited from the Russian formalists' concept of "defamiliarisation," in turn directly related to Chekhov's practice). And at the other end of the spectrum a play like Beckett's *Waiting for Godot* carries Chekhov's technique of characters in apparently idle and trivial chatter to its extreme, creating a dramatic structure without action and completely open-ended. Here the trappings of Realism have fallen away, but the Chekhovian principle remains triumphant.

Chekhov's renunciation of high-flown poetic language and rhetorical explicitness (which went much further than Ibsen's attempts at realistic dialogue) produced another paradoxical consequence: the need to orchestrate the seemingly casual conversations, and the silences and hesitations in the characters' speech produced a new kind of poetry, a lyricism in which the rhythms and pauses coalesced into a new harmony. This created an emphasis on mood, on atmosphere, that was very different from the conscious lyricism of Symbolists like Maurice Maeterlinck or Neo-Romantics like the young Hugo von Hofmannsthal, a texture of often bitter ironies and counterpoints between the overt meaning and the subtext. Chekhov's practise opened the way for a new concept of the "poetic" in the theatre, what Jean Cocteau has called the "poetry of the stage" as against mere "poetry on the stage": the formally prosaic statement that acquires its poetry from the context in which it is pronounced, its position within the rhythmic and semantic structure of a *situation*.

The new type of "lyricism" has become the main source of "the poetic" in contemporary drama, not only in stage plays but also in the cinema, where a host of great directors, from Jean Renoir and Marcel Carne to Antonioni and Robert Altmann have extracted poetry from the trivial dialogue and objects of real life situations.

By reducing the importance of overt action and "plot" Chekhov created a new focus of attention: the situation itself, the conjunction of characters, the subtle use of seemingly incongruous detail (like the map of Africa on the wall of Uncle Vania's study), the sparing use of sound (like the strumming of a guitar) put the emphasis on the complex audiovisual *image* of the stage and made the stage itself into a poetic metaphor. Chekhov was one of the pioneers in moving the theatre away from putting its main emphasis on action in the simple, literal sense. A great deal is still happening in the seemingly static stage images of Chekhov, behind the apparently trivial dialogue. But it is complex and covert rather than on the surface and direct. Much of contemporary drama derives from this use of ambivalence and irony. Sonia's last words in *Uncle Vania* in a seemingly idyllic situation, with Maria Vassilevna working on her pamphlet, Marina knitting, Telegin softly playing his guitar, and Sonia herself kneeling before Vania, "We shall rest!" seem hopeful and the situation idyllic. Yet, at the same time, Sonia may not really believe what she is saying, and the idyllic situation enshrines, in reality, the horror of endless boredom and futility. Compare this with the last line of *Waiting for Godot*: "Let's go," followed by the stage direction "(They do not move)" to see a much reduced, almost minimalist, version of the same technique.

Chekhov's refusal to depart from the mere objective delineation of people and events in their inherent inner contradictions and ambivalences made him the pioneer of another main characteristic of contemporary drama: the emergence of the *tragicomic* as its prevailing mode. That the "death of tragedy" derives from the loss of moral certainties and metaphysically grounded principles is clear enough. Chekhov was one of the first to see this and to embody its consequences in devising a new genre of drama. As Friedrich Duerrenmatt has argued, modern people are far too deeply enmeshed in society's organisational framework ever to exercise the heroic privilege of assuming full and proud responsibility for their acts, to allow their misfortunes ever to be more than mere mishaps, accidents. Chekhov was the first to cast his drama in this mode of tragicomic ambivalence; the three sisters' inability to get to Moscow, the ruination of their brother's talents, the death of Tuzenbakh—all are prime examples of just such socially determined inevitabilities, such mishaps and accidents. Vania's failure to hit the professor is comic, although the situation is tragic. But even if Vania did shoot the professor it would still not be tragedy, merely a regrettable incident. If Harold Pinter speaks of his plays as being meant to be funny up to that point where they cease to be funny, he was formulating a perception of the tragicomic that directly derives from Chekhov.

There is only a small step from Chekhov's images of a society deprived of purpose and direction to the far more emphatic presentation of a world deprived of its "metaphysical dimension" in the plays of Beckett, Genet, Adamov, or Ionesco. Admittedly, the dramatists of the Absurd have left the solid ground of reality behind and have taken off into dreamlike imagery and hallucinatory metaphor. Yet it can be argued that Chekhov himself, by his very realism, blazed even that trail. In creating so convincing a picture of the randomness and ambivalence of reality, he, more than any other dramatist before him, opened up the question about the nature of reality itself. If every member of the audience has to find his or her own meaning of what he or she sees by decoding a large number of signifiers, each spectator's image of the play will be slightly different from that which his or her neighbour sees, and will thus become one's own private image, not too far removed from being one's own private dream or fantasy. The Theatre of the Absurd merely builds on that foundation by posing, less subtly, more insistently than Chekhov, the question: "What is it that I am seeing happening before my eyes?"

The Brechtian theatre, insisting as it does on the solid material basis of the world, also requires the audience to decode the signifiers of its parables by themselves. It also derives its poetic force from the ironic juxtaposition of ambivalent and contradictory signs to produce an ultimately tragicomic world view. While it is almost certain that Brecht was not consciously or directly influenced by Chekhov, his ideas pervaded the atmosphere of theatrical and literary modernism and, indeed, more complex lines of interconnectedness can be traced. Brecht's "Verfremdungseffekt," as has already been mentioned, owed a great deal to the Russian formalists' concept of *ostranenie* (defamiliarisation). Moreover, Brecht was a great admirer of Vsevolod Meierkhold, who, before he broke away from Stanislavskii and the Moscow Art Theatre had been the first Treplev in Stanislavskii's *Seagull* and the first Tuzenbakh in the *Three Sisters* (it is said that Chekhov had written the part for him). Meierkhold's modernism thus derives indirectly from, and is an extrapolation into more daring innovation of, the demand for ruthless objectivity and open forms in the theatre. Meierkhold once sent Chekhov a photograph of himself, inscribed: "From the pale-faced Meierkhold to his God."

The greatest and most directly discernible impact of Chekhov's innovation on the modern theatre, however, is undoubtedly to be found in the field of dialogue. The concept of the "subtext" has become so deeply embedded in the fabric of basic assumptions of contemporary playwriting and acting that, literally, there can be hardly a playwright or actor today who does not unquestioningly subscribe to it in his or her practice.

Chekhov's ideas have not only been assimilated, but they have also been further developed by dramatists like Harold Pinter, whose use of pauses, silences, and subterranean currents of meaning clearly derives from Chekhov but goes far beyond him in the exploration of the implied significance of a whole gamut of speech-acts, from the use of trade jargon to that of tautology, repetition, solecisms, and delayed repartee.

Pinter's linguistic experiments, so clearly derived from Chekhov, have engendered a host of followers in Europe and the United States (where perhaps David Mamet is the foremost practitioner of this type of linguistic exploration).

The concept of the "subtext" has also led to attempts to bring onto the stage characters whose linguistic ability is so low that they are unable to express themselves clearly. Here the playwright, through the rudiments of a vocabulary they may still possess, has to show what goes on in their minds and emotions. The English playwright Edward Bond, in a play like *Saved* (1965), made extremely successful use of a technique clearly derived from Chekhov, by making fragments of illiterate speech and silences reveal the characters' thoughts and feelings.

In the German-speaking world the Bavarian playwrights Franz Xaver Kroetz and Martin Sperr, the Austrians Wolfgang Bauer and Peter Turrini, have also become masters of this type of highly laconic dialogue in which silences and half-sentences are used to uncover the mental processes of tongue-tied individuals.

It is only since the end of World War II that Chekhov has been received, by general consensus, into the canon of the world's greatest dramatists that extends from the Greek tragedians to Shakespeare, Lope de Vega, Calderon, Racine, Corneille, Moliere, to the great moderns—Ibsen and Strindberg. Today Chekhov may well be regarded as being even more important and influential than Ibsen and Strindberg.

His output of only four major, mature plays may be much smaller than theirs, but, in the long run, its originality and innovative influence may well prove much greater.

Chekhov's determination to look at the world not merely with the cool objectivity of the scientist but also with the courage to confront the world in all its absurdity and infinite suffering (without flinching or self-pity and with a deep compassion for humanity in its ignorance and helplessness) led him to anticipate, far ahead of all his contemporaries, the mood and climate of our own time. That is the secret of his profound and all-pervading influence on the literature, and, above all, the drama of the century that opened so soon after his early death.

CHARLES E. MAY

Chekhov and the Modern Short Story

Anton Chekhov's short stories were first welcomed in England and America just after the turn of the century as examples of late nineteenth-century realism, but since they did not embody the social commitment or political convictions of the realistic novel, they were termed "realistic" primarily because they seemed to focus on fragments of everyday reality. Consequently, they were characterized as "sketches," "slices of life," "cross-sections of Russian life," and were often said to be lacking every element which constitutes a really good short story. However, at the same time, other critics saw that Chekhov's ability to dispense with a striking incident, his impressionism, and his freedom from the literary conventions of the highly plotted and formalized story marked the beginnings of a new or "modern" kind of short fiction that combined the specific detail of realism with the poetic lyricism of romanticism.

The primary characteristics of this new hybrid form are: character as mood rather than as either symbolic projection or realistic depiction; story as minimal lyricized sketch rather than as elaborately plotted tale; atmosphere as an ambiguous mixture of both external details and psychic projections; and a basic impressionistic apprehension of reality itself as a function of perspectival point of view. The ultimate result of these characteristics is the modernist and postmodernist focus on reality itself as a fictional construct and the contemporary trend to make fictional assump-

From *A Chekhov Companion.* © 1985 by Toby W. Clyman.

tions and techniques both the subject matter and theme of the novel and the short story.

Character as Mood

The most basic problem in understanding the Chekhovian shift to the "modern" short story involves a new definition of the notion of "story" itself, which, in turn, involves not only a new understanding of the kind of "experience" to be embodied in story but a new conception of character as well. Primarily this shift to the modern is marked by a transition from the romantic focus on a projective fiction, in which characters are functions in an essentially code-bound parabolic or ironic structure, to an apparently realistic episode in which plot is subordinate to "as-if-real" character. However, it should be noted that Chekhov's fictional figures are not realistic in the way that characters in the novel usually are. The short story is too short to allow for character to be created by the kind of dense detail and social interaction through duration typical of the novel.

Conrad Aiken was perhaps the first critic to recognize the secret of Chekhov's creation of character. Noting that Chekhov's stories offer an unparalleled "range of states of consciousness," Aiken says that whereas Poe manipulates plot and James manipulates thought, Chekhov "manipulates feeling or mood." If, says Aiken, we find his characters have a strange way of evaporating, "it is because our view of them was never permitted for a moment to be external—we saw them only as infinitely fine and truthful sequences of mood." This apprehension of character as mood is closely related to D. S. Mirsky's understanding of the Chekhovian style, which he described as "bathed in a perfect and uniform haze," and the Chekhovian narrative method, which Mirsky says "allows nothing to 'happen,' but only smoothly and imperceptibly to 'become'."

Such a notion of character as mood and story as a hazy "eventless" becoming is characteristic of the modern artistic understanding of story. It is like Conrad's conception in *Heart of Darkness*, for to his story-teller Marlowe, "the meaning of an episode was not inside like a kernel but outside, enveloping the tale which brought it out only as a glow brings out a haze." More recently, Eudora Welty has suggested that the first thing we notice about the short story is "that we can't really see the solid outlines of it—it seems bathed in something of its own. It is wrapped in an atmosphere." Once we see that the short story, by its very shortness, cannot deal with the denseness of detail and the duration of time typical of the novel, but rather focuses on a revelatory break-up of the rhythm of everyday reality, we can see how the form, striving to accommodate "realism" at the end of the nineteenth century, focused on an experience under the influence of a particular mood and therefore depended more on tone than on plot as a principle of unity.

In fact, "all experience" phenomenologically encountered, rather than "experience" discursively understood, is the primary focus of the modern short story, and, as John Dewey makes clear, "an experience" is recognized as such precisely because it has a unity, "a single *quality* that pervades the entire experience in spite of the variation of its constituent parts." Rather than plot, what unifies the modern short story is an atmosphere, a certain tone of significance. The problem is to determine the source of this significance. On the one hand, it may be the episode itself, which, to use Henry James's phrase, seems to have a "latent value" that the artist tries to unveil. It is this point of view that governs James Joyce's notion of the epiphany—"a sudden spiritual manifestation, whether in the vulgarity of speech or of gesture or in a memorable phase of the mind itself."

On the other hand, it may be the subjectivity of the teller, his perception that what seems trivial and everyday has, from his point of view, significance and meaning. There is no way to distinguish between these two views of the source of the so-called "modern" short story, for it is by the teller's very choice of seemingly trivial details and his organization of them into a unified pattern that lyricizes the story and makes it seem natural and realistic even as it resonates with meaning. As Georg Lukács has suggested, lyricism in the short story is pure selection which hides itself behind the hard outlines of the event; it is "the most purely artistic form; it expresses the ultimate meaning of all artistic creation as *mood*."

Although Chekhov's conception of the short story as a lyrically charged fragment in which characters are less fully rounded realistic figures than they are embodiments of mood has influenced all twentieth century practitioners of the form, his most immediate impact has been on the three writers of the early twenties who have received the most critical attention for fully developing the so-called "modern" short story—James Joyce, Katherine Mansfield, and Sherwood Anderson. And because of the wide-spread influence of the stories of these three writers, Chekhov has thus had an effect on the works of such major twentieth-century short story writers as Katherine Anne Porter, Franz Kafka, Bernard Malamud, Ernest Hemingway, and Raymond Carver.

The Minimal Story

The most obvious similarity between the stories of Chekhov and those

of Joyce, Anderson, and Mansfield is their minimal dependence on the traditional notion of plot and their focus instead on a single situation in which
everyday reality is broken up by a crisis. Typical of Chekhov's minimalist
stories is the often-anthologized "Misery," in which the rhythm of the old
cab driver's everyday reality is suggested by his two different fares, a rhythm
Iona himself tries to break up with the news that his son is dead. The story
would indeed be only a sketch if Iona did not tell his story to his uncomprehending little mare at the end. For what the story communicates is the comic
and pathetic sense of the incommunicable nature of grief itself. Iona "thirsts
for speech," wants to talk of the death of his son "properly, very carefully."
He is caught by the primal desire to tell a story of the break-up of his
everyday reality that will express the irony he senses and that, by being deliberate and detailed, will both express his grief and control it. In this sense,
"Misery" is a lament—not an emotional wailing, but rather a controlled
objectification of grief and its incommunicable nature by the presentation of
deliberate details.

The story therefore illustrates one of the primary contributions
Chekhov makes to the modern short story; that is, the expression of a
complex inner state by presenting selected concrete details rather than by
presenting either a parabolic form or by depicting the mind of the character.
Significant reality for Chekhov is inner rather than outer reality, but the
problem he tried to solve is how to create an illusion of inner reality by
focusing on external details only. The answer for Chekhov, and thus for the
modern short story generally, is to find an event that, if expressed "properly,"
that is, by the judicious choice of relevant details, will embody the complexity
of the inner state. T. S. Eliot later termed such a technique an "objective
correlative"—a detailed event, description, or characterization that served as
a sort of objectification or formula for the emotion sought for. Modern story
writers after Chekhov made the objective correlative the central device in
their development of the form.

Like Chekhov, whom she greatly admired, Katherine Mansfield was
often accused of writing sketches instead of stories because her works did not
manifest the plotted action of nineteenth-century short fiction. The best
known Mansfield story similar in technique and theme to "Misery" is "The
Fly." The external action of the story is extremely slight. The unnamed
"boss" is visited by a retired friend whose casual mention of the boss's dead
son makes him aware of his inability to grieve. The story ends with the boss
idly dropping ink on a fly until it dies, whereupon he flings it away. Like
"Misery," the story is about the nature of grief; also like Chekhov's story,
"The Fly" maintains a strictly objective point of view, allowing the details of
the story to communicate the latent significance of the boss's emotional state.

However, Mansfield differs from her mentor, Chekhov, by placing more dependence on the symbolism of the fly itself, regardless of whether one perceives the creature as a symbol of the death of the boss's grief, his own manipulated son, or the trivia of life that distracts us from feeling. Moreover, instead of focusing on the inarticulate nature of grief that goes deeper than words, "The Fly" seems to emphasize the transitory nature of grief—that regardless of how much the boss would like to hold on to his grief for his son, he finds it increasingly difficult to maintain such feelings. Such an inevitable loss of grief does not necessarily suggest that the boss's feelings for his son are negligible; rather it suggests a subtle aspect of grief—that it either flows naturally or else it must be self-consciously and artificially sought after. The subtle way that Mansfield communicates the complexity of the boss's emotional situation by the seemingly irrelevant conversation between the boss and his old acquaintance and by his apparently idle toying with the fly is typical of the Chekhovian device of allowing objective detail to communicate complex states of feeling.

Chekhov's "Aniuta" also depends on a rhythm of reality being momentarily broken up by a significant event, only to fall back once again. The story opens with the medical student walking to and fro cramming for his anatomy examination, repeating his lessons over and over as he tries to learn them by heart, while Aniuta silently does her embroidery to earn money to buy him tea and tobacco. The fact that she has known five others before him who left her when they finished their studies indicates that the story depicts a repetitive event just as his sounding out his lines is repetitive. When the young medical student tries to learn the order of ribs by drawing them on Aniuta's naked flesh, we have an ironic image of the typical Chekhov device of manifesting the internal as external. After she is used for the sake of "science," she is then used for the sake of "art" when the artist borrows her for his painting of Psyche.

The fact that the story ends as it began with the student walking back and forth repeating his lessons seems to reaffirm the usual charge against Chekhov—that "nothing really happens" here. But what has happened is that by the means of two objectifications it is revealed that Aniuta is used both body and soul. The doctor tries to "sound" Aniuta's body, just as the artist tries to capture her soul, but neither is able to reveal her; only Chekhov can "sound" her by his presentation of this significant episode. We know nothing about Aniuta in any realistic detail, nor do we know the workings of her mind, but we know everything we need to know about her to understand her static situation.

Many of the stories of twentieth-century writers after Chekhov depend on this same use of objective detail and significant situation to reveal subtle moral and emotional situations. For example, in Joyce's "Clay," it is not through introspection that we know Maria, but rather by the seemingly simple details and events of the story itself. However, Joyce goes beyond Chekhov's use of simple detail to reveal a subtle emotional state by making all of his apparently "realistic" references to Maria ironic revelations of her manipulated and lonely situation. Joyce, like Mansfield, also depends more on the use of a central symbol than Chekhov does, in this case, the clay itself, which is an objective correlative not only of Maria's malleable nature, but of the decay of her possibilities. Similarly, Joyce's "Eveline" depends solely on homey details such as dusty curtains, the photo of a priest, and the sound of an organ-grinder's song to objectify Eveline's entrapment by the paralysis of the past.

One of the most reticent of Chekhov's stories, a story so pure and clean that it presages the lucid limitations of Ernest Hemingway, is "The Lady with a Lapdog"—a paradigm for the story of the illicit affair. It is never clear in the story whether Gurov truly loves Anna Sergeevna or whether it is only the romantic fantasy that he wishes to maintain. What makes the story so subtle and complex is that Chekhov presents the romance in such a limited and objective way that we realize that there is no way to determine whether it is love or romance, for there is no way to distinguish between them. Although Gurov feels that he has a life open and seen, full of relative truth and falsehood like everyone else, he knows he has another life running its course in secret, a true life, and the false only was open to others. "All personal life," he feels, "rested on secrecy."

However, there is no way to determine which is the real life and which is the false. At the end of the story, Gurov and Anna wonder how they can free themselves from their intolerable bondage, but only Chekhov and the reader are aware that there is no way to free themselves, for the real bondage is not the manifest one, but the latent bondage all human beings have to the dilemma of never knowing which is the true self and which is the false one. Although it seems to the couple that they would soon find the solution and a new and splendid life would begin, at the same time it is clear to them that they had a long way to go and that the most complicated part of it was only just beginning. Indeed, what seems so simple is indeed complicated. This device of presenting a seemingly simple external situation in such a way as to suggest emotional complexities beneath it is typical of the best of Hemingway's short stories.

Hemingway's debt to Chekhov lies in the radical limitation of authorial comment and the complete dependence on situation, a situation often so limited, with so much of what we usually expect in narrative left out, that all we have is dialogue and description. "Hills Like White Elephants" is perhaps the best example of Hemingway's use of the Chekhov device of allowing the bare situation to express a complex emotional dilemma. Beneath the surface level of "Hills Like White Elephants," a story made up mostly of silences, lies a complex emotional conflict between what the man thinks is "reasonable" and what the girl wants emotionally. The key to the silences of the story is the seemingly irrelevant detail announced at the beginning that the train will arrive in forty minutes. If delivered dramatically, the actual dialogue of the story would actually take only about fifteen minutes. Consequently, the story contains approximately twenty-five minutes of silence, a silence more telling in many ways than the dialogue itself. Moreover, the exposition of the story—that is, what the couple's life is like, what the girl wants, and what the man wants—is communicated by simple details such as the man looking at their bags which have labels from all the hotels where they had spent nights and the girl looking at the dry hills and the fertile hills on the two sides of the valley. The bare situation and the seemingly trivial dialogue reveal a complex moral and emotional problem about the girl's proposed abortion which cannot be talked about directly.

Hemingway's focus on radically realistic events and his minimal description of such events seem obviously influenced by Chekhov. In his famous iceberg analogy, Hemingway echoes the typical Chekhovian idea about limiting his stories: "If a writer of prose knows enough about what he is writing about he may omit things that he knows and the reader, if the writer is writing truly enough, will have a feeling of those things as strongly as though the writer had stated them. The dignity of movement of an ice-berg is due to only one-eighth of it being above water." Hemingway's seemingly inconclusive stories such as "Hills Like White Elephants" and his highly detailed stories such as "Big, Two-Hearted River" are Chekovian in their use of concrete details to reflect complex states of mind. What critics have referred to as Hemingway's "objective magic" and his creation of stories that seem like "nightmares at noonday" derive from Chekhov's use of the objective correlative, his objective style, and his love of irony and under-statement.

Between Dream and Reality

Such Chekhov stories as "Sleepy" and "The Bishop" make use of another significant modern short story technique: focusing on reality as an ambiguous mixture of the psychic and the external. "Sleepy" marks a sort of realistic half-way point between the symbolic use of the hypnogogic state by Poe and its being pushed to surrealistic extremes by Kafka. Chekhov presents a basically realistic situation of the young Varka being literally caught in a hypnogogic state between desirable sleep and undesirable reality. The two realms blend indistinguishably in her mind until the hallucination takes over completely and she strangles the baby so she can sleep as "soundly as the dead." Although the irony of the ending is obvious, it is the hypnotic rhythm of the events and the hallucinatory images that blend dream and reality which makes the story a significant treatment of the short story device of dissolving the rhythm of everyday reality into the purely psychic.

The two modern short story writers who have pushed this technique to extremes are Katherine Anne Porter and Franz Kafka—Porter by using illness and the approach of death to create dream-like realms of psychic reality and Kafka by making use of crisis situations to transform everyday states into nightmarish and surrealistic experiences. In "Pale Horse, Pale Rider," Miranda is caught up in a dual world of dream and delirium made up both of the real world of war and death and the fantasy world of her illness and her love for the young man Adam. Porter takes Chekhov's use of the hallucinatory state and pushes it to ritualistic extremes to embody Miranda's death wish. Similarly, Kafka's "The Judgement" begins in a realistic way, until as a result of a crisis confrontation between father and son, it turns into hallucinatory unreality which dramatizes suppressed emotional forces finally bursting forth. What makes this movement from phenomenal reality into the hallucination of dream so different from the early nineteenth-century use of the motif is that the dream-like reality is presented as "realistically" and as concretely as external reality itself.

With "The Bishop," Chekhov blurs the lines between fantasy and reality for a more serious thematic purpose than in the relatively simple "Sleepy." For here he links it with a theme that forms the center of one of his most frequently discussed works, "A Dreary Story," a theme which also preoccupies the stories of Porter and Kafka, as well as the stories of many other modern short story writers later on—the conflict between the presentational self and the problematical "real" self; the result is a lack of genuine communication and sympathy between the central character and others. The Bishop feels that the whole time he has been a Bishop, "not one person had spoken to him genuinely, simply, as to a human being. . . . he still felt that he had missed what was most important, something of which he had dimly dreamed in the past." (I, 46–47). Caught in the rhythm of his professional reality, the Bishop searches for his real self in reverie and hallucinatory memory. In this story, Chekhov moves closer to the kind of grotesque distortion of nightmare reality characteristic of Kafka. From the Bishop's sense of confusion, it its only a relatively small step to Kafka's country doctor, who in "great perplexity" is caught between external reality and psychic nightmare.

Katherine Anne Porter, in "The Jilting of Granny Weatherall," inten-sifies the hallucinatory effect of illness and impending death that we see in "The Bishop" by centering her story on Granny on her deathbed, hovering between hallucination and memory and trying to justify her past presenta-tional self. Both the crucial past event of Granny's life and her present situa-tion are so blended together that it is difficult for the reader to separate them. Like "The Bishop," the story mingles past and present, but Porter exceeds Chekhov's use of the technique by presenting seemingly discon-nected and irrelevant details of Granny's physical and psychic experience in such a fragmented way that the reader must tie the various details together in order to understand the overall pattern of Granny's failure and the cause of her final jilting.

The best known story of Franz Kafka which presents the theme of the presentational self within a framework of nightmarish situation and detail is of course "Metamorphosis." Here Kafka pushes the hallucinatory device of Chekhov to its utmost extreme by forcing Gregor Samsa to face his real self in a metaphor that must be taken as reality. The drastic step Kafka takes is to make the transformation of the psychic into the physical the precipitating premise which the entire story follows. The only suspension of disbelief required in the story is that the reader accept the premise that Gregor Samsa awakes one morning from uneasy dreams to find himself transformed into a giant dung beetle. Once one accepts this event, the rest of the story is quite prosaic and realistic. The transformation of Gregor indicates the objectifica-tion of an inner state; the basic tension in the story that makes the reader not sure whether to laugh or to cry is between the horrifying yet absurd content and the matter-of-fact realistic style.

Impressionism and Art as Reality

In Chekhov's "A Dreary Story," Professor Stepanovitch, like the Bishop, searches for his real self in the face of his impending death. Also like the Bishop, he desires to be loved not for his fame or label, but as an ordi-nary man. In the climactic moment of realization, similar to that epiphanic moment of Gabriel in Joyce's "The Dead," the professor, striving to know himself, comes to the realization that there is no common bond to connect all his thoughts, feelings, and ideas. "Every feeling and every thought exists apart in me; and in all my criticisms of science, the theatre, literature, my pupils, and in all the pictures my imagination draws, even the most skillful analyst could not find what is called a general idea, or the god of a living man. And if there is not that, then there is nothing" (I, 529). Although this lack of a general idea is often cited as the professor's ultimate negative characteristic as a man, as well as reflective of Chekhov's own most negative characteristic as an artist, such a critical judgment reveals a failure to understand Chekhov's modern point of view and indeed the modern short story. The professor's lack of a general idea ironically is the basis for his one means of salvation, the acceptance of the relativistic and impressionistic view via art which his young ward Katia objectifies. But as Katia tells him, he has no instinct or feeling for art, and his philosophizing about it only reveals he does not understand it.

Chekhov's adoption of such a relativistic and impressionistic point of view is what makes him both a master of short story and an innovator of its modernity. As Nadine Gordimer has said about short story writers: "theirs is the art of the only thing one can be sure of—the present moment. . . . A discrete moment of truth is aimed at—not *the* moment of truth, because the short story doesn't deal in cumulatives." Peter Stowell has made a strong case for understanding Chekhov's modernism as a result of his impressionistic point of view. The ambiguous and tenuous nature of experience perceived by the impressionist, says Stowell,

> drives the author to render perceptually blurred bewilderment, rather than either the subject or the object. What is rendered is the mood, sense, feel, and atmosphere that exists between perceiver and perceived, subject and object. Literary impressionists discovered a new way to depict a new way of seeing and knowing. Literary impressionists discovered modernism."

More recently, Suzanne C. Ferguson has attempted to show that the so-called modern short story is not a discrete genre at all, but rather a manifestation of impressionism. As Ferguson points out, "when all we have in the world is our own experience of it, all received knowledge becomes suspect, and the very nature of knowledge becomes problematic" and we must "confront the possibility that we cannot know anything for certain, that the processes we follow in search for truth may yield only fictions."

Although indeed Ferguson's suggestion may reflect the negative side of the modernist temperament, there is also a positive aspect to such relativism which has been explored by such so-called postmodernist writers as Jorge Borges, John Barth, Robert Coover, and others; that is, that if reality is a fictional construct and the writer wishes to focus on the nature of reality, then he has little choice but to focus on the nature of art and fiction-making itself. If reality is a fiction, an artistic construct, then art perhaps provides the only means to experience reality. Both sides of this modernist predisposition can be seen in such Chekhov stories as, on the one hand, "The House with an Attic" and on the other hand, "Easter Eve" and "The Student."

For Chekhov, art as a means to experience true reality is a complex religious, aesthetic, and sympathetic process. Like the professor in "A Dreary Story," the artist in "The House with an Attic" is too bound by "general ideas," too wedded to philosophizing and rhetoric to truly enter into the human realm of art and participate in its mysterious unity. He says a man should feel superior even to what is beyond his understanding; otherwise he is not a man but a mouse afraid of everything. "Phenomena I don't understand," he tells the young Genia, "I face boldly, and am not overwhelmed by them. I am above them" (I, 545). Unlike Olga in "The Grasshopper" who only knows the external trappings of art, Genia, nicknamed "Misuc," genuinely wishes the artist to initiate her into the domain of the "Eternal and the Beautiful." But it is a realm that the artist knows only through rhetoric.

The central scene in the story is the artist's confrontation with Genia's older sister, Lida, who scorns him for not portraying the privations of the peasants. While she insists that the highest and holiest thing for a civilized being to do is to serve his neighbors, he says the highest vocation of man is spiritual activity—"the perpetual search for truth and the meaning of life." Becoming carried away with his own rhetoric, he insists: "When science and art are real, they aim not at temporary, private ends, but at eternal and universal—they seek for truth and the meaning of life, they seek for God, for the soul" (I, 552). While both Lida and the artist are individually right in their emphases on serving the other and searching for the eternal, neither actually genuinely embodies these ideals, any more than the artist and the doctor embody them in "Aniuta." Their failure is reflected by contrast with Genia whom they both misuse and manipulate for their own ends.

For Chekhov, the only way that the eternal can be achieved is aesthetically through a unification with the human. It is best embodied in his two most mystic stories which deal with the nature of art: "Easter Eve" and "The Student." Both stories focus on the tension between disorder and harmony, between separation resulting from everyday reality and unity achieved by means of story and song. In an in-between time between death and resurrection, in an in-between place on the ferry between darkness and chaos, Ieronim tells his story of Brother Nikolai and his extraordinary gift of writing hymns of praise. Chekhov comes as close here as anywhere in his letters and notes to describing his own aesthetic. As Ieronim says, canticles are quite a different thing from writing histories or sermons; moreover, it is not enough to know well the life of the saint or the conventions that govern the writing of canticles. What matters, he says, is the beauty and sweetness of it.

Everything must be harmonious, brief and complete. There must be in every line softness, graciousness and tenderness; not one word should be harsh or rough or unsuitable. It must be written so that the worshipper may rejoice at heart and weep, while his mind is stirred and he is thrown into a tremor. (I, 464)

In contrast to the silence of the dark river and the remembered beauty of Nikolai's songs is the chaos and restlessness of the celebration the narrator enters, where everyone is too caught up in the "childishly irresponsible joy, seeking a pretext to break out and vent itself in some movement, even in senseless jostling and shoving" to listen to the songs of Nikolai. The narrator looks for the dead brother but does not regret not seeing him. "God knows, perhaps if I had seen him I should have lost the picture my imagination paints for me now" (I, 468). Indeed, it is the creation of Nikolai in the narrator's imagination that justifies Ieronim's story, just as it is Nikolai's songs that sustain Ieronim. For the key to the eternal for Chekhov is the art work which serves to unify human experience; thus Ieronim sees the face of his brother in the face of everyone.

"The Student" begins with a sense of disorder and lack of harmony. However, it is once again song or story that serves to heal a fractured sense of reality. After the student tells the story of the Last Supper and Peter's denial of Christ, which itself takes up about one third of this very short story, he says he imagines Peter weeping, "The garden was deathly still and very dark, and in the silence there came the sound of muffled sobbing." And with this final imaginative projection, the power of the story affects the two listeners. The student says the fact that they are affected must mean that what happened to Peter has some relation to them, to the present, to the desolate village, to himself, and to all people. The widow wept not because of the way he told the tale, but "because her whole being was deeply affected by what happened in Peter's soul."

Although it may not be the manner of the student's oral telling which affects the two women, it is indeed the story itself. For, although the story does not reveal what is passing through Peter's soul, it compels the reader/ listener to sympathetically identify with Peter in his complex moment of realization. Indeed the revelation of character by means of story presentation of a crucial moment in which the reader must then imaginatively participate is the key to Chekhov's much discussed "objectivity" and yet "sympathetic" presentation. The student thus feels joy at the sense of an unbroken chain running from the past to the present. He feels that "truth and beauty" which had guided life there in the garden had continued without interruption: "always they were the most important influences working on human life and everything on the earth . . . and life suddenly seemed to him enchanting, ravishing, marvelous and full of deep meaning." As in "Easter Eve," here we see the only means by which Chekhov feels that the eternal can be achieved, through the aesthetic experience and sense of unity that story and song create.

Both Sherwood Anderson and James Joyce similarly focus on the significance of the aesthetic experience as being the means both for a religious participation with the "eternal" and a sympathetic participation with the other. For example, Joyce's "The Sisters" focuses on story and art as a religious/aesthetic experience which dominates the collection *The Dubliners*, and Anderson's "Death in The Woods" centers around "story" as the only means to know the other. "The Sisters," like both "Easter Eve" and "The Student," emphasizes the religious-like nature of the aesthetic experience which the old priest has communicated to the young boy while he was alive and which he embodies to him now in his death. "Death in the Woods" is particularly like "The Student" in its emphasis on how only story itself can reveal the mysterious nature of human communion.

Like Chekhov, both Anderson and Joyce focus on the central themes of isolation and the need for human sympathy and the moral failure of inaction which dominate the modernist movement in the early twentieth century; both abjure highly plotted stories in favor of seemingly static episodes and "slices" of reality; both depend on unity of feeling to create a sense of "storyness"; and both establish a sense of the seemingly casual out of what is deliberately patterned, creating significance out of the trivial by judicious selection of detail and meaningful ordering of the parts. The result is an objective-ironic style which has characterized the modern short story up to the present day. It is a style that, even as it seems realistic on its surface, in fact emphasizes the radical difference between the routine of everyday reality and the incisive nature of story itself as the only means to know true reality. Contemporary short story writers push this Chekhovian realization to even more aesthetic extremes.

The Contemporary Short Story

The contemporary short story writer most influenced by the Chekhovian objective/ironic style is Bernard Malamud, and the Chekhov story that seems most similar to Malamud's stories is "Rothschild's Fiddle," not only because the central conflict involves a Jew, but because of its pathetic/comic ironic tone. Iakov Ivanov's business as a coffinmaker is bad in his village because people die so seldom. His unjustified hatred for the Jewish flautist Rothschild who plays even the merriest tunes sadly, and his feeling of financial loss and ruin align Iakov with all those figures that Malamud's

Manischevitz identifies in "The Jewbird" when he says to his wife, "A wonderful thing, Fanny. Believe me, there are Jews everywhere." Chekhov's attempt to capture the sense of Yiddish folktale in "Rothschild's Fiddle" makes the story closer to a parable than most of his other best known stories.

Iakov feels distressed when his wife dies, for he knows that he has never spoken a kind word to her and has shouted at her for his losses. That Iakov has always been concerned with profit and loss rather than his family is also revealed when his wife asks him if he remembers when they had a baby and it died. He cannot remember and tells her she is dreaming. Iakov's epiphanic realization comes after his wife's death when he goes to the riverbank and remembers the child his wife had mentioned. But Chekhov's irony is more complex here than the simple sentimentality that such a realization might have elicited. Even as Iakov becomes lost in the pleasure of the pastoral scene, he wonders why he has never come here before and thinks of ways he could have made money at the riverbank. He laments once again his losses and thinks that if people did not act from envy and anger, as he has with his wife and Rothschild, they could get great "profit" from one another.

When he becomes ill and knows that he is dying, Iakov thinks that one good thing about it is that he will not have to eat and pay taxes. Thus he thinks life is a loss while death is a gain, for since we lie in the grave so long, we may realize immense profits. As he is dying, only Rothschild is there to pity him, and thus Iakov leaves Rothschild his fiddle. As Rothschild later tries to play the tune Iakov played, the result is so sad that everyone who hears it weeps. The new song so delights the town that the merchants and government officials vie with each other to get Rothschild to play for them. Thus, at the end, a profit is realized from Iakov's death.

"Rothschild's Fiddle" is an ironic parable-like story about the common Chekhov theme of loss and the lack of human communion which Malamud typically makes his own. Malamud's short stories are often closer to the oral tradition of parable than they are to the realistic fiction of social reality. However, although one can discern traces of the Yiddish tale in Malamud, one also realizes that his short stories reflect the tight symbolic structure and ironic and distanced point of view that we have come to associate with the short story since Chekhov. Malamud's stories move inevitably toward a conclusion in which complex moral dilemmas are not so much resolved as they are frozen in a symbolic final epiphany or ironic gesture. His characters are always caught in what might be called the demand for sympathy and responsibility. But the moral/aesthetic configuration of his stories is such that the reader is not permitted the luxury of an easy moral judgment.

The fact that Jews, that is, those who are alienated and suffering, are everywhere, which seems so obvious in "Rothschild's Fiddle," is of course a common theme in such Malamud stories as "The Mourners" in which the landlord Gruber, after trying to evict the unwanted and self-centered Kessler, finally pulls a sheet over himself and kneels to the floor to become a mourner with the old man. It is the central dilemma in "The Loan" in which Kobotsky arrives to ask for a loan from his old friend, Lieb the baker. When Lieb's wife Bessie, who has her own history of woes to recite, will not allow the loan, the two old friends can only embrace and part forever as the stench of the corpse-like burned bread lingers in their nostrils. Like "Rothschild's Fiddle," these stories present one sufferer who can understand the suffering of another. The bitter-sweet conclusions of most of Malamud's tales are typical of his Chekhovian refusal to give in to either sentimentality or condescension.

However, perhaps the contemporary short story writer who is closest to Chekhov is Raymond Carver. In Carver's most recent collection of stories, *What We Talk About When We Talk About Love*, language is used so sparingly and the plots are so minimal that the stories seem pallidly drained patterns with no flesh and life in them. The stories are so short and lean that they seem to have plot only as we reconstruct them in our memory. Whatever theme they may have is embodied in the bare outlines of the event and in the spare dialogue of characters who are so overcome by event and so lacking in language that the theme is unsayable. Characters often have no names or only first names and are so briefly described that they seem to have no physical presence at all; certainly they have no distinct identity but rather seem to be shadowy presences trapped in their own inarticulateness.

The charge lodged against Carver is the same one once lodged against Chekhov, that his fiction is dehumanized and therefore cold and unfeeling. In a typical Carver story, "Why Don't You Dance," plot is minimal; event is mysterious; character is negligible. A man puts all his furniture out in his front yard and runs an extension cord out so that things work just as they did when they were inside. A young couple stop by, look at the furniture, try out the bed, have a drink, and the girl dances with the owner. The conversation is functional, devoted primarily toward making purchases in a perfectly banal, garage-sale way. At the conclusion, the young wife tells someone about the event. "She kept talking. She told everyone. There was more to it, and she was trying to get it talked out. After a time, she quit trying." The problem of the story is that the event cannot be talked out; it is completely objectified in the spare description of the event itself. Although there is no exposition in the story, we know that a marriage is over, that the secret life of the house has been externalized on the front lawn, that the owner has made a desperate metaphor of his marriage, that the hopeful young couple play out a mock scenario of that marriage which presages their own, and that the event itself is a parody of events not told, but kept hidden, like the seven-eighths of the iceberg that Hemingway said could be left beneath the surface of prose if the writer knew his subject well enough.

The Will To Style

From its beginnings as a separately recognized literary form, the short story has always been more closely associated with lyric poetry than with its overgrown narrative neighbor, the novel. Regardless of whether short fiction has clung to the legendary tale form of its early ancestry, as in Hawthorne, or whether it has moved toward the presentation of the single event, as in Chekhov, the form has always been a "much in little" proposition which conceals more than it reveals and leaves much unsaid. However, there are two basic means by which the short story has pursued its movement away from the linearity of prose toward the spatiality of poetry—either by using the metaphoric and plurasignative language of the poem or by radically limiting its selection of the presented event.

The result has been two completely different textures in short fiction—the former characterized by such writers as Eudora Welty in the forties and fifties and Bernard Malamud in the sixties and seventies whose styles are thick with metaphor and myth, and the latter characterized by such writers as Hemingway in the twenties and thirties and Raymond Carver in the seventies and eighties whose styles are thin to the point of disappearing. This second style, which could be said to have been started by Chekhov, became reaffirmed as the primary mode of the "literary" or "artistic" short story (as opposed to the still-popular tale form) in the twenties by Mansfield, Anderson, and Joyce; and it was later combined with the metaphoric mode by such writers as Faulkner, Katherine Anne Porter, Flannery O'Connor, and others to create a modern short story which still maintains some of the characteristics of the old romance form even as it seems to be a radically realistic depiction of a single crucial episode.

The charge often made against the Chekhovian story—that it is dehumanized and therefore cold and unfeeling—has been made about the short story as a form since Hawthorne was criticized for his "bloodless" parables. However, such a charge ignores the nature of art that has characterized Western culture since the early nineteenth century and which Ortega y Gasset so clearly delineated in *The Dehumanization of Art*. In their nostalgia for the bourgeois security of nineteenth-century realism, critics of the short story forget that the royal road to art, as Ortega delineates is, "the will to style." And to stylize "means to deform reality, to derealize: style involves dehumanization." Given this definition of art, it is easy to see that the short story as a form has always embodied "the will to style." The short story writer realizes that the artist must not confuse reality with idea, that he must inevitably turn his back on alleged reality and, as Ortega insists, "take the ideas for what they are—mere subjective patterns—and make them live as such, lean and angular, but pure and transparent."

The lyricism of the Chekhovian short story lies in this will to style in which reality is derealized and ideas live solely as ideas. Thus Chekhov's stories are more "poetic," that is, more "artistic" than we usually expect fiction to be; they help define the difference between the loose and baggy monstrous novel and the taut, gemlike short story. One final implication of Chekhov's focus on the "will to style" is the inevitable self-consciousness of fiction as fiction. If the term "modernism" suggests, as most critics seem to agree, a reaction against nineteenth-century bourgeois realism, which, a la Chekhov, Joyce, Anderson, and others, manifested itself as a frustration of conventional expectations about the cause-and-effect nature of plot and the "as-if-real" nature of character; then postmodernism pushes this movement even further so that contemporary fiction is less and less about objective reality and more and more about its own creative processes.

The primary effect of this mode of thought on contemporary fiction is that the story has a tendency to loosen its illusion of reality to explore the reality of its illusion. Rather than presenting itself "as if" it were real—a mimetic mirroring of external reality—postmodernist fiction makes its own artistic conventions and devices the subject of the story as well as its theme. The underlying assumption is that the forms of art are explainable by the laws of art; literary language is not a proxy for something else, but rather an object of study itself. The short story as a genre has always been more apt to lay bare its fictionality than the novel, which has traditionally tried to cover it up. Fictional self-consciousness in the short story does not allow the reader to maintain the comfortable cover-up assumption that what is depicted is real; instead the reader is made uncomfortably aware that the only reality is the process of depiction itself—the fiction-making process, the language act.

Although Anton Chekhov could not have anticipated the far-reaching implications of his experimentation with the short story as a seemingly realistic, yet highly stylized, form in the work of John Barth, Donald Barthelme, Robert Coover, and Raymond Carver, it is clear that the contemporary short story, for all of its much complained-of "unread-ability," owes a significant debt to the much-criticized "storyless" stories of Chekhov. For it is with Chekhov that the short story was liberated from its adherence to the parabolic exemplum and fiction generally was liberated from the tedium of the realistic novel. With Chekhov, the short story took on a new respectability and began to be seen as the most appropriate narrative form to reflect the modern temperament. There can be no understanding of the short story as a genre without an understanding of Chekhov's contribution to the form. Conrad Aiken's assessment of him in 1921 has yet to be challenged: "Possibly the greatest writer of the short story who has ever lived."

PETER SZONDI

The Drama in Crisis: Chekhov

In Chekhov's plays the characters live under the sign of renunciation—renunciation of the present and of communication before all else, renunciation of the happiness arising from real interaction. This resignation, in which passionate longing and irony mix to prevent any extreme, also determines the form of Chekhov's plays and his position in the development of modern theater.

To renounce the present is to live with memories and utopian dreams; to do without human interaction is to be lonely. *The Three Sisters*, perhaps the most fully realized of Chekhov's plays, is exclusively a presentation of lonely individuals intoxicated by memories and dreaming of the future. Their present, overwhelmed by the past and future, is merely an interim, a period of suspended animation during which the only goal is to return to the lost homeland. This theme (around which, moreover, all romantic literature circles) becomes concrete in *The Three Sisters* in terms of the bourgeois world at the turn of the century. Thus Olga, Masha and Irina, the Prozorov sisters, live with their brother, Andrei Sergeovitch, in a large garrison town in East Russia. Eleven years earlier they had left their home in Moscow to go there with their father, who had taken command of a brigade. The play begins a year after their father's death. Their stay in the provinces has lost all meaning; memories of life in Moscow overflow into

From *Theory of the Modern Drama*. © 1987 by the University of Minnesota.

the boredom of their daily existence and grow into a single despairing cry: "To Moscow!" The wait for this return to the past, which is also supposed to be a wonderful future, absorbs the three sisters completely. They are surrounded by garrison officers who are consumed by the same fatigue and longing. For one of these officers, though, that moment in the future which is the intended goal of the Prozorov sisters has expanded into a utopian vision. Alexander Ignatyavitch Vershinin says:

> And then, in another two or three hundred years, life on earth will be beautiful and wonderful beyond anything we can imagine. Man needs such a life and while we don't have it yet, we must become aware of its impending arrival, wait for it, imagine it, and prepare the way for it.

And later,

> It seems to me that everything on earth is bound to change, little by little, and in fact it's already changing right before our eyes. Two or three hundred years or a thousand years from now—its immaterial how long—a new happy life will come about. Of course, we'll have no part in that life, but nevertheless even today, we live for it, work for it, well yes, suffer for it, and thus we are bringing it about. And that alone is the purpose of our existence and, if you like, in it lies our happiness.

> We're not meant to be happy . . . we won't be happy. . . . We must just work and work and work and someday our descendants will he happy. If I can't be happy, at least my grandchildren's grandchildren. . . .

Even more than this utopian orientation, the weight of the past and the dissatisfaction with the present isolate the characters. They all ponder their own lives, lose themselves in memories, and torment themselves by analyzing their boredom. Everyone in the Prozorov family and all their acquaintances have their own problems—problems that preoccupy them even in the company of others and, therefore, separate them from their fellow beings. Andrei is crushed by the discrepancy between a longed-for professorship in Moscow and his actual position as secretary to the rural district council. Masha married unhappily when she was seventeen. Olga believes that "in the four years [she has] been teaching at the school, [she has] felt [her] strength and youth draining away drop by drop." And Irina, who has plunged into her work to overcome her dissatisfaction and sadness, admits:

> I'm going on twenty-four already; I've worked for years now and my brain's all dried up. I've grown old and thin and unattractive without having ever found anything the slightest bit satisfactory or rewarding and time goes by and I feel I'm going farther and farther away from a real, beautiful life, slipping down into some sort of an abyss. I've lost all hope and I don't even understand how it is that I'm still alive and haven't killed myself yet.

The question is, then, how does this thematic renunciation of the present in favor of memory and longing, this perennial analysis of one's own fate, fit with a dramatic form in which the Renaissance creed of the here and now. of the interpersonal, was once crystallized? The double renunciation that marks Chekhov's characters seems inevitably to necessitate the abandonment of action and dialogue—the two most important formal categories of the Drama and, thus, dramatic form itself.

But one senses only a tendency in this direction. Despite their psychic absence from social life, the heroes of Chekhov's plays live on. They do not draw any ultimate conclusions from their loneliness and longing. Instead, they hover midway between the world and the self, between now and then, so the formal presentation does not have to reject completely those categories necessary for it to be dramatic. They are maintained in a deemphasized, incidental manner that allows the real subject negative expression as a deviation from traditional dramatic form.

The Three Sisters does have the rudiments of traditional action. The first act, the exposition, takes place on Irina's name day. The second presents transitional events: Andrei's marriage, the birth of his son. The third takes place at night while a great fire rages in the neighborhood. The fourth presents the duel in which Irina's fiancé is killed—on the very day the regiment moves out of town, leaving the Prozorovs to succumb completely to the boredom of provincial life This disconnected juxtaposition of active moments and their arrangement into four acts (which was, from the first, thought to lack tension) clearly reveals their place in the formal whole. They are included, although they do not actually express anything, to set the thematic in motion sufficiently to allow space for dialogue.

But even this dialogue carries no weight. It is the pale background on which monologic responses framed as conversation appear as touches of color in which the meaning of the whole is concentrated. These resigned self-analyses—which allow almost all the characters to make individual statements—give life to the work. It was written for their sake.

They are not monologues in the traditional sense of the word. Their source is not in the situation but in the subject. As G[eorg] Lukács has demonstrated, the dramatic monologue formulates nothing that cannot be communicated otherwise. Hamlet hides his feelings from the people at court for practical reasons. Perhaps, in fact, because they would all too readily understand that he wishes to take vengeance for his father—that he must the vengeance. The situation is quite different in Chekhov's play. The lines are spoken aloud in front of others, not while alone, and they isolate the speaker. Thus, almost without notice, empty dialogue turns into substance-filled monologue. These are not isolated monologues built into a work structured around the dialogue. Rather it is through them that the work as a whole departs from the dramatic and becomes lyric. In lyric poetry, language is less in need of justification than in the Drama. It is, as it were, more formal. In the Drama, speech, in addition to conveying the concrete meaning of the words, also announces the fact that something is being spoken. When there is nothing more to say or when something cannot be expressed, the Drama is reduced to silence. In the lyric, on the other hand, silence speaks too. Of course words are no longer "exchanged" in the course of a conversation; instead, all is spoken with a naturalness that is inherent in the nature of the lyric.

This constant movement from conversation into the lyrics of loneliness is what gives Chekhov's language its charm. Its origins probably lie in Russian expansiveness and in the immanent lyric quality of the language itself. Loneliness is not the same thing as torpor here. What the Occidental most probably experiences only while intoxicated—participation in the loneliness of the other, the inclusion at individual at loneliness in a growing collective loneliness—seems to be a possibility inherent in the Russian: the person and the language.

This is the reason the monologues in Chekhov's plays fit comfortably into the dialogue. It also explains why the dialogue creates so few problems in these plays and why the internal contradiction between monologic thematic and dialogic declaration does not lead to the destruction of the dramatic form.

Only Andrei, the three sisters' brother, is incapable of even this mode of expression. His loneliness forces him into silence: therefore, he avoids company. He can speak only when he knows he will not be understood.

Chekhov manages this by making Ferapont, the watchman at the district council offices, hard of hearing.

Andrei: How are you old friend? What can I do for you?
Ferapont: The council chairman sends you a book and some

papers. Here . . . (*Hands him a book and a packet.*)

Andrei: Thanks, that's fine. But why did you come over so late? It's after eight already.

Ferapont: What say?

Andrei (*louder*): I said, you came over very late. It's after eight.

Ferapont: That's right. It was still light when I got here, but they wouldn't let me in to see you. . . . (*Thinking Andrei has said something.*) What?

Andrei: I didn't say a thing. (*Looks over the book.*) Tomorrow's Friday and I'm off, but I'll come over anyway and do some work. I get bored at home. (*Pauses.*) Ah, old fellow, how life changes: what tricks it plays on us! Today I had nothing to do so I picked up this book here—it's an old collection of university lectures—and I felt like laughing. Good lord, here I am, secretary of the Rural Council, the council, mind you, of which Protopopov is chairman, and the most I can hope for is to become a member one day. Imagine, me a member of the local council, when every night I dream that I'm a professor at Moscow University and a famous scholar of whom all Russia is proud!

Ferapont: I wouldn't know . . . I don't hear so good.

Andrei: Its just as well, because I hardly would've spoken to you like this if you could hear. I need someone to talk to, since my wife doesn't understand me and I'm afraid that my sisters would laugh in my face. . . . I don't like bars but let me tell you, old man, right now I'd give anything to be sitting at Testov's or in the Great Moscow Inn.

Ferapont: And me, I heard some contractor over at the Council telling them that he'd seen some merchants in Moscow eating pancakes. And there was one of 'em ate forty, and it seems he died. Either forty or fifty. I can't say for sure.

Andrei: You can go into a big Moscow restaurant where you don't know anyone and no one knows you, and yet you feel perfectly at home there. Now, here, you know everyone and everyone knows you, and yet you feel like a stranger among them.— And a lonely stranger at that.

Ferapont: What? (Pause) Well, that same contractor was saying that they're stretching a big rope right across the whole of Moscow—but maybe he was lying at that!

Although this passage seems to be dialogue—thanks to the support given by the motif of not hearing—it is really a despairing monologue by Andrei. Ferapont provides counterpoint with his own equally monologic speech. Whereas elsewhere there is the possibility of real understanding because of a common subject, here its impossibility is expressed. The impression of divergence is greatest when the speeches simulate convergence. Andrei's monologue does not arise out of the dialogue. It comes from the negation of dialogue. The expressivity of this cross-purpose speaking is rooted in a painful, parodistic contrast with real dialogue, which it removes into the utopian. But dramatic form itself is called into question at this point.

Because the collapse of communication is motivated in *The Three Sisters* (Ferapont's inability to hear), a return to dialogue is still possible. Ferapont is only an occasional figure on stage. But everything thematic, the content of which is larger and weightier than the motif that serves to represent it, struggles toward precipitation as form. And the formal withdrawal of dialogue leads, of necessity, to the epic. Ferapont's inability to hear points the way to the future.

DAVID COLE

Chekhov, The Sea Gull

Near the opening of act 4 of *The Sea Gull* there occurs the following exchange:

> ([PAULINE] *goes to the desk. Leaning on her elbows she gazes at the manuscript. A pause.*) . . .
>
> PAULINE: (*Gazing at the manuscript*) Nobody ever thought or dreamed that some day, Kostya, you'd turn out to be a real author. But now, thank God, the magazines send you money for your stories. (*Passing her hand over his hair*) And you've grown handsome . . . dear, good, Kostya, be kind to my little Masha.
>
> MASHA: (*Making the bed*) Let him alone, Mama.
>
> PAULINE: She's a sweet little thing. (*A pause*) A woman, Kostya, doesn't ask much . . . only kind looks. As I well know.
>
> (TREPLEFF *rises from the desk and without speaking goes out.*)
>
> MASHA: You shouldn't have bothered him.
>
> PAULINE: I feel sorry for you, Masha.
>
> MASHA: Why should you?
>
> PAULINE: My heart aches and aches for you. I see it all.
>
> MASHA: It's all foolishness! Hopeless love . . . that's only in novels.

From *Acting As Reading: The Place of the Reading Process in the Actor's Work.* © 1992 by the University of Michigan Press.

Chekhov abounds in episodes of, and references to, reading; *The Sea Gull* alone provides many examples. Nina is "always reading" Trigorin's stories (act 1, p. 17). Arkadina and Dorn read Maupassant to each other (act 2, p. 23). Trigorin enters reading a book (act 2, pp. 30–31), enjoys reading proofs (act 2, p. 34), hates reading bad reviews (act 2, p. 31). Nina gives Trigorin a medal engraved with a page and line reference to a passage in his own writings (act 2, p. 38); Trigorin reads the inscription (act 2, p. 39), then looks up the passage (act 2, p. 45). Trigorin brings Trepleff a magazine containing stories by each of them, though the uncut pages reveal he has only read his own (act 4, pp. 59–60). Trepleff rereads and revises his own work-in-progress (act 4, p. 63). And so on.

With such a wealth of reading scenes to choose from it may seem perverse to focus on a scene of apparent *non*reading: Pauline merely "gazes" at Trepleff's manuscript while speaking of something else. I am going to argue, however, that such gazing on a text while speaking of something else is an image of the particular kind of reading required of an actor working on a Chekhov script—is, in fact, Chekhov's characteristic image of acting as reading. How it becomes so will perhaps be clearer if, contrary to our usual practice, we begin not with the scene itself but, instead, with an overview of reading in Chekhov's four major plays.

Though the act of reading is everywhere present in Chekhov, it is everywhere problematic, its very pervasiveness the symptom of a pervasive cultural problem.

Sometimes the problem is clearly with the texts themselves. Trepleff's symbolist play (*Sea Gull*, act 1) or Kulygin's "history of our high school covering fifty years, written by me" (*Three Sisters*, act 1, p. 155), are "unreadable" exercises in self-absorption which cannot speak to a reader. Often enough, though, the texts a Chekhovian character encounters have plenty to say to him. In *The Three Sisters*, especially, some text or other is constantly giving the Prozoroff family the truth of their situation. The lines of Pushkin which Masha cannot get out of her head—"By the curved seashore a green oak, a golden chain upon that oak" (act 1, pp. 144, 161)—is an image of *happiness there for the taking*. The French minister's prison diary, which Vershinin cites as an illustration that "happiness we have not. . . , we only long for it" (act 2, pp. 175–76), exposes the essential emptiness of the sisters' Moscow fantasy. Even the bit of newspaper filler read out by Tchebutykin— "Balzac was married in Berdichev" (act 2, p. 173)—contains a valuable perspective. If a great writer like Balzac could find happiness in a backwater like Berdichev, how much the more should *you, here. . . ?*

In all these instances—Pushkin, the minister's diary, the newspaper— the text itself is profitable; it is the reader who fails to profit. This suggests that the problem lies not in texts but, rather, in the transaction readers have, or fail to have, with them. "I read a great deal," says Vershinin, "but don't know how to choose books, and read, perhaps, not at all what I should" (act 2, p. 172). In particular, Chekhovian characters seem to have difficulty establishing a relation between *reading* and *subsequent action*. Either the character is unable to take any action at all in response to the text he reads:

> LOPAHIN: (*turning the pages of a book*) Here I was reading a
> book and didn't get a thing out of it. Reading and went to sleep.
> (*Cherry Orchard*, act 1, p. 228)

Or else the character is unable to take the particular action the text prescribes:

> ELENA: It is only in sociological novels they teach and cure
> sick peasants, and how can I suddenly for no reason go to curing
> and teaching them?
> (*Uncle Vanya*, act 3, p. 105)

(Compare, in our scene, Masha's "Hopeless love . . . that's only in novels.") Or else the character reads and takes action, but some action wholly unrelated to what he reads:

> (*Enter* MARIA VASILIEVNA *with a book; she sits down and*
> *reads; she is served tea and drinks it without looking up.*)
> (*Uncle Vanya*, act 1, p. 79)

Particularly frequent in Chekhov are moments when, as in our *Sea Gull* excerpt, the reader looks at a text and brings forth *something else*. Like the student in Kulygin's anecdote who misreads his teacher's marginal comment "Nonsense!" as "consensus" (*Three Sisters*, act 4, p. 207), Chekhovian readers are forever coming out with something other than the words on the page before them. Masha Prozoroff peers into a book—and whistles (*Three Sisters*, act 1, p. 140). Tchebutykin takes a newspaper out of his pocket—and begins to sing (*Three Sisters*, act 4, p. 222). Dorn leafs through a magazine—and announces Trepleff's suicide (*Sea Gull*, act 4, pp. 169–70). Conversely, Chekhov's characters are forever coming out with texts from which, at the moment, they do not read: for example, Kulygin's classical catchphrases, Masha's "chain on the oak" refrain, and the lines from Trigorin and Turgenev which keep flashing across Nina's mind in the midst of her final conversation with Trepleff (*Sea Gull*, act 4, pp. 65–68). The one thing that does not often

happen in a Chekhov reading scene is the one thing that we are accustomed to
think happens as a matter of course between an actor and a script, namely, that
a reader reads of an action and performs it. "I read all kinds of remarkable
books," broods Epihodoff in *The Cherry Orchard*, "but the trouble is I cannot
discover my own inclinations, whether to live or to shoot myself" (act 2, p.
250). There speaks the true voice, and true dilemma of Chekhovian reading.

Undoubtedly, such a breakdown in the reading process is an image and
symptom of a larger cultural situation: a historical moment when books are
no longer regarded as capable of telling people what to do now, how to act.
This unfeasibility of reading "at present" is thematized in Chekhov as a
banishment of authentic reading from the present of the play's action. True
reading belongs to the *past*:

> TCHEBUTYKIN: Since I left the University, I haven't lifted
> a finger, I've not read a single book even, but just read the news-
> papers. . . . (*taking another newspaper out of his pocket*).
> > (*Three Sisters*, act 1, p. 144)

or to the *future*:

> ANYA: We'll read in the autumn evenings, read lots of books,
> and a new, wonderful world will open up before us—
> (*daydreaming*).
> > (*Cherry Orchard*, act 4, p. 289)

Even when reading takes place onstage now it tends to look ahead or back
from the present moment. Uncle Vanya's mother, who "with one eye . . .
looks into the grave and with the other . . . rummages through her learned
books for the dawn of a new life" (act 1, p. 77), reads of a future she will never
see. Andrei Prozoroff, thumbing through his old university lectures (*Three
Sisters*, act 2, p. 165), reads of a past he will never see again.

But if such a crisis in reading implies a general cultural dilemma, it also
has—as our Greek and medieval examples have shown us an era's view of
reading tends to have—implications for acting. Or rather: In Chekhov's
depictions of reading we see what acting must *become* in a cultural situation
where texts can no longer be trusted to tell readers what scripts have always
told actors, namely, what to do next.

That such a crisis in reading as Chekhov represents might have consequences for the actor-reader is not a mere matter of speculation. Two of the
principal characters in *The Sea Gull*, Arkadina and Nina, *are* actors, and both
are represented as having difficulty establishing a link between the reading

they do and the actions they perform. With Arkadina this takes the form of outright denial that she so much as works from the "script" upon which her actions are plainly based. Near the beginning of act 2 she reads aloud and comments disapprovingly on a passage from Maupassant:

> ARKADINA: "And so when a woman has picked out the author she wants to entrap, she besieges him with compliments, amenities and favors." Well, among the French that may be, but certainly here with us there's nothing of the kind, we've no set program.
>
> (act 2, p. 23)

Yet in act 3, faced with the prospect of Trigorin's desertion, she avails herself of this very "set program":

> ARKADINA: Oh, it's impossible to read you without rapture! Do you think this is only incense? I'm flattering you? Come, look me in the eyes. . . . Do I look like a liar? There you see, only I can appreciate you; only 1 can tell you the truth, my lovely darling . . . You are coming? Yes? You won't leave me?
> TRIGORIN: I have no will of my own. . . . I've never had a will of my own. Flabby, weak, always submitting! Is it possible that might please women? Take me, carry me away, only never let me be one step away from you.
> ARKADINA: (*to herself*) Now he's mine.
>
> (act 3, p. 47)

Her final aside indicates that Arkadina is perfectly conscious of pursuing the Maupassant scenario. How, then, are we to understand her earlier disavowal of Maupassant? Arkadina claims to relish the reading aspect of the actor's work:

> It's good to be here with you, my friends, delightful listening to you, but . . . sitting in my hotel room, all by myself, studying my part . . . how much better! (act 2, p. 26)

Yet her refusal to acknowledge the hidden "scenario" behind her "performance" with Trigorin amounts to a dismissal of the ties between acting and reading. Her position seems to be: "Yes, I have read the text and, yes, I now take the very action prescribed by the text. But, for all that, I deny that I enact the text." Arkadina, in other words, installs at the heart of *acting* that

very discontinuity between reading and subsequent action which is, we have
seen, the essential dilemma of Chekhovian *reading*.

Nina's difficulties as an actor-reader at first appear quite different. Far
from seeking, like Arkadina, to deny all dependency on scripts, she is openly
trying to enact two scripts at once. On the one hand, she has been appearing
in Trigorin's drama of the abandoned girl/gull literally from the moment of
its conception:

> NINA: I'm a sea gull. No, that's not it. Do you remember, you
> shot a sea gull? *A man comes by chance, sees it, and out of nothing else
> to do, destroys it.* That's not it. . . .
>
> (act 4, p. 67, italics added)

(The italicized words are those in which Trigorin first presented to Nina the
idea for his not yet written story [act 2, p. 36].) On the other hand, she has
never quite relinquished her act 1 role as Trepleff's symbolist earth spirit; its
opening words—"Vainly now the pallid moon doth light her lamp. In the
meadows the cranes wake and cry no longer" (act 1, p. 13; and, again, act 4,
p. 68)—are the last words we hear Nina speak.

The situation of performing two scripts at once is already a perplexed
image of the relation between acting and reading. But there is the further
suggestion that, for Nina, authenticity as an actor will ultimately consist in
following *neither* script, in *turning* from scripts. Her impulse to fall in with
the Trigorin scenario ("I'm a sea gull") is followed by her denial: "No, that's
not it. I'm an *actress*" (act 4, p. 67, italics added). And her impulse to reassume
the earth spirit role in Trepleff's monodrama is followed by her departure for
her next *acting* job. While Nina's decision to step free of the two male "playwrights" who between them would confine her forever to the roles of *victim*
or *goddess* no doubt bodes well for her as a woman and an artist, the implications of such a move for the relation between reading and acting are not so
hopeful. For, in each case, while acting *ensues* upon the impulse to follow a
script, it ensues as a *cancellation* of that impulse. She will be an actress *rather
than* play Trigorin's sea gull, go off to her next acting job *rather than* perform
Trepleff's *Erdgeist*. To choose to act, it is implied, is to choose to have nothing
further to do with the text one has been reading. As with Arkadina, the
familiar Chekhovian disjunction between reading and subsequent action
once again appears at the heart of, as the truth of, acting.

Unlike Arkadina and Nina, Pauline in our scene—to which, after this
long detour, I now return—is not an actress. She is also, strictly speaking, not
a reader: All she does is "gaze" at the text in her hand while speaking of other
things. Nonetheless, I would argue that, in this apparent nonreading by an

apparent nonactor, Chekhov images an acting-reading relation that gets beyond the disjunction between reading and subsequent action so characteristic of both Chekhov's readers and his actor-readers.

Not surprisingly, in view of all the difficulties associated with reading, *refusals to read* are quite common in *The Sea Gull*. Arkadina has not read her son's play (act 1, p. 6), and, even after he becomes a published author, she claims she cannot find time to read him (act 4, p. 62); Nina declines Masha's request to read a selection from Trepleff's script (act 2, p. 24); Trepleff asserts he has not read the works of Trigorin (act 1, p. 11), and Trigorin does not bother to read the writings of Trepleff (act 4, p. 62). Is there any reason why Pauline's behavior with the manuscript here should not be added to this list? On what conceivable view of reading is gazing at a text in one's hand and speaking words other than those it contains a possible image of reading, rather than the image of reading *avoided*, reading *refused*, which it appears to be?

First of all, notice that the words Pauline speaks, while not those of the Trepleff text she gazes at, are not unrelated to that text. In fact, they reflect what she understands the significance of that text to be:

> PAULINE: (*gazing at the manuscript*) Nobody ever thought or dreamed that some day, Kostya, you'd turn out to be a real author. But now, thank God, the magazines send you money for your stories. . . . dear, good Kostya, be kind to my little Masha.
>
> (act 2, p. 52)

This we may paraphrase as follows: "As the latest production of a recognized author, this manuscript of yours will be treated far better than your works used to be. In the neglect you formerly showed my daughter, you were, I believe, 'passing on' society's neglect of you. Perhaps now that the world is paying you more attention, you in turn will feel able to pay more attention to her." In other words, what Pauline "reads" in Trepleff's manuscript is a prospect of better treatment for her daughter.

Is this a "good" reading? Pauline doesn't even notice what the manuscript says! Or, rather, "what it says" has been reduced to what the fact of its existence "says" to her. When someone reads this way in real life we are likely to dismiss his reading as "wholly subjective." But there is one situation where the wholly subjective reading is the appropriate one, and that situation is acting. Pauline is a type of the actor reading with a stake—or, perhaps, of reading narrowed and intensified to the *finding* of a stake.

Pauline, in other words, is reading for what Stanislavski was later to call the "subtext." And the mere gaze she bestows on Trepleff's manuscript is an image of the kind of attention which an actor reading for subtexts bestows on a text—attention within which the words become transparent (i.e., "disappear"), allowing the actor-reader to see through the verbal surface to "the inwardly felt expression of a human being in a part, which flows uninterruptedly beneath the words." Stanislavski's principle that "the words come from the author, the subtext from the actor," exactly describes the transaction between the "author"-character (Trepleff) and the "actor"-character (Pauline) in our scene. But this amounts to saying that the Stanislavskian conception of acting as reading for subtext is already inscribed in this Chekhovian scene of reading as *its* image of reading per se. And, one must quickly add, the Chekhovian *mistrust* of acting as a reading for subtext is also already inscribed there.

This mistrust manifests itself in several ways—for one thing, in the fact that Pauline, unlike Nina and Arkadina, is *not an actor*. Conceivably, this could be taken as implying that acting has something to learn from the self-absorbed, self-seeking (but therefore, at least, *absorbed* and *seeking*) approach of the ordinary, nontheatrical "bad reader." But there is also the distinct suggestion that what ⌐he is doing *isn't acting*. A more important indication of Chekhov's mistrust of acting as subtextual reading is that Pauline never actually brings forth the text. According to Stanislavski, "It is the subtext that makes us say the words we do." Pauline, however, does not get around to speaking the words on Trepleff's page. In this regard she is, as a reader, no great improvement on Masha Prozoroff gazing into a book and whistling or Tchebutykin unfolding his newspaper and bursting into song.

Now, as a critique of subtextual acting, this cannot be meant literally; even the most subtext-oriented actor does not omit to deliver his lines. Nevertheless, there is an emblematic truth here. Subtextual reading does, indeed, "make away with" the words of the script, not in the sense that they are henceforth no longer present but in the sense that they are henceforth present only as the crust or veil—the "outside"—of another, more authentic "inner" discourse. The subtext is a prime example of the Derridean *supplement*: a supposed "mere addition," which, in fact, supplants that which it claims to be only supplementing. In our scene this supplanting *in importance* of the text by the subtext becomes a *literal* supplanting of the former by the latter: Instead of delivering the text (i.e., reading Trepleff's manuscript) with the subtext somehow "behind" it, Pauline actually *delivers the subtext*.

It may seem outrageous to propose Chekhov as the source of the Stanislavskian concept of "subtext," even with the proviso that he is also a source of misgivings about it. Chekhov—who never wearied of complaining that Stanislavski's approaches distorted his work? Chekhov—who was forever telling the Moscow Art players, "you'll find it all in the text"? And, yet, alongside this last dictum must be placed another very different pronouncement of Chekhov's on reading:

> When I write, I count upon my reader fully, assuming that he himself will add the subjective elements that are lacking in the telling.

While Chekhov seems to be speaking primarily about readers of his fiction ("in the *telling*"), to wish for a reader who, like Pauline, will "add the subjective elements that are lacking" is to wish for the Stanislavski actor. A search outside the text and inside the reader for emotional material that "makes [characters] say the words [they] do" was Chekhov's model of the reading process long before it was Stanislavski's theory of subtexts.

But I want to go further and argue that the whole encounter of the Stanislavski actor with the Chekhov script is already inscribed in that script, that the actual trouble Stanislavski is known to have had as actor-reader of Chekhov's plays is anticipated in those plays' own images of troubled reading.

For all the affinity he professed to feel for them, Stanislavski did not find Chekhov's scripts easy to read. "I am used," he wrote the playwright, "to receiving rather confused impressions from the first reading of your plays." And, indeed, the first time through, *The Sea Gull* struck him as "monotonous" and insufficiently "scenic." "Are you sure," he asked Nemirovich-Danchenko, "it can be performed at all?" This last comment reveals Stanislavski, as reader *of* Chekhov, grappling with what we have seen to be the characteristic dilemma of readers *in* Chekhov: inability to *imagine taking action* on the basis of what one has read. Moreover, the solution Stanislavski found to this dilemma is also anticipated in at least one moment of Chekhov's writing, namely, our scene. *Unable to read in and act from the text, one reads into the text something which, as already one's own, it is possible to act upon*—this sentence describes the Chekhovian reader, the Stanislavskian actor as forecast by Chekhov, and the figure of Pauline, in whom these meet.

In other words the "distortion" that Chekhov complained the Stanislavski actor inflicted upon his plays is nothing other than *reading itself*, as Chekhov's own plays present reading. Chekhov's misgivings about Stanislavski's techniques merely repeat the misgivings about reading which the plays themselves dramatize. Or alternately: Stanislavski's work methods merely enact the problematic view of reading already present in Chekhov's texts. Ironically, Stanislavski's actors heeded all too well Chekhov's injunction to "find it all in the text." For what they found in Chekhov's text were images of how problematic an act "finding in a text" must be, on such a view of reading as Chekhov's.

In this chapter I have advanced the conjecture that any script's scenes of reading forecast what will be the eventual rehearsal experience of actors working on that script. In the present case we possess some information on the actual rehearsal experience of a particular group of actors who worked on the material in question, and the information confirms the conjecture. The treatment that Chekhov's scenes of reading predict for themselves at the hands of actors is the very treatment they received from the Moscow Art players. The Chekhovian scene of reading has seen the future—and it is Stanislavski.

MICHAEL C. FINKE

"At Sea": A Psychoanalytic Approach to Chekhov's First Signed Work

With the publication of "The Requiem" (Panikhida) in February 1886, Anton Chekhov made his first appearance in *Novoe vremia*, a Petersburg daily published by Aleksei Suvorin. He had submitted the story under the pseudonym Antosha Chekhonte but was persuaded by the paper's editors to attach his real name. That this moment receives special mention in biographies of Chekhov is natural, given the significance Suvorin was to have in the development of Chekhov's career and the meaning commonly attached to the signing of one's proper name. But it is in equal measure odd that so little attention has been afforded the first story published under the name of A. Chekhov at the author's own initiative. This was "At Sea," a very short tale published in *Mirskoi tolk* in 1883. Two more stories signed by Chekhov, "He Understood" and "The Swedish Match," soon also appeared in different journals.

"At Sea" has an interesting publication history, as told by the editors of Chekhov's complete works. Soon after its submission, Chekhov apparently grew anxious enough about the provocative subject matter to write a letter to the editors asking that they return the story; he was told it was too late, although the editors would be happy in the future to receive "less spicy" tales. A short time later, in the letter of December 25, 1883, to Nikolai Leykin, Chekhov complained of the tactics of unscrupulous publishers regarding his name. He explained: "I sign with my full family name only in

From *Reading Chekhov's Text*. © 1993 by Northwestern University Press.

Priroda i okhota [where "He Understood" appeared], and once I put it under a large story in *Strekoza* [this was "The Swedish Match"]." Less than two months after "At Sea" appeared in *Mirskoi tolk*, Chekhov neglected to mention it when listing the few stories he had published under his own name to date—a striking indication of his ambivalence regarding the story.

Almost two decades later Ivan Bunin asked Chekhov to contribute somthing to an almanac projected by the publishing house Skorpion. Chekhov, who had been revising his early pieces for the Marks edition of his collected works, offered a slightly reworked "At Sea" under a new title, "At Night"; but he was then appalled by the decadent company in which he found himself printed. He was also irritated at the sloppy proofs Skorpion sent him to correct, and he was angry that the proofs arrived with postage due. What seems to have especially provoked Chekhov, however, was the overprominent use of his name to advertise the almanac in the newspaper *Russkie vedomosti*. As happens to the narrator of "A Boring Story" (1889), Chekhov saw his name detached from his self and circulated as a coin of exchange. His letter of complaint to Bunin (March 14, 1901) ended with a pun: "Having read this announcement in *Russkie vedomosti*, I swore never again to become involved with scorpions, crocodiles, or snakes."

If the first publication of a story under Chekhov's own name involved a great deal of anxiety, then republication of the same story many years later became an occasion for manifestly hostile feelings; in both instances the issue of Chekhov's name was central. When revising the story, Chekhov did not disturb its spicy plot, nor did he remove some astonishingly suggestive erotic imagery. Indeed, Skorpion's editor, Valery Bryusov, complained in his diary that Chekhov had intentionally sent a story that would be unlikely to pass the censors. What Chekhov suppressed—what, perhaps, he wished he had suppressed before he sent the story in eighteen years before—were, first, overt signals of intertextual connections with Victor Hugo's *Toilers of the Sea* and Shakespeare's *Hamlet* and, second, details about the relationships between the story's sailor-narrator, his father, and his late mother.

Chekhov normally cut material when making revisions. But the anxiety and ill will that accompanied each publication of this tale, together with the singular fact of Chekhov's signature, lead one to suspect an excessive degree of emotional, even unconscious, involvement. Might not something in the story be at least partially responsible for both Chekhov's signature and his discomfort? The following assay at a psychoanalytic approach to "At Sea" reveals a deep nexus between the story's most remarkable features: its provocative erotic plot and imagery and the author's revisions, anxieties, and signature. But first we will briefly examine the story's plot and Chekhov's revisions.

The Plot

The plot tension of "At Sea" is explicitly based on the dynamics of erotic desire: the sailors aboard a steamer have drawn lots to determine which two of them will spy on a newly wed English pastor and his young wife in the bridal suite. The winners are father and son, and the son is also the tale's first-person narrator. Since both the debauched sailors and the story's reader anticipate as payoff or denouement the culmination of two others' sexual act, the reader's position here is no less voyeuristic than the narrator's. The familial relationship between the two peeping Toms creates additional expectations: scenes of mastery and initiation will occur on both sides of the wall.

The two sailors take their places at the peepholes, but there is a hitch in the bridal suite: the bride appears to be reluctant. When she does finally assent, we peeping Toms, who were unable to hear the husband's words, assume that he was pleading for himself and that the marriage's consummation will follow. In the surprise denouement, a banker with whom the couple had been socializing earlier enters, gives the pastor some money, and is left alone with the bride. The stunned sailors leave the peephole without witnessing the sexual act, thereby also depriving the reader of the voyeuristic titillation promised earlier.

The denouement provokes a moral reevaluation of the sailors, earlier self-described by the narrator as "more disgusting than anything on earth." For had the peepers' desires been strictly pornographic, the exchange of privileges for money should have been no cause for them to give up their stations. At the same time, a man of the cloth is the last husband we would expect to be pimping his own bride. Finally, the roles of father and son are reversed: the son, whom his father addresses as "laddie" or "little boy" (*mal'chishka*), becomes father to his own father as he helps him up the stairs.

Every detail in this miniature relates to the denouement, either as anticipated by the sailors or as it actually takes place. The setting at sea and at night—both of which Chekhov underlined in various published versions by alternately using them as titles for the story—suggests a space, cut off from the normal world, where anything might happen; it is a space tailor-made for liminal states. Each of the first three short paragraphs culminates in images that, if interpreted with the story's anticipated denouement in mind, suggest erotic culmination: the heavy clouds wishing to let go of their rain in a burst; the joking sailor who, as lots are drawn to determine who will spy on the newlyweds, crows like a rooster; and this bold image— "A little shudder ran from the back of my head to my very heels, as if there were a hole in the back of my head from which little cold shot poured down my naked body. I was shivering not from the cold, but from other reasons."

Next follows a digression that sets up an opposition between the debauched seaman's world and the virginal world of the newly wed pastor, his bride, and idealized love. This opposition, which will be reversed in the denouement, is later made explicit in the passage juxtaposing the space where the peepers stand with the space of the bridal suite. At the moment, however, the narrator focuses on the sailor's world. His view of his own and his comrades' moral state is summed up by the special kind of space they inhabit. Both literally and figuratively, it is the vertical space necessary for a fall: "To me it seems that the sailor has more reasons to hate and curse himself than any other. A person who might every moment fall from a mast and be immersed forever under the waves, who knows God only when he is drowning or plunging headfirst, needs nothing and feels pity for nothing in existence." Here the sailor embodies man in his fallen state, man who falls all the time, compulsively. In the denouement the narrator jumps back from his peephole "as if stung" or bitten, as by a serpent (the Russian word here, *uzhalennyi*, would be used for a snake bite). The father's face is described as "similar to a baked apple"; this motif has special resonance in the context of a story about falls, carnal knowledge and egregious sin. The inhabitants of this anti-Eden are compelled to repeat forever the moment of the Fall.

The digression ends: "We drink a lot of vodka, we are debauched, because we don't know who needs virtue at sea, and for what." Yet the antic- ipated coupling between pastor and bride is special precisely because of its aura of idealized love and virtue, while the sailors' reactions in the denoue- ment demonstrate that virtue is necessary to them, even if they do not expect to take part in it. Here we might compare the way negotiations are carried out between the banker and the pastor with the sailors' method of deciding who among them will receive voyeuristic satisfaction of their erotic desires. The latter cast lots; they rely on luck, God's will, to decide the matter. For the pastor, God's representative, he who can pay gets what he wants. The woman whom the sailor idealizes as a love object becomes a commodity for the pastor and the banker.

"At Sea" begins as a story about the depravity of the sailor's world but ends as a tale depicting the depravity of the "aristocratic bedroom"—a reversal perhaps banally moralistic, but not untypical of the early Chekhov. The last image is one of the father and son moving upward in space.

Subtexts

Now we return to the question of Chekhov's revisions. These can be divided into three chief areas: his handling of subtextual references to Hugo, his handling of references to Shakespeare, and his decision to drop certain details regarding the familial relations of the two peepers.

The characters and setting of "At Sea" are quite exotic for Chekhov, and one suspects from the start that they have been imported. The Russian scholar R. G. Nazirov recently revealed the story to be a parody of Victor Hugo's *Toilers of the Sea* (Les travailleurs de la mer, 1866). "At Sea" picks up where *Toilers* leaves off: the English pastor, Ebenezer, is departing on a steamer with his bride, Deruchette. Left behind in despair is the extraordinary seaman, Gilliatt, who once saved Ebenezer's life and to whom Deruchette was promised. Chekhov's story echoes the opposition between the coarse laborer of the sea and the refined representative of God, and it repeats certain central motifs, such as that of peeping: the lovesick Gilliatt spies on Deruchette for four years before he takes action to win her; he is spying on her when the pastor declares his love and kisses her for the first time; and even at the novel's melodramatic end, as Gilliatt commits suicide by allowing the rising tide to cover him where he sits, he is watching Deruchette and Ebenezer hold hands on the deck of a departing steamer. To the echoes Nazirov notes can be added Chekhov's handling of the plot device of reversal: men whose exemplary virtue is remarked on by Hugo's narrator repeatedly turn out to be utter scoundrels.

One effect of Chekhov's revisions was to distance "At Sea" from Hugo's novel. Here the customary strategy of improving the rhythm of his prose, shortening dialogues, and pruning some of the melodramatic imagery eliminated the excesses so characteristic of Hugo's style and thereby weakened the links between this parody and its target text. In particular, "Chekhov cut a direct 'bibliographic key'—an allusion to the original object of parody: 'the loud, drunken laughter of *toilers of the sea*." It has been suggested that Chekhov's diminution of "stylistic mimicry" of Hugo was meant to place greater emphasis on the story's critique of romantic aestheticism. Debunking romantic love, however, is a theme that has lent itself to lighthearted narrative treatment for ages (e.g., in the fabliau), and it is a staple of the early Chekhov. It is highly improbable that when Chekhov returned to this story while editing his early stories for the Marks edition of his works he revised it to further a project of setting the world straight on the issue of romantic love. Rather, he likely found the story unsatisfactory in form and no less unsettling in content than when it was first published.

The second subtext obscured in the revisions was *Hamlet*. Chekhov's career-long involvement with Shakespeare, especially with *Hamlet*, certainly deserves the epithet *obsessive*. As one Russian critic has put it, "Shakespeare is mentioned so often in the stories and plays of Chekhov that one could call him one of Chekhov's heroes." In the 1883 version of "At Sea," the steamer's name, *Prince Hamlet*, is mentioned five times—this in a work of under five pages. Such an underlining of the *Hamlet* motif leads one to look for other allusions, and several can be found.

The cock's crow and the narrator's shudder, discussed above, recall the appearance of the ghost of Hamlet's father:

> BARNARDO: It was about to speak when the cock crew.
> HORATIO: And then it started like a guilty thing
>   Upon a fearful summons.

For the sailor imitating the sound and those who are amused by it, the cock's crow is an erotic allusion; for the narrator, however, who has been contemplating his fallen state and is full of self-reproaches, it is also a "fearful summons" heard by a "guilty thing." In the Gospel tale of Peter's denial, retold in Chekhov's short masterpiece of 1894, "The Student," the rooster's call has a similar meaning.

In *Hamlet* this shudder at the recollection of one's guilt is repeated when Claudius sees his crime portrayed in Hamlet's mousetrap. The moment is paralleled in "At Sea" in the narrator's reaction during the dumb show of the wedding night: if the crime of treating the bride as an object to be bought and sold stuns him, this is perhaps because it echoes what he and his shipmates did when they created and raffled the use of the peepholes.

In the original version of the story, the narrator goes on deck and previews in fantasy the scene to be staged in the bridal suite:

> I lit a pipe and began looking at the sea. It was dark, but there must have been blood boiling in my eyes. Against the night's black backdrop I made out the hazy image of that which had been the object of our drawing lots.
>   "I love you!" I gasped, stretching my hands toward the darkness.
>   This expression "I love" I knew from books lying around in the canteen on the upper shelf.

As he utters "I love you" and stretches his hands toward the phantasm he has conjured, the narrator imagines himself in the place of the one man who in reality has the right to utter these words and embrace the woman—the bridegroom. In a sense, this fantasy places the narrator on the other side of the wall at which he will soon be standing. The motifs of dreaming and reading also associate the narrator with Hamlet; in particular, they recall act II, scene ii, where Hamlet enters reading, in which he utters the line "Words, words, words," and which ends with a torrent of self-reproaches, including his calling himself "John-a-dreams." As we have seen, the narrator of "At Sea" is no less liberal with criticism of himself. It is also in act II, scene ii, that Hamlet calls Polonius "Jephthah, judge of Israel," thereby accusing the father of sacrificing Ophelia to gain favor with Claudius. There is a clear thematic connection with "At Sea," where the bridegroom sacrifices his wife for financial gain.

Chekhov's recourse to *Hamlet* in this story appears distinctive when compared with references in his other early narrative works. There allusions to Shakespeare are usually comically distorted citations that sharpen a character's speech characteristics, reveal a farcically pretentious character's lack of culture, or lampoon Russian pseudo Hamlets and latter-day superfluous men. Something more substantial is taking place in "At Sea." And yet Chekhov chose to obscure the story's connection with *Hamlet* when revising it.

The third area of changes in Chekhov's revision of "At Sea" involves suppressing all mention of the narrator's late mother and toning down the hostility between the narrator and his father. In the 1883 version, the elder sailor addresses his son after they win the lottery:

"Today, laddie, you and I have gotten lucky," he said, twisting his sinewy, toothless mouth with a smile.

"You know what, son? It occurs to me that when we were drawing lots your mother—that is, my wife—was praying for us. Ha-ha!"

"You can leave my mother in peace!" I said.

The "that is" (in Russian, the contrastive conjunction *a*) separating the two designations "your mother" and "my wife" underlines the different functions this one woman held for the two men. (The erotic connotations that can be associated with "getting lucky" work in Russian as well as in English translation.) In the 1901 version this exchange is replaced by the father's words: "Today, laddie, you and I have gotten lucky. . . . Do you hear, laddie? Happiness has befallen you and me at the same time. And that means something." What this odd coincidence means, perhaps, is what it has displaced from the story's earlier version: the mother.

In addition to leaving the mother in peace, Chekhov cut out explicit motifs of antagonism between father and son. In the original version, when the father asks the son to switch peepholes so that he, with his weaker eyes, might see better, the son strikes his father. "My father respected my fist," he says.

The Primal Scene

"At Sea" is so laden and ready to burst with motifs of Oedipal strivings that, had the story not been written some sixteen years prior to Freud's first public discussion of Oedipus and Prince Hamlet in *The Interpretation of Dreams*, one would be sorely tempted to conjecture about Freud's influence on Chekhov. To the extent that Chekhov departed from the situations and configurations of characters given him in Hugo's *Toilers* and, at a deeper level, *Hamlet*, his alterations of these subtexts in the original version of "At Sea" directly parallel Freud's interpretation of Shakespeare's play: they superimpose direct conflict with the father onto an impossible erotic desire.

The story's English characters and Shakespearean steamer led the censors to take its original version as a translation from English; "At Night," the version rewritten for Ivan Bunin in 1901, was received as an imitation of Maupassant. Perhaps this helps explain why, in spite of Bryusov's concerns, the story was passed by the censors: giving works non-Russian settings and characters and presenting an original work as a translation or an imitation of a foreign author were long-standing techniques for evading prohibition. But if elements of foreignness acted as a screen from government censors, might this not be true of Chekhov's internal censor as well? Recourse to the exotic Hugo subtext and to *Hamlet* may have facilitated the emergence of very sensitive material. Years later, when Chekhov revised the story for Skorpion, he attenuated the agonistic relationship with the father and the Hugo and *Hamlet* connections in equal measures.

Behind the incident of voyeurism we can see many features of the "primal scene," that archetypal peeping situation, defined in psychoanalytic literature as a "scene of sexual intercourse between the parents which the child observes, or infers on the basis of certain indications, and phantasies. It is generally interpreted by the child as an act of violence on the part of the father." In "At Sea" the scene is portrayed with idiosyncrasies and distortions characteristic of the work of the defense mechanism of repression. These include splitting the father into two figures, the old sailor at the peephole and the pastor (or the reverend father), whose conjugal place the narrator has already taken in his fantasies (when he is on deck with outstretched arms in the story's first version). They also make it possible for the father and the son to share the object of desire even as they contest for her; that is, there is a transformation in which the "either me or you" or "not me but you" as rightful agents of erotic desire for the mother figure into a "both me and you." This helps explain the uncanny stroke of luck— "that means something"—by which both father and son have won the right to stand at the peepholes.

The narrator's positioning at his peephole actually begins as a dream-like image of penetration into a low and dark place: "I felt out my aperture and extracted the rectangular piece of wood I had whittled for so long. And I saw a thin, transparent muslin, through which a soft, pink light penetrated to me. And together with the light there touched my burning face a suffocating, most pleasant odor; this had to be the odor of an aristocratic bedroom. In order to see the bedroom, it was necessary to spread the muslin apart with two fingers, which I hurried to do." The Russian here for orifice, *otverstie*, can refer to an orifice in the anatomical sense as well. The aristocratic bedroom, with its ambivalently perceived scent, is revealed only after a parting of the hymeneal "muslin"; the notion of hymen is, after all, what makes the anticipated coupling of newlyweds special.

The dialogue between father and son as they are waiting in anticipation at their stations vocalizes, after a process of displacement, thoughts belonging to the situation of the primal scene: "Let me take your place," and "Be quiet, they might hear us." In theory it is the child who can be traumatized by his lack of potency in the Oedipal stage; here the old man complains of his weak eyes. We can interpret the "stung" reaction of the narrator at the denouement—once again, on a different plane of meaning—as just such a castrating trauma, with potency redefined in pounds sterling and the idealized pastor-father exposed in his lack of it. The shock is all the more effective when juxtaposed with the images of excessive and impatient potency at the story's start. At the same time, the exchange represents the uncanny event of a wish fulfilled: the narrator's investment in this scene is predicated on a fantasy of taking the pastor-father's place, and now, before his eyes, just such a substitution is made. Once again, on the model of Hamlet's mousetrap, the sailor's conscience has been captured—with the difference that his most serious crime was no more than a transgressive wish. The narrator's sudden solicitous attitude toward his father—helping him up the stairs— may be interpreted as an attempt to undo this fantasy, a mechanism typical of obsessional neurosis. Earlier, the sailor's reaction was interpreted as revealing an essential morality; now it appears to be a neurotic symptom. The two traits are deliberately entangled in Chekhov's 1889 story "An Attack of Nerves" (Pripadok).

A full-scale psychoanalytic interpretation of the story would only be beginning at this point. In tracing the vicissitudes of the peeping compulsion, Freud treats scopophilia and exhibitionism as inextricably linked opposites "which appear in ambivalent forms." This is certainly the case in "At Sea," where Chekhov can be said to expose himself in a story depicting scopophilia. Indeed, Chekhov himself consciously associated publishing and exhibitionism when he told I. I. Yasinsky that he wrote under a pen name to avoid feelings of shame: "It was just like walking naked with a large mask on and showing oneself like that to the public." The narrator's fantasies and voyeurism are fundamentally autoerotic acts, while the contradictory situation of father and son peeping together, which then culminates with the father's order to desist, could at once dramatize a wish for union with the father and the father's injunction against autoerotic activity, both features of ambivalent Oedipal dynamics. The narrator portrays his father as laying down the moral law and so impinging on his natural process of maturation: "Let's get out of here! You shouldn't see this! You are still a boy." By now, however, this gesture of paternal authority appears ludicrous.

Chekhov

Chekhov wrote "At Sea" as a twenty-two-year-old medical student, who at the time, incidentally, was following a patient in a clinic for nervous disorders. The past few years had seen a "tangling up of the family sequence" in which Chekhov had become in a sense the father of his own brothers, sister, and parents. This was chiefly a result of his ability to bring money— that same signifier of authority that displaces the Bible in "At Sea"—into the clan after his father's disastrous bankruptcy. In Chekhov's own family, moreover, the Bible can be associated with Chekhov's pedantically religious father, who was fond of reading religious texts aloud. Just what Chekhov's new status meant to him is hinted at in Tatyana Shchepkina-Kupernik's retelling of a favorite story of Chekhov's mother: still a student, Chekhov came to her and announced, "Well, Mama, from this day on I myself will pay for Masha's schooling!"

The definite antierotic strain in Chekhov's life and works may well bespeak an inadequate resolution of the issues glimpsed in "At Sea." Chekhov's coy, ironic, at times even sadistic bearing toward women with whom he skirted serious involvement, notably Lika Mizinova, recalls Hamlet's treatment of Ophelia and his mother, the women he claims to love. It happens that the measure by which Hamlet quantifies his love for the dead Ophelia—more than "forty thousand brothers" (V.i.269)—was a favorite citation of the early Chekhov; in humorous paraphrasings it became a synonym for "a lot." More to the point, some of Chekhov's later, full-length stories that are notable for their representation of psychopathological states—in particular "Ward Six" (1892)—very carefully situate certain characters' psychological problems in respect to their relations with their fathers.

Psychoanalytic theory has it that the son's identification with the father, his accession to the father's name, closes the Oedipal stage. This comes about after acquiescence to what is perceived as the father's threat of castration and the renunciation of erotic desire for the mother. Fully one-third of "At Sea" involves the narrator's self-reproaches, all of which are based on his sailor's calling, that is, the professional identity shared with and given him by his father. It is clearly an uneasy identity. For Chekhov, too, any identification with his real father would have been terribly problematic.

Chekhov's very first ambitious literary attempt, the play he wrote while still in Taganrog and subsequently destroyed, was titled *Fatherless* (Bezottsovshchina). The first story Chekhov signed with the name of his father, "At Sea," depicts a son overtaking the father; in subsequent years Chekhov was to sign his own name only when he had already become a prominent literary figure and when his ascendancy over the family of his father was beyond dispute. Later in life, just after his father died—when he must have been meditating on his relationship with his father—Chekhov made an oblique association between his own family and that of Oedipus. On receiving a telegram of condolence from V. I. Nemirovich-Danchenko on behalf of Konstantin Stanislavsky and the others in the Moscow Art Theater, Chekhov replied in a letter of October 21, 1898: "I am waiting for *Antigone*. I'm waiting, for you promised to send it. I really need it. I'm waiting for my sister, who, as she has telegraphed, is coming to me in Yalta. Together we'll decide how to arrange things now. After the death of our father, our mother will hardly want to live alone in the country. We've got to think up something new." Chekhov sets up a parallelism ("I'm waiting for *Antigone*. . . . I'm waiting for my sister") that casts the shadow of Oedipus's family onto his own, and the upshot of his comment is. Now that my father is dead, my mother will want to live with me.

But there may be more at issue than the Chekhov family dynamics and their reflection in the author's psyche. The allusions in "At Sea" to Hugo and Shakespeare—and their elimination in the story's revision— invite consideration of Chekhov's relations with his literary fathers. "At Sea" juxtaposes two subtexts of vastly different literary value. In parodying Hugo's melodramatic situations and stylistic excesses (as Chekhov had done in the 1880 spoof "One Thousand and One Horrors," dedicated to Victor Hugo), Chekhov treats this predecessor as does the sailor-narrator his own father. Hugo may be openly and easily displaced; Shakespeare, however, is another matter. Whether imitated by would-be authors, misquoted by pretentious buffoons, or performed by untalented actors, Shakespeare in Chekhov's works is a benchmark against which pretension stands revealed, very often to comic effect. And this notion of pretension might apply equally to the ill-equipped youngster who boldly advances an erotic claim on his parent and to the young author who declares his identity as an author for the first time by signing his proper name.

When Chekhov wrote "At Sea," the figure of Prince Hamlet had served Russian literature as a paradigm for the inability to translate desires and talents into action for decades. The allusion to *Hamlet* in "At Sea" is a kind of a joke about that paradigm, but one that perhaps nevertheless indicates anxiety about failure and a wish to forestall it. By the time Chekhov revised the story in 1901, however, his place as an author was secure. There is even evidence that he had become a conscious theorist of Oedipal anxieties and their implication in the problems of authorship: in *The Sea Gull* (1896), the young writer Treplev, who laces his speech with citations from *Hamlet*, must contest an established author of the preceding generation for both the affection of his mother and recognition as an author.

In any case, the early Chekhov repeatedly associated the fateful moment of asserting one's identity in spite of feelings of inadequacy and probable failure with *Hamlet*. In "Baron" (1882), the seedy prompter, a failed actor who had shown great talent but lacked courage, is carried away during a performance of *Hamlet* and begins declaiming the lines he should have been whispering to the red-haired youth playing the Prince. It is his end. He is kicked out of the theater altogether, but at least for once in his life he has shown boldness; he has declaimed. How appropriate that the story in which Chekhov decides to be Chekhov, to sign his own name, should be engaged with *Hamlet*.

ROBERT LOUIS JACKSON

"The Enemies": A Story at War with Itself?

Die Botschaft hor'ich wohl,
allein mir fehlt der Glaube.
—Goethe, *Faust*

The principle of symmetry governs Chekhov's story "The Enemies." Oddly enough, it is symmetry itself that is disturbing to the reader. Are there no imbalances in the story?

The title, "Vragi" (Enemies), carries us into one of the oldest and most disturbing realms of human experience. There are two protagonists who become enemies: Kirilov and Abogin. Kirilov's name has its root in the Greek *kyrios* ("Lord," "master") and echoes, incidentally, the name of a missionary who brought Christianity to Russia, St. Cyril (Constantine). Kirilov is a doctor, we are told, who has "experienced need and ill fortune." Abogin is a wealthy gentleman, the root of whose name appears in *bog*, Russian for "god," or *bogatyi*, "wealthy," "rich"; and in *obozhat'*, "to worship," "to adore." Indeed, we learn, Abogin worships his wife like a slave. Chekhov also may have meant the name Abogin to be understood as a Greek-Russian hybrid in which the Greek alpha privitive *a* combines with the Russian word *bog*, thus suggesting the Greek *atheos* (*a-*, "without"+ *-theos*, "god"), atheist.

From *Reading Chekhov's Text*. © 1993 by Northwestern University Press.

197

Both of these men suffer misfortunes at the same time: Kirilov endures the death of his only child; Abogin experiences what he first takes to be the serious illness of his wife, but then turns out to be the deception of a woman who feigns mortal illness in order to run off with another man.

The story divides neatly into two parts. In the first part we are in Kirilov's house and learn how he meets his misfortune. Abogin arrives barely five minutes after the death of Kirilov's child. Terribly upset, he pressures the reluctant Dr. Kirilov into visiting his presumably sick wife. "I understand perfectly your situation," Abogin tells Kirilov several times. "You are in sorrow, I understand." In fact, in the blindness of his distress, he does not understand Kirilov's suffering. Every word he uses seems to violate it.

A transitional episode occurs in which both characters are on the road together traveling to Abogin's house. For one moment they seem joined in their misery. Even the crows, awakened by the noise of the carriage wheels, nonjudgmentally give out "an anxious pitiful wail, as if they knew that the doctor's son was dead and Abogin's wife was ill." Does nature, too, have a premonition that what unites these two men in their misery is their inability to communicate? "In all of nature one felt something hopeless, sick." Yet paradoxically these two men are closest to each other in their silence. Not without reason does the narrator early in the story observe that "the highest expression of happiness or unhappiness most often is silence; lovers understand one another better when they are silent." The equilibrium established through silence, however, is not long lasting. The carriage crosses a river, a line that seems to divide not only the two territories the men inhabit but also their social and psychic habitations.

The second part of the story takes place in Abogin's house. We discover how he meets his real misfortune, his wife's flight from the house with her lover. Abogin rages over this deception. It is now Kirilov's turn not to understand the suffering or distress that afflicts Abogin. "I do not understand," Kirilov keeps repeating as Abogin recounts the banalities of his bedroom melodrama, one in which, it turns out, he is the cuckold. "I do not understand." In fact, Kirilov does understand something of the world of Abogin, though what he understands he cruelly caricatures.

There is a stormy clash between the two men: Kirilov is outraged at being called upon to participate in what he calls a "vulgar [family] comedy" or "melodrama," and Abogin, who is mortally offended at the violent insults of Kirilov, likewise rages. These differences explode in class hatred. With the contempt of a man who obviously has faced the harsh realities of lower-class existence in his own and other people's lives, Kirilov compares the suffering of the wealthy Abogin to that of a contented "capon." In turn, Abogin, reaching back into the dark class history of Russia, responds furiously: "For such words people are thrashed! Do you understand?"

The story ends with Abogin and Kirilov going their separate ways, as enemies. Abogin drives off "to protest, to do foolish things." Kirilov drives off, not thinking of his wife nor of (his son) Andrei, full of "unjust and inhumanly cruel thoughts" about Abogin, his wife, and her lover, Papchinsky. Kirilov, the narrator tells us, condemns all three of them and "all people who live in rosy subdued light and smell of scent. All the way home he hated and despised them to the point of pain in his heart. And a firm conviction concerning those people took shape in his mind. Time will pass, Kirilov's sorrow will pass, but this conviction, unjust, unworthy of the human heart, will not pass and will remain in the doctor's mind to the very grave." The final words of the story, then, speak of Kirilov's permanent failure to overcome his deep hostility toward Abogin, that is, to reach out to him. The scales, it would seem, have tipped in favor of Abogin. Have they been tipping in that direction in the second half of the story? Do the prestigiously located words at the end of the story signal that on the deeper ethical plane of the story's meaning a reversal of roles has taken place, one in which the "godless" Abogin has overtaken the "Christian" Kirilov in the sympathies of the reader? So much for the symmetries and neat pattern of reversals on which this story and its conventional interpretation thrive.

The narrator himself interprets in a very judicious way the events he narrates: the "egoism of suffering," he observes, drives people apart. "The unhappy are egoistic, spiteful, unjust, cruel, and less capable of understanding each other than fools. Unhappiness does not bring people together but draws them apart." Suffering divides Kirilov and Abogin. Both are bearers of a certain measure of truth, but only as it relates to their own unhappiness; with respect to the whole truth both are blind.

The protagonists, then, are victims of a fundamental misunderstanding, the kind that lies at the root of so many divisions between human beings. Only Chekhov and his narrator—the narrator in this interpretation *is* Chekhov—are aware of the full and complex truth involving Kirilov and Abogin. Thus Chekhov emerges as a kind of arbiter: he holds in his hands the scales of justice, and they are balanced. Suffering is suffering, Chekhov appears to be saying. There is no such thing as a hierarchy of suffering, no foundation for anybody to say, "My suffering is deeper than yours," any more than there is a basis for somebody to say that "what I call beauty is beauty, but what you call beauty is ugliness."

There is much to recommend this interpretation of the story. Yet I find something—not everything, but *something*—wanting in this interpretation. Or rather, I accept it with my head—I see the design very well—but I do not wholly feel it with my heart. Chekhov does not appear to me to approach his two protagonists in an evenhanded way. His sympathies seem to lie with Kirilov, and his antipathies with Abogin. Let me be absolutely clear: Chekhov, the narrator, and the reader, I think, are all agreed that both men as they exchange insults at the end of the story really are equally at fault. Yet in the course of the story Chekhov presents the misunderstanding between the two men in the context of radical differences between these men in their personalities, modes of suffering, and life-styles. Approaching the story from this direction, we are inclined to say that the men part as "enemies" not only because an extraordinary coincidence of circumstances has plunged them into the "egoism of suffering" but also because they are enemies in some deeper sense. The crisis only brings into broad relief certain underlying realities. It is on this deeper level of their misunderstanding—a misunderstanding, as it were, between two different realities—that I find Chekhov's sympathies and my own leaning toward Kirilov.

Whether or not we subscribe to the view that these two men are divided on a deeper level of enmity, Chekhov's near-caricature of Abogin's language and personality complicates an exclusively ecumenical understanding of the story, an understanding well formulated in Beverly Hahn's view that "the story is primarily concerned with the intersecting needs of different lives and consequently with the relativity of moral claims"; that the story is "a plea for understanding, against prejudice"; and that, finally, in this story Chekhov moves "beyond his instinctive sympathies and antipathies to defend the rights and dignity of a comparatively shallow man." The apparent direction of Chekhov's effort is well stated here, and one might say that the design is brilliantly executed. Yet I would argue that Chekhov's instinct and intent are to some extent at cross-purposes with one another. Indeed, it is this fact that awakens the story, for me at least, from its ecumenical dream and makes it at once intriguing, enigmatic, and ambiguous, as so many of Chekhov's stories are.

I am not the first person seriously to raise some of these questions, though I may be the second. More than forty years ago the Soviet ideologist V. V. Yermilov, a heavy-handed but not unintelligent critic, suggested that Chekhov views were not expressed directly in the text: "They live as it were *under* the text, in the deep subterranean current of the story," in its "subtext." Chekhov's sympathy for the little man, Yermilov believed, was expressed in the poetic detail of the text. Yermilov, however, had no patience with what he called the "conciliatory" element in the story. Loudly blowing his class trumpet, he discovered only a repressed message of class antagonisms in the story, what he felt to be Chekhov's hatred of the "parasitical" and "banal" Abogin. "The 'conciliatory' element introduced by Chekhov in the story,"

Yermilov insisted, "is clearly alluvial, alien to the poetry of the work, and can be explained by the 'pacifist' influence of Tolstoy's teachings that Chekhov was experiencing just at this moment."

The concept of class enemies, which was implemented in a grim way in the Soviet Union, seems to have unbalanced Yermilov's critical mind. But we must give the devil his due: Yermilov rightly calls attention to Chekhov's tendency, on the one hand, to elevate Kirilov and his suffering and, on the other hand, to undercut Abogin. We may object to reducing the conflict of Abogin and Kirilov to a Marxist class struggle, but we cannot avoid treating the question of Chekhov's uneven treatment of his two protagonists.

What is the problem here? Perhaps it is only an aesthetic one. We need only imagine the problem a theatrical adaptation of "The Enemies" would present to a director who understood the story exclusively in its ecumenical dimension. How should one depict Abogin? How does one convey two realities: the fact that on the subjective plane of experience Abogin really does suffer the apparent illness of his wife and then her deceit (suffering is suffering), and the fact that on the objective plane of expression, where the spectacle of suffering and personality is concerned, Abogin comes across as slightly foppish, certainly shallow, and in some respects even comic? In his major plays, Chekhov resolved this kind of problem through characterizations that combine in miraculous ways the comic and the lyrical, the tragic and the ridiculous. There is no trace of such an approach here.

Let us now turn our attention to the question of imbalances in Chekhov's characterization of Kirilov and Abogin. "The most lofty beauty is not without but within," Dostoevsky once observed. Unattractive and ungainly in looks and shape, harsh and embittered in manner, seemingly indifferent to life and people through prolonged contact with a bitter reality, Kirilov nonetheless emerges as a person of dark strength and integrity, one who has lived his values. "Looking at his desiccated figure," the narrator remarks, "one would not believe that this person had a wife, that he could weep over a child."

The opening two lines of the story introduce us to the Kirilovs' suffering. The first sentence is like a terse comunique: "At around ten o'clock on a dark September evening the district doctor Kirilov's only child, the six-year-old Andrei, died of diphtheria." Words here seek not to express an attitude toward the event, but simply to convey stark, terrible fact. Comment is superfluous. The second sentence is dominated by one image, that of the Pieta. "Just as the doctor's wife sank on her knees by the dead child's bed and was overwhelmed by the first wave of despair, there came a sharp ring at the bell in the entry." The bell that breaks the silence of the Kirilovs' suffering announces the arrival of Abogin and, as we shall see, the intrusion into the story of a radically different expression of suffering, one that announces itself at every turn and is full of superfluous commentary.

Abogin's first wave of words, his appeal to the doctor for assistance, is met by silence. "Kirilov listened and was silent, as though he did not understand Russian speech." Abogin's second attempt to break through the silence is met by a recapitulation of the story's terse opening line: "Excuse me, I can't go . . . Five minutes ago . . . my son died . . ." Abogin, stunned, momentarily seems to consider leaving; nevertheless, he continues to press the doctor to come. But "a silence ensued." In the moments that follow (a page and a half of the text) the reader is drawn into the bleak and tragic world of the death scene. Every detail speaks mutely of the catastrophe: Kirilov standing with his back to Abogin; his unsteady, mechanical walk; the unlighted lamp; Kirilov's glance into an unidentified "thick book" lying on the table (one may presume, perhaps, that the book is the Bible); the reference to a "stranger" in the entry. The stranger is not only Abogin; as in Chekhov's story "Kashtanka," the stranger is also death, as dark as the unlighted lamp that Kirilov abstractedly touches as he passes into the bedroom.

"Here in the bedroom reigned a dead silence," writes the narrator. "Everything to the smallest detail spoke eloquently of the storm that had just been experienced, about exhaustion, and everything was at rest." Again, the details are singular: the candle, the bottles, the large lamp illuminating the room, the mother kneeling down before the bed, and on the bed "a boy with open eyes and an expression of wonder on his face." Death is closure, but the open eyes of wonder erase the line that separates life from death. Only at the end of this silent scene does the narrator speak directly of the ensemble of death, suffering, and beauty we have witnessed.

> That repellent horror that people think of when they speak of death was absent from the bedroom. In the pervading numbness, in the mother's pose, in the indifference on the doctor's face, there was something that attracted and touched the heart, precisely that subtle, almost elusive beauty of human sorrow that it will take men a long time to learn to understand and describe, and that it seems only music can convey. Beauty was also felt in the somber stillness; Kirilov and his wife were silent and not weeping, as though besides the anguish of their loss they were conscious, too, of all the poetry of their condition.

The reader thinks the obvious: that Chekhov has learned to understand and paint such suffering, that "the elusive beauty of human sorrow" such as we find in this first scene of "The Enemies" is like music. The reader could think further that although there is absolutely no basis for anybody to say, "What I call beauty is beauty, and what you call beauty is ugliness," nonetheless Chekhov in "The Enemies" has presented to us in this tableau his own conception of the "beauty of human sorrow," his own "feeling of beauty," his own poetics of suffering. Whether or not Chekhov's own tableau of sorrow, anymore than Botticelli's or Michelangelo's, carries any objective weight is a matter for each reader to decide. What is certain, however, is that Chekhov stands in intimate relation to the Pietà he has created.

"I myself am profoundly unhappy," Abogin tells the increasingly disturbed and angry Kirilov after he, Abogin, has learned of his wife's betrayal. Kirilov responds scornfully, "Unhappy? Do not touch this word; it does not concern you." In any ordinary sense Kirilov's remark is absurd. Suffering is suffering. Abogin, our head tells us, suffers in his own way. Yet Chekhov depicts the suffering Abogin in a way that demeans his suffering. The spectacle of suffering of the Kirilovs is lyrical, tragic. The spectacle of suffering of Abogin is melodramatic and lowered by the details of his personality and surroundings.

Let us go back, for a moment, to the first scene in which the narrator introduces Abogin to us. "Is the doctor at home?" asks the person who enters the room. "I am at home," answers Kirilov. "What do you want?" "Oh, it's you? I'm very glad!" rejoiced the newcomer (*ochen' rad, obradovalsia voshedshii*), and he began feeling in the dark for the doctor's hand, found it, and squeezed it tightly in his own. "I'm very . . . very glad! [*Ochen', ochen' rad*] We are acquainted! I'm Abogin . . . and I had the pleasure of seeing you in the summer at Gnuchev's. I'm very glad [*ochen' rad*] that I found you in . . . For God's sake [*Boga radi*] don't refuse to come with me now . . . My wife is dangerously ill . . . And I've a carriage. . . . On the way to you I suffered terribly [*isstradalsia dushoi*]."

Abogin is distressed. The narrator notes in his shaking voice "an unaffected sincerity and childlike uncertainty." Frightened and overwhelmed, he spoke in brief, jerky sentences and "uttered a great many unnecessary, irrelevant words." His selection of words, indeed, contradicts the seriousness and urgency of his mission. The word *rad* (glad) is repeated often, by itself and within words: *obradovalsia, isstradalsia*. It produces a strangely incongruous effect, in view of Abogin's distress. Finally, his *Boga radi* and *radi Boga* almost pass into *radi Abogina* (for Abogin's sake). And indeed this is how Abogin incongruously comes across to us. It is a fact worth noting that the word *Bog* (God) in one form or another is repeatedly on Abogin's lips, in his name, A-bog-in, *Boga radi, radi Boga, Bozhe moe, vidit Bog, Ei-Bogu*, and *Dai-to Bog*. By contrast, the name of God only once passes the lips of Kirilov. Only the "thick book" hints at Kirilov's relationship to God. No words about love or sacrifice pass his lips. On the other hand, we learn that Abogin loved his wife "fervently like a slave" (*Ja liubil nabozhno* [the root of this word is *bog*, or god] *kak rab*), that "he sacrificed the civil service and music" (*brosil sluzhbu i muzyku*) for his wife. Indeed, there is no music in his life, or perhaps, religion—if we choose to remember the double meaning of *sluzhba* (both "service" as in civil service and "service" as in religious services).

The "irrelevant" words *rad* (glad, happy) and *udovol'stvie* (pleasure) that crop up in Abogin's speech are signal words: they are not merely expressions of a distressed man who has lost control of his language, but they point to a residual sense of self-satisfaction and egoism that characterizes the man. The narrator speaks of Abogin's "contentedness [*sytost'*], health, and assurance." Even before his quarrel with Abogin, Kirilov early observes in Abogin's house "a stuffed wolf as substantial and content [*sytyi*] as Abogin himself." This expression of "contentedness" (*sytosti*), the narrator notes, only disappears when Abogin learns of his wife's deception. But as he waits for his carriage a short while later, we are told, "he regained his expression of contentedness [*sytosti*] and refined elegance."

There is, indeed, something childishly, naively, egotistically *radi Abogina* (for the sake of Abogin) about Abogin and his use of words. "Doctor, I'm not made of wood [*doktor, ja ne istukan*], I understand your situation perfectly. . . . I sympathize with you." But there is something oddly unfeeling about Abogin. We have translated the word *istukan* as "piece of wood"; it also means "idol" or "statue," figuratively, a person without feeling. Whether we ascribe it to his distress, to something basic in his personality, or to both, there is something out of place in Abogin's way of expressing himself: "My God," he says pleadingly to Kirilov, "You have suffering, I understand, but really I am inviting you not to do some dental work or to a consultation, but to save a human life! . . . A life is higher than any personal suffering! Really, I'm asking for courage, for heroism! in the name of humanity!"

Without any question, Abogin is terribly upset. He is out of touch with his words; it may even be said that Abogin's tone contradicts his words. Yet our words, even in crises, say something about ourselves. There is something banal and shallow about this man. "You never love those close to you as when you are in danger of losing them," Abogin says to Kirilov when, at last, the two men are on their way to Abogin's house. There is some truth in this observation. Yet it is a truth that is not usually uttered by one who directly faces the loss of a loved one. Authentic love does not comment on itself. "If something happens [to her]," Abogin exclaims in the carriage, "I won't survive it!" (*Esli chto sluchitsia, to . . . ia ne perezhivu*). The focus here is oddly upon himself. Later when he learns of his wife's deception, he more truthfully declares: "Oh, God, better that she should have died! I won't be able to bear it! I won't be able to bear it!" (*Ia ne vynesu! Ne vynesu ia!*). Again the focus is upon himself.

"Abogin was sincere," the narrator remarks early in the story about Abogin's way of expressing himself, "but it was remarkable that whatever words he uttered all sounded stilted, soulless, and inappropriately flowery and even seemed to do violence to the atmosphere of the doctor's home and to the woman who was somewhere dying. He felt this himself, and therefore, fearing to be misunderstood, did everything possible to give his voice a softness and tenderness, so that at least sincerity of tone, if not his words, would take effect." Abogin is by no means a man without genuine feelings. He is arguably sympathetic in his tortured naïveté; he reaches out to Kirilov (he presses his hand on meeting him, touches him several times as though to establish human contact and to awaken Kirilov from the numbness of grief). Yet Chekhov makes it difficult for us to respond sympathetically to him: "In general the phrase, however lofty and profound it may be, acts only on the indifferent but cannot always satisfy those who are happy or unhappy; therefore the highest expression of happiness or unhappiness is most often silence; lovers understand each other better when they are silent, while a feverish, passionate speech spoken at the grave moves only bystanders, whereas to the widow or children of the deceased it seems cold and insignificant."

The classical Greek view was that every character is at the root of his own fate. In the case of Abogin, the style is the man. This slightly foppish and contented man—this naive and shallow man who abandoned music and the service slavishly to attend to a capricious and fast-living wife—is the kind of banal character to whom banal things happen. The more we learn about him and see him in his own environment, the more we find some connection between his character and his bedroom melodrama. Just as his eyes "laugh with pain," so his suffering has a touch of the burlesque. Here is how the narrator describes Abogin at the time he discovers his wife's betrayal: The sound *a!* (is it only a coincidence that the first letter of Abogin's name announces his grotesque entry?) echoes from the room in which he first realizes that his wife has absconded with Papchinsky. If, as suggested at the outset of our discussion, Chekhov indeed intended the name Abogin to be understood as a Greek-Russian hybrid (with the *a* in his name representing the Greek alpha privitive meaning "without"), then the sound that he despairingly utters when he discovers that his wife has deceived him may conceal a Chekhovian joke: Abogin, who has worshiped his wife like a slave, is suddenly "without" his deity, his god.

Abogin enters the living room.

His expression of satiety and refined elegance had disappeared; his face, hands, his whole stance, were contorted by a repulsive expression combining horror and the torment of physical pain. His nose, his lips, his moustache—all his features were moving and seemed to be trying to tear themselves from his face; his eyes looked as though they were laughing with pain. . . . Abogin took a heavy and wide step into the middle of the drawing room, bent forward, moaned, and shook his fists. "She has de*ceiv*ed me!" he cried, strongly accenting the second syllable. "She's gone off! . . . with that clown Papchinsky! My God!" Abogin stepped heavily toward the doctor, thrust his white soft fists to his face, and shaking them continued to wail: "She has gone off! Deceived me! But why this lie?! My God! My God! . . . What did I do to her? She's gone off!" Tears gushed from his eyes. . . . Now in his short coat and his fashionable narrow trousers in which his legs looked disproportionately slim, and with his big head and mane, he extraordinarily resembled a lion. . . . "A sick person! a sick person!" cried out Abogin, laughing, weeping, all the while shaking his fists.

Echoes of the irrelevant *rad* appear, of course, in this last reference to "laughing, weeping." Indeed, the melodramatic scene before us, like Abogin's suffering, seems to border on tragicomedy or even farce. "If you marry big-rich, rage around big-rich, and then act out a melodrama, what has this got to do with me?" exclaims Kirilov after listening to Abogin pour out his family secrets. "Who gave you this right to mock another man's sorrow?" Kirilov blindly observes. Yet what has Abogin's suffering got to do with Kirilov's? And can we—how much are we supposed to empathize with Abogin? We remember well Kirilov's gratuitous and cruel dismissal of Abogin as a clown, his characterization of Abogin's bedroom drama as farce, his savage comparison of Abogin's unhappiness or suffering to that of a capon who is unhappy because it is overweight. "Worthless people!" Of course, Kirilov, like Abogin in the first scene, has lost control of his words, his touch with reality; his portrait of Abogin is a gross caricature. We forget, however, that Chekhov has provided us with an image of Abogin and his suffering that lends a certain credibility to this cruel caricature. In this connection, it is noteworthy that toward the end of the story the narrator suggests that had the doctor been able to listen to Abogin instead of heaping abuse on him, Abogin "might have reconciled himself to his sorrow without protest." The suggestion here is that a more sympathetic response on Kirilov's part might have helped assuage Abogin's grief. Yet it appears that such a gesture was not necessary. We are informed a little later that when Abogin leaves his house his usual "expression of satiety and refined elegance" have returned to him.

Beverly Hahn maintains that "it is Abogin who progressively gains the story's sympathy and Kirilov, in his arrogant rejection of Abogin's suffering, who loses some of it." I do agree that this is what should happen. Unfortunately, I do not think Abogin rises very much in our estimation at the end of the story or that Kirilov appreciably suffers. In short, I do not think that Chekhov succeeds wholly in overcoming a certain residual lack of sympathy for Abogin. More important, the reader is ill prepared for the sermonic words with which the narrator reproaches Kirilov at the end of the story. Chekhov's message is clear. The point is that it is too clearly a message.

Sisyphus in the eponymous myth is condemned to roll a stone to the top of the mountain only to have it roll down again to the foot of the mountain, and so on. I see Chekhov in "The Enemies" in the same position as Sisyphus. More than any other Russian writer in the nineteenth century Chekhov approaches humankind "with malice toward none, with charity for all" (to borrow our words from Lincoln). But Chekhov was also human. Had there not been a bit of the *vrag*, or "enemy," in him, there would have been no charity. I think Chekhov understood this when he wrote "The Enemies."

LIZA KNAPP

Fear and Pity in "Ward Six": Chekhovian Catharsis

In the middle of "Ward Six (Palata No. 6, 1892), Chekhov notes in passing that "people who are fond of visiting insane asylums are few in this world." And yet Chekov has conspired to make the reader of his story feel like an actual visitor in the mental ward of a provincial hospital. After an initial paragraph describing the exterior of the hospital, he invites the reader to enter the hospital premises with him as a guide: "If you are not afraid of being stung by the nettles, let us go along the narrow path." As soon becomes apparent, these nettles are not all the visitor to ward 6 or the reader of "Ward Six" need fear. Warnings of the perils and hardships of a journey to this godforsaken place recall the beginning of Dante's *Divine Comedy*, for to enter ward 6 is indeed to "abandon all hope."

Chekhov found himself writing this story, one he considered uncharacteristic and in some ways unappealing, since it "stinks of the hospital and mortuary," in 1892, less than two years after his journey to the penal colony of Sakhalin. As he worked on "Ward Six," a fictional "visit" to an insane asylum, Chekhov had for various reasons interrupted work on the factual, scholarly account of his visit to the penal colony. Still, in many ways, "Ward Six" was a response to the trip, a response more indirect, in form, than *The Island of Sakhalin*, but, in essence, perhaps just as immediate.

That mental wards and penal institutions were associated in Chekhov's

From *Reading Chekhov's Text*. © 1993 by Northwestern University Press.

mind is demonstrated by a series of comparisons made in the story. In the first paragraph he mentions "that particular desolate, godforsaken look which is exclusive to our hospital and prison buildings." When Dr. Ragin first puts on his hospital *khalat*, he feels "like a convict." At one point, ward 6 is called a "little Bastille." Repeated references to the bars over the windows of ward 6 emphasize its likeness to a prison: lack of physical freedom and of human dignity is suffered in both places.

Chekhov directly formulates the link between these two locales in a letter he wrote to Suvorin, explaining his motivation for visiting Sakhalin. "The much-glorified sixties," writes Chekhov, "did *nothing* for the sick and for prisoners and thereby violated the chief commandment of Christian civilization." Chekhov believed that he and others shared a collective responsibility for eliminating, alleviating, or at the very least acknowledging the suffering that takes place, with an exceptionally high concentration, in these two locales, penal institutions and hospitals, places that nobody wants to visit, much less, of course, to inhabit.

In this spirit, Chekhov visited the island of Sakhalin, this "place of unbearable suffering of the sort only man, whether free or subjugated, is capable of." Chekhov visited Sakhalin partly because he felt that it was time that Russia stopped ignoring the suffering that went on there. He wrote: "It is evident that we have let *millions* of people rot in jails, we have let them rot to no purpose, unthinkingly and barbarously. We have driven people through the cold, in chains, across tens of thousands of versts, we have infected them with syphilis, debauched them, bred criminals and blamed it all on red-nosed prison wardens. Now all educated Europe knows that all of us, not the wardens, are to blame." Furthermore, he tells Suvorin that were he a "sentimental man, [he'd] say that we ought to make pilgrimages to places like Sakhalin the way the Turks go to Mecca."

"Ward Six" stands as the literary equivalent of a pilgrimage, not to a penal colony, but to an analogous place, a mental ward, with its own "red-nosed warden," whose guilt, Chekhov would have us believe, we all share. The point of a pilgrimage, be it that of a Muslim to Mecca, a Christian to Golgotha, a Russian subject to Sakhalin, or Chekhov's reader to ward 6, is to gain greater understanding of another's experience and suffering (Muhammad's, Christ's, an inmate's) by imitating the experience and suffering of another, by following physically in another's footsteps. Pilgrims do whatever they can to make the other's experience their own. They may not be able to duplicate what the other has lived through, but they can try to find out what it is like. The experience of a pilgrimage becomes the empirical equivalent of a simile.

The premise of Chekhov's story, like that of a pilgrimage, is that suffering cannot be understood in the abstract. One needs to have it made as immediate as possible. That reading Chekhov's story has the effect of making one feel as if one were in ward 6 has been attested by many of its readers, prominent among them being Vladimir Lenin, who commented: "When I finished reading the story last night, I started to feel literally sick; I couldn't stay in my room. I got up and went out. I felt as if I, too, had been incarcerated in Ward 6." Such a statement suggests more than the notion that, as Leskov put it, "Ward 6 is everywhere. It's Russia," for it also reveals what seems to have been Chekhov's intent in the story: to play on the reader's emotions so that he or she feels what it is like to be locked up in ward 6.

In evoking in the reader a response to the suffering that is witnessed in ward 6, Chekhov aims at evoking pity and fear, the same emotions that, according to Aristotle, a good tragedy will evoke in its audience. In his *Poetics*, Aristotle defines *pity* as the emotion we feel for undeserved suffering and *fear* as the emotion we feel when we witness the suffering of someone like ourselves." Aristotelian pity and fear at times cease to be two discrete emotions, since, as one scholar puts it, "we pity others where under like circumstances we should fear for ourselves. Those who are incapable of fear are incapable also of pity." Both emotions are related to the concept of *philanthropia*, or love for one's fellow man, which for the Greeks meant that one should have sympathy for one's fellow man, this sympathy stemming from a recognition of solidarity with others. One should take another's "misfortunes as a warning of one's own insecurity." Tragic events reveal "the precariousness of the human condition" and thus "make men fear for themselves." At the root of the fear is a recognition that one is much like the tragic protagonist, that one is "endowed with similar capacities and exposed to similar dangers."

Fear, as understood by Aristotle, is predicated upon the recognition, however subliminal, of a similarity between the self and the other whose suffering is witnessed. The basic mental operation involved is the same as that described by Aristotle elsewhere in the *Poetics* when he discusses similes and metaphors, which are based on the intuition of similarites between different phenomena. In recognizing similarities between disparate phenomena, we should not go so far as to equate them. At the same time that we recognize similarities, we must bear the differences in mind. We need not have lived through what tragic heroes live through; rather, we, as audience, put ourselves in their place and fall into a mood in which, according to Butcher, "we feel that we too are liable to suffering." Tragedy thus has the effect of making the public less complacent and of reminding them that their own good fortune may be precarious.

A strategy to be learned from Greek tragedy and epic is that if you want another to take pity on you and do something for you—for example, to give your father asylum (Antigone in *Oedipus at Colonus*) or to surrender your son's body for burial (Priam in *The Iliad*)—the best way is to make that person fearful. You make that person realize that what you are suffering could happen to him or her. Hence, Antigone tells the people of Colonus who were shunning her and her father to look on her "as if [she] were a child of [theirs]" and to "take pity on [her] unhappiness." By bringing her plight home to them in this manner, Antigone gains their sympathy. Similarly, Priam, trying to get Achilles to give him Hector's body, tells him: "Take pity upon me remembering your father." He creates fear in Achilles by reminding him that his own father will be in an analogous situation, since Achilles is fated to die soon. The strategy works, for, as "he spoke, [Priam] stirred in [Achilles] a passion of grieving for his own father," and this, in turn, moved Achilles to relinquish Hector's body. These Greek heroes implicitly realize that fear for oneself serves as a catalyst for bringing about pity for another, insofar as people use themselves as a point of reference.

Chekhov demonstrates his understanding of the dynamics of Aristotelian fear and pity in "The Duel," written in 1891, a year before 'Ward Six.' We are told that earlier when Laevsky loved Nadezhda Fedorovna, her suffering (in the form of her illness) "evoked pity and fear in him (*vozbuzhdala v nem zhalost' i strakh*), whereas once that love has been obscured, he no longer responds empathetically to her suffering." Although Chekhov mentions these Aristotelian concepts in a seemingly casual way, they appear to be central to "The Duel," especially to the moments of tragic recognition it describes.

In "Ward Six" Chekhov explores the mechanics of pity and fear on two levels: not only does he seek to arouse these emotions in his readers as they witness the suffering of the inmates, but he also makes pity and fear dynamic forces within the story, by having the main drama result from the fact that neither of the two protagonists can respond adequately when he witnesses the suffering of others. In Dr. Ragin, the capacity for experiencing fear and pity has atrophied, whereas in Gromov it has hypertrophied.

Already an inmate of ward 6 when the action begins, Ivan Dmitrich Gromov suffers from a "persecution mania." Although a series of personal misfortunes had left him in an unstable mental state, excessive fear, leading to his mental collapse and incarceration, was triggered when he found himself the chance witness to the misfortune of others. We are told that Gromov was going about his business one autumn day when "in one of the side streets, he came upon two convicts in chains accompanied by four armed guards. Ivan Dmitrich had often encountered convicts and they always aroused in him feelings of pity and discomfort, but this time he was strangely and unaccountably affected. For some reason he suddenly felt that he *too* could be clapped in irons and led in this same way through the mud to prison." At the sight of the convicts, Gromov realizes that he is exposed to similar dangers, and the result is fear. But his anxiety then develops into a persecution complex that debilitates him and threatens to engulf all else, even his pity for other people.

> At home he was haunted all day by these convicts and soldiers with rifles, and an inexplicable mental anxiety prevented him from reading or concentrating. He did not light his lamp in the evening and at night he was unable to sleep, but kept thinking that he too could be arrested, clapped in irons, and thrown into prison. He knew of no crime in his past and was confident that in the future he would never be guilty of murder, arson or theft, but was it not possible to commit a crime by accident, without meaning to, and was not calumny too, or even a judicial error, conceivable?

Gromov's feeling of "there but for the grace of God go I," his initial sympathetic pity for the convicts, and the concomitant fear for himself quickly give way to a nearly psychopathic self-pity as he imagines his own arrest for a crime he did not commit. In a dangerous mental leap, Gromov goes from a wise recognition that such misfortune is something that could happen to him to the unhealthy delusion that it was happening to him, or was about to.

To a certain degree, Chekhov may be using Gromov's fear of judicial error to draw attention to the prevailing lack of faith in Russian justice. Indeed, in Sakhalin, Chekhov had learned of many cases of people being convicted of crimes they did not commit. Gromov's fears of incarceration become a self-fulfilling prophecy when he ends up imprisoned in ward 6. From the Aristotelian point of view, were Gromov nothing more than the innocent victim of the obviously flawed Russian system, his situation would shock the reader but not evoke the deeper emotions of fear and pity; in the *Poetics*, Aristotle argues that the misfortune of a completely innocent man is more "shocking" than "fearful and pitiful." Chekhov appears to make Gromov into something of a tragic hero, one whose particular flaw may be seen as his tendency to excess in his response to the world. In what may be a reference to Aristotle's ethical ideal of the golden mean, we are told that, with Gromov, "there was no middle ground" (*serediny zhe ne bylo*). Gromov's tragic flaw lies in his immoderate response to the suffering of others.

In contrast, Dr. Andrei Efimych Ragin, who is in charge of the ward, shut his eyes to the suffering he witnesses. At one point, Gromov notes that heartlessness may be an occupational hazard afflicting judges, physicians, and police, that is, people who "have an official, professional relation to other men's suffering." Dr. Ragin's callousness may be related to this phenomenon. The doctor's indifference to suffering manifests itself in his motto, "It's all the same" (*vsë ravno*). He elevates this colloquial verbal tick to the status of a general philosophical view that nothing matters. But the phrase literally means that it is all the same, that all is equivalent, that everything is like everything else, that there is no difference between one thing and another. In other words, Ragin sees false similarities or equivalencies. When he asserts the similarity between a comfortable study and ward 6, between a frock coat and an inmate's smock, the doctor vilely abuses the capacity for contemplating likenesses that, according to Aristotle, is the tool of the philosopher.

Dr. Ragin, in insisting that everything is equivalent, recalls the "philosopher" Chekhov refers to in *The Island of Sakhalin* when he writes of convicts that "if he is not a philosopher, for whom it is all the same where and under what conditions he lives, the convict can't, and shouldn't, not want to escape." In Chekhov's lexicon, the term *philosopher* stands as a pejorative epithet for someone who has withdrawn into his mind. The blind assertion of similarities between disparate phenomena, such as Dr. Ragin practices, constitutes a disregard for the physical world and for life itself.

At the time he wrote "Ward Six," Chekhov had been reading the *Meditations* of Marcus Aurelius, who preached a mix of philanthropy and retirement within the self. "If you are doing what is right," claims Marcus Aurelius, "never mind whether you are freezing with cold or beside a good fire; heavy-eyed or fresh from a sound sleep." In his long conversations with Gromov, Dr. Ragin echoes this notion of the equivalence of all physical states and the primacy of the inner world of the self. When Ragin presents Gromov with such platitudes as "In any physical environment you can find solace within yourself" or "The common man looks for good or evil in external things: a carriage, a study, while the thinking man looks for them within himself," Gromov counsels him to "go preach that philosophy in Greece, where it's warm and smells of oranges; it's not suited to the climate here." His point is that the doctor, in asserting the equivalence of all external things, uses his own comfortable existence as his point of reference. The more Gromov argues that there is a difference in climate between Russia and Greece, that there is a difference between being hungry and having enough to eat, that there is a difference between being beaten and not, the more it becomes apparent that Ragin's tragic flaw lies in his unwillingness to concede these differences.

For Chekhov, such differences were quite real, and philosophical pessimism such as Ragin's was anathema to him. In a letter of 1894, in which he reveals his views on some of the issues explored in "Ward Six," Chekhov directly suggests that his own commitment to progress results from the fact that differences between various physical states (differences of the kind ignored by Ragin) mattered to him. He writes: "I acquired my belief in progress when still a child; I couldn't help believing in it, because the difference between the period when they flogged me and the period when they stopped flogging me was enormous." Life had schooled him in such a way that he strove to improve physical conditions in an attempt to alleviate suffering. Dr. Ragin, in maintaining that "it is all futile, senseless," and that "there is essentially no difference between the best Viennese clinic and [this] hospital," violates the values of the medical profession, since, from Chekhov's point of view, doctors ought to believe in material progress.

In "Ward Six" Chekhov points out the root meaning of the doctor's indifference: as he ceases to perceive the differences among real phenomena, the world becomes one big, senseless simile where everything is like everything else, or one big, senseless tautology. In keeping with this worldview, he fails to respond to the suffering around him. The phrase that he keeps repeating to Gromov, "What is there to fear? (*chego boiat'sia?*), is the Aristotelian corollary of "It's all the same" (*vsë ravno*). Dr. Ragin does nothing to alleviate the suffering he witnesses because he is indifferent to it; he feels no fear and consequently no pity. Whereas Gromov was overcome by manic fear and self-pity, Ragin shows an exaggerated indifference to the suffering of others. But for both, the net result is the same: incarceration in ward 6. Gromov suggests that Ragin fails to respond to the suffering of others because he has never suffered himself. According to Gromov, Ragin's acquaintance with reality (which for Gromov is synonymous with suffering) has remained theoretical. Having never been beaten as a child, having never gone hungry, the doctor has had no firsthand knowledge of suffering and no conception of what it is to need.

All this changes when Dr. Ragin himself becomes an inmate in ward 6. At first, as Nikita takes away his clothes, Ragin clings to his indifference: "'It's all the same [*vsë ravno*] . . .' thought Andrei Efimych [Ragin], modestly drawing the dressing gown around him and feeling that he looked like a convict in his new costume. 'It's all the same [*vsë ravno*] . . . Whether it's a frockcoat, a uniform, or this robe, it's all the same [*vsë ravno*]' . . . Andrei Efimych was convinced even now that there was no difference between Byelova's house [his former residence] and Ward No. 6." But soon, the physical differences that the doctor had so long denied become apparent:

> Nikita quickly opened the door, and using both hands and his
> knee, roughly knocked Andrei Efimych to one side, then drew

back his fist and punched him in the face. Andrei Efimych felt as though a huge salty wave had broken over his head and was dragging him back to his bed; there was, in fact, a salty taste in his mouth, probably blood from his teeth. Waving his arms as if trying to emerge, he caught hold of somebody's bed, and at that moment felt two more blows from Nikita's fists in his back.

Ivan Dmitrich [Gromov] screamed loudly. He too was evidently being beaten.

Then all was quiet. The moon shed its pale light through the bars, and on the floor lay a shadow that looked like a net. It was terrible. Andrei Efimich lay still, holding his breath, waiting in terror to be struck again. He felt as if someone had taken a sickle, thrust it into his body, and twisted it several times in his chest and bowels. He bit the pillow and clenched his teeth with pain; and all of a sudden out of the chaos there clearly flashed through his mind the dreadful, unbearable thought that these people, who now looked like black shadows in the moonlight, must have experienced this same pain day in and day out for years. How could it have happened that in the course of more than twenty years he had not known, had refused to know this? Having no conception of pain, he could not possibly have known it, so he was not guilty, but his conscience, no less inexorable and implacable than Nikita, made him turn cold from head to foot.

Only when he himself experiences physical pain does Dr. Ragin know what fear is: He waited "in terror to be struck again." The question, "What is there to fear?" (*chego boiat'sia?*) is no longer a rhetorical one; one answer is pain. Only now does he sense his true kinship with Gromov and others, for now he understands the suffering that he had witnessed day in and day out for years (or which he would have witnessed had he gone to work every day as he was supposed to).

In this story, Chekhov explores the epistemology of suffering and seems to suggest that the surest route to an understanding of suffering is to experience it directly, for yourself. This is ultimately what happens to Dr. Ragin at the end of "Ward Six." But by the time Dr. Ragin gets an idea of what the inmates of ward 6 have endured day in and day out, he is about to die, having, in a sense, been destroyed by his realization, and he can do nothing about it.

Chekhov outlines a tragic situation for which there are many precedents. For example, what happens to Ragin is similar to what happens to King Lear, who takes pity on what he refers to as "houseless heads and unfed sides" only after he, too, finds himself homeless and hungry. Lear realizes that when he had been in a position to help those in need, he had "ta'en / Too little care of this!" If you want to know what suffering is like, then you should "expose [your]self to feel what wretches feel." But the physical suffering of feeling what powerless wretches feel, combined with mental anguish, kills Lear. Like Lear, Ragin realizes that he had neglected both his professional and his human duties only when it is too late to do anything about them.

Although he presents tragic situations of this sort, Chekhov refuses to romanticize suffering. It may heighten consciousness, or as Ragin argues, it may indeed differentiate man's life from that of an amoeba, but at the same time it destroys the physical organism, and under such circumstances the enlightenment serves little practical purpose. An essential difference exists between the fear experienced by the witness of mimetic suffering and that experienced by the witness (and especially by the victim) of actual suffering. The latter debilitates, whereas the former, according to Aristotle, does not. As one critic puts it, "Tragic fear, though it may send an inward shudder through the blood, does not paralyze the mind or stir the senses, as does the direct vision of some impending calamity. And the reason is that this fear, unlike the fear of common reality, is based on the imaginative union with another's life. The spectator is lifted out of himself. He becomes one with the tragic sufferer and through him with humanity at large." For the inmates of ward 6, fear stuns, paralyzes, and even kills. But the reader who "visits" ward 6 may, by being "lifted out of himself," learn from the fear witnessed through the medium of art. The reader may even be motivated to act on behalf of the sick and prisoners, thereby fulfilling what Chekhov referred to as "the chief commandment of Christian civilization."

According to Aristotelian scholars, "the purpose of the catharsis of pity and fear is not to drain our emotional capacities so that we are no longer able to feel these emotions; instead it is to predispose us to feel emotion in the right way, at the right time, towards the right object, with the right motive, and to the proper degree." The protagonists of Chekhov's story fail to undergo catharsis upon witnessing the actual suffering of others. The pity and fear Gromov experienced as he watched the convicts' suffering became pathological, developed into a mania, and found no outlet, whereas Ragin for years exhibited a pathological inability to feel pity and fear upon witnessing the suffering of others. He fears and pities only when the suffering becomes his own. But these emotions are not purged; on the contrary, they, combined with the physical pain they accompany, destroy the doctor.

Chekhov arouses fear and pity in his reader by making the suffering of others seem real and matter to the reader, who in this way is spared the actual trip to ward 6, spared actually putting on an inmate's smock, and, above all, spared actually being beaten by Nikita. To this end, Chekhov makes the fictional (mental) visit to ward 6 as vivid as possible. He concentrates on physical details, on the stench of the place that makes you feel as though "you've entered a menagerie," on the bars on the window, and so forth, lest the reader ever try to ignore the difference between a comfortable study and ward 6.

In trying to evoke fear and pity in the reader, Chekhov employs many similes, the simile itself being the poetic device that, by suggesting a physical image for something, "undoes the withdrawal from the physical world of appearances—which characterizes mental activities." Since "Ward Six" is about, among other things, the perils of withdrawing from the physical world into an abstract world of mental activity, the simile becomes a particularly important literary device. Chekhov uses the simile to rouse the reader and force him or her back into the physical world. He uses it as an antidote to the indifference resulting from withdrawal into one's self. In the passage describing the doctor's first beating and the tragic recognition it brings about within him, Chekhov uses a series of similes: the taste of blood in Ragin's mouth is compared to a salty wave breaking over his head, the pain of being beaten is compared to that of having a sickle thrust into his body; more interestingly, Ragin's conscience is compared to Nikita. Chekhov uses these similes to make what Ragin undergoes more vivid and real to the reader, who may never have been beaten and who may also be tempted to use ignorance as a moral subterfuge. "Ward Six" is affective and effective largely because Chekhov makes proper, judicious, and artistic use of the very faculty that is impaired in his two heroes, Gromov and Ragin, the faculty for contemplating similarities. Their respective disorders, which are two extremes of the same continuum, prevent them from experiencing fear and pity in a healthy, moderate, cathartic fashion.

Chekhov uses his literary skills, especially his artistic faculty for contemplating likenesses, to encourage his readers to empathize with the inmates of ward 6, to recognize the full horror of ward 6 by feeling that there is a kinship between them and the inmates. He does not lose sight, however, of the fact that differences exist. One difference is that the fictional visitor to ward 6, unlike the inmate, may have the actual power, freedom, and/or strength to fight to eliminate senseless suffering. The inmate is locked in ward 6, but the reader is not. The reader should not, in Chekhov's words, simply "sit within [his] four walls and complain what a mess God has made of creating man."

GARY SAUL MORSON

Uncle Vanya *as Prosaic Metadrama*

Solyony: I have never had anything against
you, Baron. But I have the temperament
of Lermontov. [Softly] I even look like
Lermontov . . . so they say . . .
   —Chekhov, *The Three Sisters*

Theater of Theatricality

It might be said that the fundamental theme of Chekhov's plays is theatricality itself, our tendency to live our lives "dramatically." In Chekhov's view, life as we actually live it does not generally conform to staged plots, except when people try to endow their lives with a spurious meaningfulness by imitating literary characters and scenes. Traditional plays imitate life only to the extent that people imitate plays, which is unfortunately all too common. There are Hamlets in life primarily because people have read *Hamlet* or works like it. The theater has been realistic only when people have self-consciously reversed mimesis to imitate it.

Such reverse mimesis is typical of Chekhov's major characters. His plays center on histrionic people who imitate theatrical performances and

From *Reading Chekhov's Text*. © 1993 by Northwestern University Press.

model themselves on other melodramatic genres. They posture, seek grand romance, imagine that a tragic fatalism governs their lives, and indulge in utopian dreams while they neglect the ordinary virtues and ignore the daily processes that truly sustain them. Such virtues—the prosaic decencies in which Chekhov deeply believed—are typically practiced by relatively undramatic characters who do not appreciate their own significance. In the background of the play and on the margins of its central actions, truly meaningful prosaic life can be glimpsed.

Because histrionics is Chekhov's central theme, his plays rely to a great extent on metatheatrical devices. Those devices show us why the world is *not* a stage and why we should detect falsity whenever it seems to resemble a play. Metatheatricality is most obvious in *The Sea Gull*, Chekhov's first major dramatic success. Indeed, Chekhov's use of the technique in this play borders on the heavy-handed. We have only to recall that one major character, an actress, behaves as theatrically with her family as she does on the stage; that her son is a playwright who devotes his life to romantic longing and *ressentiment*; that an aspiring young actress tries to reenact the romance of a famous novel by sending its author a quotation from it; that citizens from *Hamlet* suffuse the action; and, of course, that a play-within-a-play provides the point of reference for all other events. *Uncle Vanya* dispenses with much of this overt machinery while still maintaining the metatheatrical allusions it was designed to create. In effect, the internal play expands to become the drama itself. Like a committee of the whole, *Uncle Vanya* becomes in its entirety a sort of play-within-a-play.

As a result, the work reverses the usual foreground and background of a drama. In most plays people behave "dramatically" in a world where such behavior is appropriate. The audience, which lives in the undramatic world we all know, participates vicariously in the more interesting and exciting world of the stage. That, indeed, may be one reason people go to the theater. In *Uncle Vanya* the characters carry on just as "dramatically" as anyone might expect from the stage, but they do so in a world that seems as ordinary and everyday as the world of the audience. Consequently, actions that would be tragic or heroic in other plays here acquire tonalities of comedy or even farce. Chekhov never tired of reminding Stanislavsky and others that his plays were not melodramas but precisely (as he subtitled *The Sea Gull* and *The Cherry Orchard*) comedies. Chekhov gives us dramatic characters in an undramatic world order to satirize all theatrical poses and all attempts to behave as if life were literary and theatrical. Histrionics for Chekhov was a particularly loathsome form of lying, which truly cultured people avoid "even in small matters."

Chekhov's toying with, the dramatic frame may be seen as a particularly original use of a traditional satiric technique. Like his great predecessors in parody, he transforms his main characters into what might be called "generic refugees." That is, he creates characters who would be at home in one genre but places them in the world of another. So Don Quixote, Emma Bovary, and Ilya Ilych Oblomov become comic when forced to live in a realistic world rather than the chivalric adventure story, the romantic novel, or the idyll of which they dream. *War and Peace* places its epic hero, Prince Andrei, in a novelistic world where epic heroism is an illusion; *Middlemarch* confers refugee status on Dorothea in its Prelude about how she, like Saint Theresa, needed an "epic life" to realize her potential but, in the nineteenth century, could find only prosaic reality. As these examples show, this technique does not preclude an admixture of sympathy in the satire.

Chekhov's main characters think of themselves as heroes or heroines from various genres of Russian literature, which is ironic, of course, because they are characters in Russian literature. Having read the great authors, they, like many members of the *intelligentsia*, plagiarize significance by imitating received models. Here it is worth observing that the Russian term *intelligentsia* does not mean the same thing as the English word *intelligentsia*, which underwent a shift in meaning when borrowed from the Russian. In Russian, an *intelligent* (member of the intelligentsia) was not necessarily an intellectual, and not all intellectuals were *intelligenty*. A member of the *intelligentsia* was identified as such by a particular way of living—bad manners of a specified sort were important—and above all by a complex of attitudes, including militant atheism, an opposition to all established authority, socialism, and a mystique of revolution. Prosaic virtues were regarded as unimportant, if not harmful, and a taste for the grand and dramatic was cultivated. *Intelligenty* were expected to adopt one or another grand system of thought that purported to explain all of culture and society and promised an end to all human suffering if a given kind of revolution should take place; the function of the *intelligentsia* was to adopt the right system and make sure its recommendations were put into practice. To do so, solidarity—what Chekhov despised as intellectual conformism—was needed. If by *intellectual* we mean someone characterized by independence of thought, we can see how it was easily possible for an intellectual to be an "antiintelligentsial" and for an *intelligent* to be antiintellectual. A member of an *intelligentsia* "circle," even if he never read a book, would be considered an *intelligent* more readily than Leo Tolstoy, who expressed utter contempt for this whole complex of beliefs and lived a manifestly nonintelligentsial life.

Not surprisingly, this dominant tradition of the *intelligentsia* generated a countertradition of thinkers who rejected its fundamental premises. Tolstoy's masterpieces, *War and Peace* and *Anna Karenina*, explicitly attack all grand systems of thought, all attempts to find hidden laws of history, and, consequently, all prescriptions for universal salvation. For Tolstoy, and the countertradition generally, it is not the dramatic events of life that matter, either for individuals or for societies, but the countless small, prosaic events of daily life.

It was above all this aspect of Tolstoy's thought that had the most profound influence on Chekhov, who, as we have seen, constantly expressed the deepest skepticism about the intelligentsial mentality and valued everyday virtues. Invited to join one *intelligentsia* circle, Chekhov responded with an accusation of hypocrisy and a restatement of his most cherished values—honesty and simple acts of kindness, for which "you've got to be not so much the young literary figure as just a plain human being. Let us be ordinary people, let us adopt the same attitude *toward all*, then an artificially over-wrought solidarity will not be needed." In the twentieth century this countertradition—the kind of thought I call prosaics—has been represented by that remarkable anthology of essays by disillusioned *intelligenty*, *Landmarks: A Collection of Essays on the Russian Intelligentsia* (1909); by Mikhail Zoschenko; and by the literary and cultural critic Mikhail Bakhtin.

Both Chekhov and Tolstoy understood that the prestige of the *intelligentsia* cast a shadow on educated society as a whole and predisposed people to adopt grand roles drawn from literature. Chekhov's characters imagine that they are heroes or heroines in a genre suffused with romance, heroism, great theories, and decisive action, or else they try to play the lead roles in tragic tales of paralyzing disillusionment and emptiness. They consider themselves to be either heroes or "heroes of our time." But their search for drama unfolds in Chekhov's universe of prosaics.

In its examination of histrionics, *Uncle Vanya* is in a position to exploit metatheatrical devices. *Uncle Vanya* is theater about theatricality, and so its main characters, are continually "overacting." One reason the play has proven so difficult to stage in the right tonality— as critics and directors have constantly noted—is that the actors must overact and call attention to their theatrical status but without ceasing to play real people who truly suffer. They must not over-overact. Their performance must allude to but not shatter the dramatic frame.

When we watch *Uncle Vanya*, we do not see actors playing characters. We see characters playing characters. They labor under the belief that this role-playing brings them closer to "true life," but in fact it does the opposite. The audience contemplates real people—people like themselves—who live citational lives, that is, lives shaped by literary role-playing, lives consisting not so much of actions as of allusions. We are asked to consider the extent to which our own lives are, like the title of this play, citational.

TURGENEV'S GOUT

> If criticism, the authority of which you cite,
> knows what you and I don't, why has it kept mum
> until now? Why doesn't it disclose to us the truth
> and immutable laws? If it had known, believe me,
> it would long ago have shown us the way and we
> would know what to do. . . . But criticism keeps
> pompously quiet or gets off cheap with idle,
> worthless chatter. If it presents itself to you as
> influential, it is only because it is immodest,
> insolent, and loud, because it is an empty barrel
> that one involuntarily hears. Let's spit on all this.
> —Chekhov, letter to Leontiev-Shcheglov,
>   March 22, 1890

Chekhov places members of the *intelligentsia* at the center of his play because they are especially given to self-dramatization and because they love to display their superior culture. As they cite novels, criticism, and other dramas, Chekhov shapes his metaliterary satire of histrionics and intelligentsial posing.

Old Serebryakov, we are told at the very beginning of the play, was a former theology student and the son of a sexton. These are just the roots one would choose if one's goal was to display a typical member of the *intelligentsia*. A professor of literature, he peevishly demands that someone fetch his copy of the poet Batyushkov, looks down on those with fewer citations at their disposal, and tries to illuminate his life with literary models.

He makes even his illness allusive: "They say that Turgenev developed angina pectoris from gout. I'm afraid I may have it." At the beginning of his speech to the assembled family in act III, he first asks them "to lend me your ears, as the saying goes [*Laughs*]." As is so often the case in Chekhov's plays, the line is more meaningful than he knows, for the speech he has prepared, like that of his Shakespearean model, is made under false pretenses. Appropriately enough, he continues his game of allusions by citing Gogol's famous play—"I invited you here, ladies and gentlemen, to announce that the Inspector General is coming"—evidently without having considered that its action concerns confidence games. Like *Uncle Vanya*, *The Inspector General* involves multiple layers of role-playing, mutually reinforcing poses, and self-induced self-deceptions. In his last appearance of the play, the professor proposes to transform its action into yet another occasion for professional criticism. "After what has happened, I have lived through so much, and thought so much in the course of a few hours, that I believe I could write a whole treatise for the edification of posterity." It is hard to decide whether to call this line pathetic or repulsive, but in either case it ought to disturb us professionals more than it has.

If the old professor projects ill-considered confidence in his merely citational importance, then Voinitsky, who has at last understood such falsities, can only create new ones. He realizes that for most of his life he has been content with a vicarious connection to the professor's vicarious connection to literature, but all he learns from his disillusionment is that the professor was the wrong intermediary.

Given our own views of the professor, we may take at face value Voinitsky's denunciation of his work as an uncomprehending and momentarily fashionable deployment of modish but empty jargon. But that only makes Voinitsky's desire for a better connection with literature even more misguided. Filled with all the self-pity, impotent rage, and underground *ressentiment* of a disappointed member of the *intelligentsia*, he regrets that he is too old to surpass the professor at his own game. Chekhov brilliantly merges despair and slapstick humor—we seem to check ourselves in midlaugh—when Voinitsky declares: "My life is over! I was talented, intelligent, self-confident . . . If I had had a normal life, I might have been a Schopenhauer, a Dostoevsky . . ." To put it mildly, the choice of Dostoevsky as an example of someone who lived "a normal life" suggests a rather odd (but intelligentsial) understanding of normality. And we are aware of Dostoevsky's penchant for describing the very mixture of megalomania and self-contempt that Vanya so pathetically displays.

As if to mock both Voinitsky's precarious connection to literature and his self-indulgent pleas for pity, Chekhov has the ridiculous and truly pitiful Telegin interrupt the scene of confrontation. Telegin insists on his own incredibly vicarious link to scholarship:

> TELEGIN [*embarrassed*]: Your Excellency, I cherish not only a
> feeling of reverence for scholarship, but of kinship as well. My
> brother Grigory Ilych's wife's brother—perhaps you know
> him—Konstantin Trofimovitch Lakedomonov, was an M.A. . . .
> VOINITSKY: Be quiet, Waffles, we're talking business.

In Telegin's pathetic "perhaps you know him" and in the truly Gogolian name Lakedomonov we may perhaps detect another allusion to *The Inspector General.* In Gogol's play, Pyotr Ivanovich Bobchinsky would feel his life were worthwhile if the powers that be knew of his mere existence:

BOBCHINSKY: I humbly beg you, sir, when you return to the capital, tell all those great gentlemen—the senators and admirals and all the rest—say, "Your Excellency or Your Highness, in such and such a town there lives a man called Pyotr Ivanovich Bobchinsky." Be sure to tell them, "Pyotr Ivanovich Bobchinsky lives there."

KHLESTAKOV: Very well.

BOBCHINSKY: And if you should happen to meet with the tsar, then tell the tsar too, "Your Imperial Majesty, in such and such a town there lives a man called Pyotr Ivanovich Bobchinsky."

KHLESTAKOV: Fine.

Telegin is a Bobchinsky for whom professors have replaced admirals. Voinitsky seems unaware that he treats Telegin with the same disregard that he so resents in the professor's treatment of him.

Voinitsky is undoubtedly correct that his mother's "principles" are, as he puts it, a "venomous joke." As he now sees, she can only repeat received expressions "about the emancipation of women," without being aware that her own behavior verges on an unwitting counterargument. Her actions also suggest unconscious self-parody as she, presumably like so many shallow members of the *intelligentsia*, constantly "makes notes on the margins of her pamphlet." This stage direction closes act I, and the phrase is repeated by a number of characters, so by the time the stage directions repeat it again at the very end of the play, we are ready to apply Voinitsky's phrase about the professor—*perpetuum mobile*—to her as well. Her first speech concerns these insipid pamphlets that she imagines to be, in Voinitsky's phrase, "books of wisdom."

Her devotion to intelligentsial concerns has led her to idolize the old professor; she alone remains unaware that he is not what he pretends to be. But it is not so much her vacuity as her small, incessant acts of cruelty to her son that deprive her so totally of the audience's sympathy. As her son regrets his wasted life, she reproaches him in canned phrases for not caring more about the latest intellectual movements: "You used to be a man of definite convictions, an enlightened personality." We may imagine that Voinitsky's rage at the professor's proposal to deprive him of the estate is fueled to a significant extent by resentment of his mother, who repeats, as she has evidently done so often, "Jean, don't contradict Aleksandr. Believe me, he knows better than we do what is right and what is wrong." Even the professor, who has utter contempt for her, is not so intolerable as she is. Perhaps he senses, as we do, that as Telegin is a paltry double of Voinitsky, so Maria Vasilievna farcically duplicates him.

Idleness and the Apocalypse of Squabbles

Elena Andreevna, the professor's young wife, and Astrov, the doctor who is summoned to treat him, each combine prosaic insight with melodramatic blindness. Though they often fail to live up to the standards they recommend, they do glimpse the value of everyday decency and ordinary virtues. They even understand, more or less, the danger of histrionic behavior, cited self-pity, and grand gestures, all of which nevertheless infect their own speeches. For this reason, Chekhov can use these speeches to enunciate the play's central values while simultaneously illustrating the consequences of not taking these values seriously enough.

Elena comes closest to a Chekhovian sermon as she fends off Voinitsky in act II:

> ELENA ANDREEVNA: Ivan Petrovich, you are an educated, intelligent man, and I should think you would understand that the world is being destroyed not by crime and fire, but by hatred, enmity, all these petty squabbles . . . Your business should be not to grumble, but to reconcile us to one another.
> VOINITSKY: First reconcile me to myself! My darling . . .

Elena is absolutely right: life is spoiled not by grand crises or dramatic disappointments but by "petty squabbles." It is all the more ironic, then, that in praising prosaic virtues she cannot avoid images of catastrophe and the rhetoric of apocalypse. Characteristically, her choice of words strikes Voinitsky most: "All that rhetoric and lazy morality, her foolish, lazy ideas about the ruin of the world—all that is utterly hateful to me."

Perhaps Chekhov intended Elena as an allusion to Dorothea Brooke, although Elena lacks Dorothea's unshakable integrity. Elena married the professor, just as Voinitsky worked for him, out of an intelligentsial love. Her speech about petty squabbles suggests that she has reflected on his daily pettiness and self-centered petulance, which he explicitly justifies as a right conferred by his professorial status. And so Elena, who has studied music at the conservatory, requires and does not receive permission to play the piano.

Elena understands that something is wrong, but not what would be right. We first see her in act I ignoring, almost to the point of the grotesque, the feelings of Telegin:

> TELEGIN: The temperature of the samovar has fallen perceptibly.

ELENA ANDREEVNA: Never mind, Ivan Ivanovich, we'll drink it cold.

TELEGIN: I beg your pardon . . . I am not Ivan Ivanovich, but Ilya Ilych . . . Ilya Ilych Telegin, or, as some people call me because of my pockmarked face, Waffles. I am Sonichka's godfather, and His Excellency, your husband, knows me quite well. I live here now, on your estate . . . You may have been so kind as to notice that I have dinner with you every day.

SONYA: Ilya Ilych is our helper, our right hand. [*Tenderly*] Let me give you some more tea, Godfather.

If these lines are performed as I think Chekhov meant them, one will detect no reproach, no irony, in Telegin's voice. He has so little self-esteem that he expects to be overlooked, and so he reminds people of his existence—or of his brother's wife's brother's existence—sincerely, out of a sense that he is too insignificant to be remembered even when he is constantly present. Chekhov uses Telegin as a touchstone for the basic decency of other characters: is it worth their while to be kind to someone who is obviously of no use to anyone? In this scene, Elena fails the test, and Sonya, who calls him Godfather, passes it. Voinitsky, we remember, calls him Waffles, a nickname that only the pathetic Telegin could possibly accept and even repeat.

Elena does not work but, rather, as Astrov observes, infects everyone around her with her idleness. The old nurse speaks correctly when she complains that many of the household's ills derive from the visitors' disruption of old habits, habits related to work. A schedule, arrived at over the course of decades and carefully calibrated so that the estate can be well managed, has been replaced by a purely whimsical approach to time: Marina is awakened to get the samovar ready at 1:30 in the morning.

The *intelligentsia* may view habits as numbing, but from the standpoint of prosaics, good or bad habits more than anything else shape a life. Attention, after all, is a limited resource, and most of what we do occurs when we are concentrating on something else or on nothing in particular, as the sort of action and dialogue in Chekhov's plays makes clear. And yet it is the cumulative effect of all those actions, governed largely by habit, that conditions and indeed constitutes our lives. Moreover, habits result from countless earlier decisions and therefore can serve as a good index to a person's values and past behavior. That, indeed, is one reason Chekhov emphasizes them so much and one way in which he makes even short literary forms so resonant with incidents not directly described. Chekhov's wiser characters also understand that attention can be applied to new problems that demand more than habit only if good habits efficiently handle routine concerns. They keep one's mental hands free.

Relying on beauty, charm, and high ideals—she really has them— Elena does not appreciate the importance of habits, routine, and work. For her, life becomes meaningful at times of high drama, great sacrifice, or passionate romance. That is to say it can be redeemed only by exceptional moments. Consequently, when those moments pass, she can only be bored. Sonya tries to suggest a different view. She values daily work and unexceptional moments, but Elena cannot understand:

> ELENA ANDREEVNA [*in misery*]: I'm dying of boredom, I don't know what to do.
> SONYA [*shrugging her shoulders*]: Isn't there plenty to do? If you only wanted to . . .
> ELENA ANDREEVNA: For instance?
> SONYA: You could help with running the estate, teach, take care of the sick. Isn't that enough? When you and Papa were not here, Uncle Vanya and I used to go to market ourselves to sell the flour.
> ELENA ANDREEVNA: I don't know how to do such things. And it's not interesting. Only in idealistic novels do people teach and doctor the peasants, and how can I, for no reason whatever, suddenly start teaching and looking after the peasants?
> SONYA: I don't see how one can help doing it. Wait a bit, you'll get accustomed to it. [*Embraces her*] Don't be bored, darling.

Elena significantly misunderstands Sonya. Given her usual ways of thinking in literary terms, she translates Sonya's recommendations into a speech from an "idealistic novel." That, presumably, is why she ignores the possibility of helping with the estate and singles out teaching or doctoring the peasants. She imagines that Sonya offers only a ridiculous populist idyll.

If that were what Sonya meant, Elena's objections would be quite apt. Her misunderstanding allows Chekhov to make a characteristically prosaic point about meaningful activity. In the Russian countertradition, the dynamics and significance of work—daily, ordinary work—figure as a major theme. Elena's only idea of work corresponds to a view that Levin learns to reject in *Anna Karenina*—work "for all humanity"—and she correctly rejects that choice as work "for no reason whatever." What she cannot understand is the possibility of a different sort of work that would be meaningful: prosaic work.

Thinking like a member of the *intelligentsia*, she believes that either meaning is grand and transcendent or else it is absent. Her mistake in marrying the professor has convinced her that transcendent meaning is an illusion, and so she, like Voinitsky, can imagine only the opposite, a meaningless world of empty routine extending endlessly. But Sonya's actual recommendation, like the sort of daily work Levin describes as "incontestably necessary," implicitly challenges the very terms of Elena's, and the *intelligentsia*'s, dialectic.

Sonya recommends taking care of the estate *because it has to be done*. She can draw an "incontestable" connection between getting the right price for flour and making the estate operate profitably or between not allowing the hay to rot and not indulging in waste, which is troubling in itself. Like Tolstoy, Chekhov had utter contempt for the *intelligentsia*'s (and aristocracy's) disdain of efficiency, profitability, and the sort of deliberate calculation needed to avoid waste. That is one reason the play ends with the long-delayed recording of prices for agricultural products.

When Elena characterizes caring for peasants as a purely literary pose, Sonya replies that she does not see "how one can help doing it." For Sonya, it is not a literary pose, and it serves no ideology but is part of her more general habits of caring for everyone. High ideals or broad social goals have nothing to do with her efforts on behalf of others, as we see in this very passage when she responds not with a counterargument but with a sympathetic embrace of the despairing Elena.

Sonya understands that both work and care require habits of working and caring. One has to know how they are done, and they cannot just be picked up "suddenly," as Elena correctly observes. Elena has the wrong habits, and that is her real problem. What she does not see is that she needs to begin acquiring new ones, which is what Sonya is really recommending.

WASTE BY OMISSION
those graceful acts,
Those thousand decencies, that daily flow.
—Milton, *Paradise Lost*

Least of all does Elena need romance, which is what Astrov offers. Like Elena and Voinitsky, he is obsessed with the vision of a brief, ecstatic affair in a literary setting. You are bound to be unfaithful sometime and somewhere, he tells Elena, so why not here, "in the lap of nature . . . At least it's poetic, the autumn is really beautiful . . . Here there is the plantation, the dilapidated country houses in the style of Turgenev." He might almost have said in the style of Chekhov. When this pathetic attempt at seduction fails, Astrov intones "Finita la commedia," a line that, interpreted literally, does correctly characterize his desire for romance as comic, if not farcical. When he repeats "Finita!" soon afterward, the possibility of farce grows stronger.

Astrov constantly looks for literary or theatrical images to explain his life. "What's the use?" he asks at the beginning of the play. "In one of Ostrovsky's plays there's a man with a large moustache and small abilities. That's me." In fact, these self-pitying allusions make him a good example of the "more intelligent" members of the *intelligentsia* as he describes them:

> ASTROV: . . . it's hard to get along with the intelligentsia—they
> tire you out. All of them, all our good friends here, think and
> feel in a small way, they see no farther than their noses: to put
> it bluntly, they're stupid. And those who are more intelligent
> and more outstanding, are hysterical, eaten up with analysis and
> introspection . . . They whine. . . . [*He is about to drink*]
> SONYA [*stopping him*]: No, please, I beg you, don't drink any more.

Of course, this very speech exemplifies the *intelligentsia*'s indulgence in self-pitying self-analysis. Astrov whines about whining, and what's more, he knows it. But this self-knowledge does him no good for reasons that Chekhov frequently explores.

Some self-destructive behavior can be modified by an awareness of what one is doing, but not the sort of introspection that Astrov describes. On the contrary, the more one is aware of it, the more that awareness becomes a part of it. (Perhaps that is what Karl Kraus meant when he said that psychoanalysis is the disease that it purports to cure.) The more Astrov blames himself for whining, and for whining about whining, the more he whines about it. This sort of introspective self-pity feeds on itself; so does alcoholic self-pity, which is why Chekhov has him drink while complaining.

To persuade him not to drink, Sonya reproaches Astrov for contradicting himself. "You always say people don't create, but merely destroy what has been given them from above. Then why, why, are you destroying yourself?" And in fact, Astrov has spoken powerfully about waste and the need for prosaic care; his speeches are the closest Chekhov comes to a Tolstoyan essay or to one of Levin's meditations.

Astrov's lectures on what we would now call "the environment" sound so strikingly contemporary that it is hard to see them in the context of Chekhov's play. In a way not uncommon in literary history, their very coincidence with current concerns provokes critical anachronism or the interpretation of them as detachable parts. It is worth stressing, therefore, that Astrov does not object to any and all destruction of trees. "Now I could accept the cutting of wood out of need, but why devastate the forests?" he says. "You will say that . . . the old life must naturally give place to the new. Yes, I understand, and if in place of these devastated forests there were highways, railroads, if there were factories, mills, schools, and the people had become healthier, richer, more intelligent—but, you see, there is nothing of the sort!" The chamber of commerce might well concur.

What bothers Astrov, what bothers Chekhov, is waste. And waste results from the lack not of great ideals but of daily care. The forests disappear for the same reason that the hay rots. After Sonya offers her breathless paraphrase of Astrov's ideas, Voinitsky, with his clothes still rumpled and his bad habits showing, refuses to see the point:

> VOINITSKY [*laughing*]: Bravo, bravo! . . . All that is charming,
> but not very convincing, [*to Astrov*] and so, my friend, allow
> me to go on heating my stoves with logs and building my
> barns with wood.
> ASTROV: You can heat your stoves with peat and build your
> barns with brick. . . . The Russian forests are groaning under
> the ax . . . wonderful landscapes vanish never to return, and all
> because lazy man hasn't sense enough to stoop down and pick
> up fuel from the ground.

What destroys the forests, and what destroys lives, is not some malevolent force, not some lack of great ideas, and not some social or political evil. Trees fall, and lives are ruined, because of thoughtless behavior, everyday laziness, and bad habits, or, more accurately, the lack of good ones. Destruction results from what we do not do. Chekhov's prosaic vision receives remarkably powerful expression in these passages.

Astrov and Sonya also give voice to that vision when they describe how the ruin of forests is not just an analogue for but also a cause of needlessly impoverished lives. To paraphrase their thought: the background of our lives imperceptibly shapes them, because what happens constantly at the periphery of our attention, what is so familiar that we do not even notice it, modifies the tiny alterations of our thoughts. Literally and figuratively, our surroundings temper the "climate" of our minds. Like good housekeeping and careful estate management, unwasted forests subtly condition the lives unfolding in their midst.

Where Sonya, and especially Astrov, go wrong is in their rhetoric, which, like Elena's, becomes rapidly apocalyptic or utopian. They intone lyrical poetry celebrating prosaic habits and praise undramatic care with theatrical declamation:

> SONYA: If you listen to him [Astrov], you'll fully agree with him. He says that the forests . . . teach man to understand beauty and induce in him a nobility of mind. Forests temper the severity of the climate. In countries where the climate is mild, less energy is wasted in the struggle with nature, so man is softer and more tender; in such countries the people are beautiful, flexible, easily stirred, their speech is elegant, their gestures graceful. Science and art flourish among them, their philosophy is not somber, and their attitude toward women is full of an exquisite courtesy . . .
>
> . . . .
>
> ASTROV: . . . maybe I am just a crank, but when I walk by a peasant's woodland which I have saved from being cut down, or when I hear the rustling of young trees which I have planted with my own hands, I realize that the climate is some what in my power, and that if, a thousand years from now, mankind is happy, I shall be responsible for that too, in a small way. When I plant a birch tree and then watch it put forth its leaves and sway in the wind, my soul is filled with pride, and I . . . [*seeing the workman who has brought a glass of vodka on a tray*] however . . . [*Drinks*]

They expect a lot from trees. The doctor and his admirers show enthusiasm in the sense Dr. Johnson defined the word: a vain belief in private revelation. Sonya's enthusiasm reflects her love for Astrov, but what does Astrov's reflect? In his tendency to visionary exaggeration, in his millenarian references to the destiny of all mankind, we sense his distinctly unprosaic tendency, in spite of everything, to think in the terms of drama, utopias, and romance—and to drink.

Chronology

1860   Anton Pavlovich Chekhov born January 17 in Taganrog, Crimea, to Pavel Yegorovich, a grocer, and Eugenia Morozov. Chekhov's grandfather had bought his way out of serfdom just twenty years earlier.

1875   Chekhov's father, forced into bankruptcy, flees Taganrog for Moscow. Chekhov's family is evicted from their home, but Chekhov decides to remain in Taganrog to complete his high school education.

1879   Chekhov moves to Moscow. There he rejoins his family and enrolls in the University of Moscow to study medicine.

1880   Begins contributing humorous short stories and sketches to magazines in Moscow and St. Petersburg under the penname Antosha Chekhonte.

1884   Begins medical practice.

1886   "Vanka" published. Begins fruitful correspondence with Dmitri Grigorovich, a well-established Russian writer.

1887   *Ivanov*, Chekhov's first play, is produced in Moscow to mixed reviews.

1888   Wins the Pushkin Prize for Literature from the Russian
        Academy of Sciences. "The Steppe" published.

1889   *The Wood Demon*, a early prototype for *Uncle Vanya*, closes after three
        performances. Chekhov's brother Nikolai dies of tuberculosis.

1890   Travels to Siberia to report on the Sakhalin Island penal colony.
        During his research there, he interviews up to 160 people a day.

1891   When famine hits the nearby Russian provinces, Chekhov works
        to relieve the cholera epidemic that ensues among the serf popu-
        lation. This work becomes material for his short story written
        concurrently, "The Peasants."

1892   "Ward No. 6" published.

1894   "Rothschild's Fiddle" and "The Student" published.

1896   *The Sea Gull* produced at the Alexandra Theatre in the fall to
        disappointing crowds.

1897   *Uncle Vanya* published. First diagnosed with consumption, or
        pulmonary tuberculosis, a disease that will eventually prove fatal.

1898   "Gooseberries" published.

1899   Moves to Yalta with his family after his father's death. *Uncle Vanya*
        opens in Moscow to large audiences. *The Sea Gull*, which failed in
        its first production, reopens at the Moscow Art Theater, also with
        success. "Lady with Lapdog" published.

1901   *Three Sisters* published. Marries Olga Knipper, a member of the
        Moscow Art Theater troupe.

1902   "The Bishop" published.

1903   "The Betrothal" published.

1904   *The Cherry Orchard* produced in January with great acclaim.
        Chekhov dies on July 2 in Germany, of pulmonary tuberculosis
        at age 44.

Contributors

ERIC BENTLEY was born in 1916. He is a literary critic, a translator and a writer on theater. From 1953 to 1969 he was the Brandes-Matthews Professor of Dramatic Literature at Columbia University in New York. He has published numerous dramatic and critical works including: *The Recantation of Galileo Galilei*; *The Playwright as Thinker*; *In Search of Theatre*; *The Theatre of Commitment* and, as editor and translator, *Seven Plays by Bertold Brecht* and *Naked Masks* by Pirandello.

HAROLD BLOOM is Sterling Professor of Humanities at Yale University and Berg Professor at New York University. He is an extraordinarily prolific and innovative author of many literary critical works including: *The Anxiety of Influence*; *Breaking the Vessels*; *Ruin the Sacred Truths*; *The Western Canon* and *The Book of J*. He has edited numerous collections of literature and critical essays, including the present collection.

DAVID COLE is a playwright and scholar. His plays include *The Moments of The Wandering Jew* and *The Muse of Self Absorption*. He is the author of *Acting as Reading*, winner of the George Jean Nathan Award for Dramatic Criticism, 1992–93, and of *The Theatrical Event*.

MARTIN ESSLIN was born in 1918 in Budapest, Hungary. In 1938, he fled Vienna where he was studying to become a director, to escape the Nazi invasion of Austria. He became a British citizen and worked as writer and drama critic for the BBC. His most influential book, *The Theater of the Absurd*, came out in 1961 and has been consistently reissued. Other works by him include: *Reflections: Essays on Modern Theatre; The Peopled Wound: The Work of Harold Pinter* and a collection of his radio talks for Britain's Open University, *An Anatomy of Drama*.

FRANCIS FERGUSSON is Professor of Comparative Literature at Princeton University. She has published numerous critical studies, including *The Idea of Theater: A Study of Ten Plays* and other works on Dante, Chekhov, Greek plays, dramatic literature and poetry.

MICHAEL C. FINKE is a professor of Russian language and literature at Washington University in St. Louis. He has written about Chekhov and Pushkin.

MAXIM GORKY was a Russian novelist, short-story writer and playwright. From his birth in 1868 until his early 20's Gorky lived in terrible poverty and by hard labor. After this period, he started to write and publish. He was imprisoned several times for his Marxist writings and for his participation in the Revolution of 1905. He was a friend to various famous writers in Russia, including Chekhov. After the Revolution, because of his commitment to the revolutionary principles, Gorky was able to intercede and often save the life of many literary figures. Among his numerous works are: *Mother*; his autobiographical trilogy, *Childhood, In the World* and *My Universities; Notes from a Diary; The Artamonov Business* and various plays.

ROBERT LOUIS JACKSON was born in 1923 in New York City. He is the B. E. Bensinger Professor of Slavic Languages and Literatures at Yale University. He is also the President of the International Chekhov Society. His numerous writings include: *The Art of Dostoevsky: Deliriums and Nocturnes; Dialogues with Dostoevsky: The Overwhelming Questions; Reading Chekhov's Text* and other essays on Turgenev, Gogol, Chekhov, Dostoevsky, Pasternak, Tolstoy and other writers.

LIZA KNAPP is a professor of Slavic Language and Literatures at the University of California, Berkeley. She has written on Dostoevsky, Chekhov, Tolstoy and Marina Tsvetaeva.

RUFUS W. MATHEWSON, JR. was born in 1919. He was chairman of the Department of Slavic Languages and professor of Russian and Comparative Literature at Columbia University, New York. As a teacher and writer, he significantly influenced the work of several generations of Russian scholars and teachers. Among his writings are his book, *The Positive Hero in Russian Literature* and several essays on Chekhov. He died in Brooklin, ME in 1978.

CHARLES E. MAY is a professor of English at California State University, Long Beach. Among his writings are: *Short Story Theories;* and his six-volume work-in-progress, *The Theory and History of Short Fiction* and more than 100 essays mainly concerned with the short story.

GARY SAUL MORSON was born in 1948 in New York City. He is the Frances Hooper Professor of Arts and Humanities and Professor of Slavic Languages at Northwestern University. He is author of *The Boundaries of Genre: Dostoevsky's "Diary of a Writer" and the Traditions of Literary Utopia; Hidden in Plain View: Narrative and Creative Potentials in "War and Peace"* and of other works on Tolstoy, Dostoevsky, Chekhov, Turgenev and Bahktin.

HOWARD MOSS was born in New York City in 1922. He was a poet, critic, editor and teacher. For forty years he was poetry editor for *The New Yorker*. His poetic works include *Selected Poems*, winner of the National Book Award in 1971 and *New Selected Poems*, winner of the Leonore Marshall National Prize for Poetry in 1986. His critical works include *Writing Against Time* and *Magic Lantern of Marcel Proust*. He died in 1987.

LEON (LEV) SHESTOV was a Russian existentialist philosopher and religious thinker. He was born in Kiev in 1866 and died in Paris in 1938. His translated works include. *All Things Are Possible, Penultimate Words and Other Essays* and *In Job's Balances*.

RAYMOND WILLIAMS was born in Wales in 1921. He has served as a lecturer, a fellow, a director and a reader of English Studies at Jesus College, Cambridge. He has written and edited a large number of critical works and several plays and novels. These include: *Reading and Criticism; Drama from Ibsen to Brecht; Culture and Society: 1780–1950; Keywords* and his *Border Country* trilogy.

VIRGINIA WOOLF was born in 1882 in London and committed suicide in 1941. She is recognized as one of the most innovative novelists and experimental essayists of Modernism. Numbered among her works are: *To the Lighthouse; A Room of One's Own; Mrs. Dalloway* and *Between the Acts.*

Bibliography

Bentley, Eric, and Theodore Hoffman. *The Brute, and Other Farces*. New York: Grove Press, 1958.

Bristow, Eugene K. *Anton Chekhov's Plays*. Norton Critical Edition. New York: Norton, 1977.

Dunnigan, Ann, trans. *Chekhov: The Major Plays*. New York: 1964.

Letters on the Short Story, the Drama and Other Literary Topics by Anton Chekhov. Selected and ed. by Louis S. Friedland. 2nd. ed., rpt. New York: Dover Publications, 1966.

The Letters of Anton Pavlovich Tchehov to Olga Leonardovna Knipper. Trans and ed. by Constance Garnett. New York: Benjamin Blom, 1966.

Letters of Anton Chekhov. Trans. by Micheal H. Heim in collaboration with Simon Karlinsky. New York: Harper & Row, 1973.

Hingley, Ronald. *The Oxford Chekhov*, 9 vols. Oxford: Oxford University Press, 1965–1980.

Jarrel, Randall. *The Three Sisters*. New York: Macmillan, 1969.

Matelaw, Ralph E., ed. *Anton Chekhov's Short Stories: Texts of the Stories, Background, Criticism*. New York: Norton, 1979.

Yarmolinsky, Avrahm. *The Unknown Chekhov: Stories and Other Writings*. London, 1959.

———, ed. *The Portable Chekhov*. New York: Viking, 1947; 2nd ed., 1968.

Bibliographies

Lantz, Kenneth A. *Anton Chekhov: A Reference Guide to Literature*. Boston: G. K. Hall, 1985.

Senderovich, Savely and Munir Sendich, eds. *Anton Chekhov Rediscovered. A Collection of New Studies with a Comprehensive Bibliography*. East Lansing, MI: Russian Language Journal, 1987.

Yachnin, Rissa. *The Chekhov Centennial: Chekhov in English: A Selective List of Works by and About Him, 1949–1960*. New York: Public Library, 1960.

Biographies

Chukovsky, Kornei. *Chekhov the Man.* Trans. P. Rose. London: Hutchinson and Co., 1945.
Ermilov, Victor. *Anton P. Chekhov: 1860–1904.* Trans. Ivy Litvinov. Moscow: Foreign Language Publishing House, 1953.
Hingley, Ronald. *A New Life of Anton Chekhov.* New York: Alfred A. Knopf, 1976.
Koteliansky, S. S., ed. and trans. *Anton Tchekhov: Literary and Theatrical Reminiscences.* New York: 1927; rpt. New York: Blom, 1965.
Koteliansky, S. S. and L. Woolf, trans. *Reminiscences of Anton Chekhov by M. Gorky, A. Kuprin, and I. A. Bunin.* New York: B.W. Huebsch, 1921.
Magarshack, David. *Chekhov: A Life.* 1953; rpt. Westport, CT: Greenwood Press, 1970.
Nemirovsky, Irene. *A Life of Chekhov.* Trans. E. de Mauny. London: Grey Walls Press, 1950.
Rayfield, Donald. *Anton Chekhov: A Life.* London: HarperCollins Publishers, 1997.

Criticism: Books

Barricelli, Jeane-Pierre, ed. *Chekhov's Great Plays: A Critical Anthology.* New York: New York University Press, 1981.
Bitsilli, Petr M. *Chekhov's Art: A Stylistic Analysis.* Trans. T. W. Clyman and E. J. Cruise. Ann Arbor, MI: Ardis Press, 1983.
Chudakov, Alexander P. *Chekhov's Poetics.* Trans. E. Cruise and D. Dragt. Ann Arbor, MI: Ardis Publishers, 1983.
Debreczeny, Paul, and Thomas Eekman, eds. *Chekhov's Art of Writing: A Collection of Critical Essays.* Columbus, OH: Slavica Publishers, 1977.
Debreczeny, Paul, and Roger Anderson, eds. *Russian Narrative and Visual Art: Varieties of Seeing.* 1994.
De Maegd-Soep, Carolina. *Chekhov and Women: Women in the Life and Work of Chekhov.* Columbus, OH: 1987.
Eekman, Thomas, ed. *Critical Essays on Anton Chekhov.* Boston: G. K. Hall & Co., 1989.
Emeljanow, Victor, ed. *Chekhov: The Critical Heritage.* London, Boston and Henley: Routledge and Kegan Paul, 1981.
Gottlieb, Vera. *Chekhov in Performance in Russia and Soviet Russia.* Alexandria, VA: Chadwyck Healey, 1984.
Hahn, Beverly. *Chekhov: A Study of the Major Stories and Plays.* London: Cambridge University Press, 1988.
Jackson, Robert L., ed. *Chekhov: A Collection of Critical Essays.* Englewood Cliffs, NJ: Prentice-Hall, 1967.
Jackson, Robert, L., ed. *Reading Chekhov's Text.* Evanston, IL: Northwestern University Press, 1993.
Kramer, Karl D. *The Chameleon and the Dream: The Image of Reality in Chekhov's Stories.* The Hague: Mouton, 1970.
Nilsson, Nils Ake. *Studies in Chekhov's Narrative Technique: "The Steppe" and "The Bishop".* A Univ St. Stockholm: Almqvist and Wiksell, 1968.
Pervukhina, Natalia. *Anton Chekhov: The Sense and the Nonsense.* New York: Ottawa, 1993.
Roken, Freddie. *Theatrical Space in Ibsen, Chekhov and Strindberg: Public Forms of Privacy.* Ann Arbor, MI: UMI Press, 1986.
Senderovich, Savely, and Munir Sendich, eds. *Anton Chekhov Rediscovered: A Collection of New Studies with a Comprehensive Bibliography.* East Lansing, MI: 1987.

Valency, Maurice. *The Breaking String: The Plays of Anton Chekhov.* New York: Oxford University Press, 1966.

Van der Eng, Jan, Jan M. Meijer, and Herta Schmid, eds., *On the Theory of Descriptive Poetics: Anton P. Chekhov As Story-Teller and Playwright.* Lisse: Peter de Ridder Press, 1978.

Winner, Thomas. *Chekhov and His Prose.* New York: Holt, Rinehart and Winston, 1966.

Criticism: Articles and Chapters

Bely, Andrei. "The Cherry Orchard." In L. Senelick, ed. and trans. *Russian Dramatic Theory from Pushkin to the Symbolists: An Anthology.* Austin, TX: University of Texas Press, 1981.

Bitsilli, Petr. "From Chekhonte to Chekhov." In V. Erlich, ed. *Twentieth-Century Russian Literary Criticism.* New Haven: Yale University Press, 1975.

Bogayevskaya, Ksenia. Introd. "Tolstoy on Chekhov: Previously Unknown Comments." *Soviet Literature* 1 (1980).

Brustein, Robert. "Anton Chekhov." *The Theater of Revolt: An Approach to the Modern Drama.* Boston: Little, Brown, 1964.

Calder, Angus. "Literature and Morality: Leskov, Chekhov, Late Tolstoy." Ch. 8, *Russia Discovered: Nineteenth-century Fiction from Pushkin to Chekhov.* New York: Barnes and Noble Books, 1976.

Conrad, Joseph. "Sensuality in Chekhov's Prose." *Slavic and East European Journal* 24, n.2 (Sum. 1980): 103–117.

Debreczeny, Paul. "The Device of Conspicuous Silence in Tolstoy, Chekhov, and Faulkner." In Victor Terras, ed. *American Contributions to the Eighth International Congress of Slavists.* Vol. II: *Literature.* Columbus, OH: Slavica, 1978.

Erenburg, Ilya. "On Re-reading Chekhov." In *Chekhov, Stendhal and Other Essays.* Ed. and trans. by A Bostock and Y. Kapp. Leningrad: Iskusstvo, 1962.

Frydman, Anne. "'Enemies': An Experimental Story." *Ulbandus Review* 2 (1979): 103–119.

Ganz, Arthur. "Anton Chekhov: Arrivals and Departures." In ch. 2 of his *Realms of The Self: Variations on a Theme in Modern Drama.* New York: New York University Press: 1980.

Gorky, Maxim. "What Chekhov Thought of It." *English Review* 8 (1911): 256–266.

Holland, Peter. "Chekhov and the Resistant Symbol." In J. Redmond, ed. *Drama and Symbolism.* Cambridge: Cambridge University Press, 1982.

Howe, Irving. "What Can We Do With Chekhov?." *Pequod* 34 (1992): 11–15.

Karlinsky, Simon. "Nabokov and Chekhov: Affinities, Parallels, Structures." *Cysnos* 10, n.1 (1993): 33–7.

Lavrin, Janko. "Chekhov and Maupassant." *Studies in East European Literature.* London: Constable, 1929, 156–192.

Mann, Thomas. "Anton Chekhov." *Mainstream* 12 (1959): 2–21.

Moss, Howard. "Three Sisters." *The Hudson Review* 30 (1977–78): 525–543.

———. "Chekhov." In Donald Davie, ed. *Russian Literature and Modern English Fiction: A Collection of Critical Essays.* Chicago: University of Chicago Press, 1965.

Martin, David W. "Figurative Language and Concretism in Chekhov's Short Stories." *Russian Literature* 8 (1980): 125–150.

Mathewson, Rufus W., Jr. "Thoreau and Chekhov: A Note on 'The Steppe'." *Ulbandus Review* 1 (1977): 28–40.

———. "Intimations of Mortality in Four Chekhov Stories." In W. E. Harkins, ed.

American Contributions to the Sixth International Congress of Slavists. Vol. II: *Literary Contributions.* The Hague: Mouton, 1968.

O'Connor, Frank. "The Slave's Son." Ch. 3. In *The Lonely Voice: A Study of the Short Story.* Cleveland and New York: Meridian Books, World Publishing Co., 1965.

O'Faolain, Sean. "Anton Chekhov or 'The Persistent Moralist'." *The Short Story.* London: Collins, 1948.

Pahomov, George. "Essential Perception: Chekhov and Modern Art." *Russian, Croation, Serbian, Czech and Slovak, Polish Literature* 35, n.2 (1994).

Scolnicov, Hanna. "Chekhov's Reading of *Hamlet.*" In *Reading Plays: Interpretation and Reception.* Eds. Hanna Scolnicov and Peter Holland. New York: Cambridge University Press, 1991.

Speirs, Logan. "Tolstoy and Chekhov: *The Death of Ivan Ilych* and 'A Dreary Story'." *Oxford Review* 8 (1968): 81–93.

Strongin, Carol. "Irony and Theatricality in Chekhov's *The Seagull.*" *Comparative Drama* 15 (1981): 366–380.

Styan, J. L. "The Delicate Balance: Audience Ambivalence in the Comedy of Shakespeare and Chekhov." *Costerus* 2 (1972): 159–184.

Tolstoy, Leo. "An Afterword to Chekhov's Story 'Darling'." *What Is Art? and Essays on Art.* Trans. Aylmer Maude. London: 1938.

Wilson, Edmund. "Seeing Chekhov Plain." *The New Yorker* 22 (November 1952): 180–198.

Acknowledgments

"*The Cherry Orchard*" by Virginia Woolf from *The New Statesman*, July 24, 1920.

"Fragments of Recollections" by Maxim Gorky from *Reminiscences of Anton Chekhov* by Maxim Gorky, Alexander Kuprin, and I.A. Bunin, translated by S.S. Koteliansky and Leonard Woolf, copyright 1921 by B.W. Huebsch, Inc. Reprinted by permission.

"Craftsmanship in *Uncle Vanya*" by Eric Bentley from *In Search of Theater* by Eric Bentley, copyright 1953 by Eric Bentley. Reprinted by permission.

"Anton Chekhov" by Raymond Williams from *Drama: From Ibsen to Brecht* by Raymond Williams, copyright 1968 by Raymond Williams. Reprinted by permission of Oxford University Press.

"Anton Chekhov: (Creation from the Void)" by Lev Shestov from *All Things Are Possible and Penultimate Words and Other Essays* by Lev Shestov, copyright 1977 by Ohio University Press. Reprinted by permission.

"*The Cherry Orchard*: A Theater-Poem of the Suffering of Change" by Francis Fergusson from *Chekhov's Great Plays*, edited by Jean-Pierre Barricelli, copyright 1981 by New York University Press. Reprinted by permission.

"Chekhov's Legacy: Icebergs and Epiphanies" by Rufus W. Mathewson, Jr. from *Chekhov and Our Age: Responses to Chekhov by American Writers and Scholars*, edited by James McConkey, copyright 1984 by Cornell University Center for International Studies. Reprinted by permission of Cornell University Press.

"*Three Sisters*" by Howard Moss from *Chekhov and Our Age: Responses to Chekhov by American Writers and Scholars*, edited by James McConkey, copyright 1984 by Cornell University Center for International Studies. Reprinted by permission of Cornell University Press.

"Chekhov and the Modern Drama" by Martin Esslin from *A Chekhov Companion*, edited by Toby W. Clyman, copyright 1985 by Toby W. Clyman. Reprinted by permission of Greenwood Press.

"Chekhov and the Modern Short Story" by Charles E. May from *A Chekhov Companion*, edited by Toby W. Clyman, copyright 1985 by Toby W. Clyman. Reprinted by permission of Greenwood Press.

"The Drama in Crisis: Chekhov" by Peter Szondi from *Theory of the Modern Drama* by Peter Szondi, copyright 1987 by University of Minnesota. Reprinted by permission of University of Minnesota Press.

"Chekhov, *The Seagull*" by David Cole from *Acting As Reading: The Place of the Reading Process in the Actor's Work* by David Cole, copyright 1992 by the University of Michigan Press. Reprinted by permission.

"'At Sea': A Psychoanalytic Approach to Chekhov's First Signed Work" by Michael C. Finke from *Reading Chekhov's Text*, edited by Robert Louis Jackson, copyright 1993 by Northwestern University Press. Reprinted by permission.

"'The Enemies': A Story at War with Itself?" by Robert Louis Jackson from *Reading Chekhov's Text*, edited by Robert Louis Jackson, copyright 1993 by Northwestern University Press. Reprinted by permission.

"Fear and Pity in 'Ward Six': Chekhovian Catharsis" by Liza Knapp from *Reading Chekhov's Text*, edited by Robert Louis Jackson, copyright 1993 by Northwestern University Press. Reprinted by permission.

"*Uncle Vanya* as Prosaic Metadrama" by Gary Saul Morson from *Reading Chekhov's Text*, edited by Robert Louis Jackson, copyright 1993 by Northwestern University Press. Reprinted by permission.

Index